ECONOMIC COMMISSION FC

Geneva

CLEARING THE AIR

25 years of the Convention on Long-range Transboundary Air Pollution

Editors
Johan Sliggers and Willem Kakebeeke

UNITED NATIONS
New York and Geneva 2004

Note

Symbols of United Nations documents are composed of capital letters combined with figures. Mention of such a symbol indicates a reference to a United Nations document.

*

* *

The designations employed and the presentation of the material in this publication do not imply the expression of any opinion whatsoever on the part of the Secretariat of the United Nations concerning the legal status of any country, territory, city or area, or of its authorities, or concerning the delimitation of its frontiers or boundaries.

The views expressed in this publication do not necessarily reflect those of the United Nations Economic Commission for Europe (UNECE) or any of its member States.

ECE/EB.AIR/84

Printed at United Nations, Geneva, Switzerland

UNITED NATIONS PUBLICATION

Sales No. E.04.II.E.20

ISBN 92-1-116910-0

Foreword by the Secretary-General of the United Nations

By the late 1970s, air pollution had become the main environmental problem facing many countries in Europe and North America, harming people's health and damaging historic buildings and monuments. Acid rain, brought on by contamination of the air, was taking a particularly heavy toll, killing forests and lakes even in remote places far from industrial facilities.

In 1979, the Member States of the UN Economic Commission for Europe adopted the Convention on Long-range Transboundary Air Pollution. Negotiated under UNECE's auspices, the Convention was the first international environmental agreement to address this threat to human health and well-being. After 25 years of international cooperation, its Parties are reaping the benefits of the cuts in air pollution that they have made in compliance with the Convention's provisions.

It is not just the people of Europe and North America who are benefiting. Other regions are keen to emulate the successful combination of sound science and ambitious policy-making that underpins the Convention, and adapt it to their particular needs. In addition, some of the Convention's work, for instance on persistent organic pollutants such as DDT and dioxins, has been used as a model for worldwide environmental agreements.

The Convention has also galvanized action within UNECE. Since the Convention's adoption, the Commission has become a prolific environmental-law-making forum. It has negotiated four more regional environmental conventions, covering international rivers and lakes, industrial accidents, environmental impact assessment and public participation. All four have entered into force and are contributing to making sustainable development a reality.

On the 25th anniversary of the Convention's adoption, I congratulate all the stakeholders on the achievements of the past quarter century, and encourage them to continue their efforts to find innovative approaches to protecting the purity of the air we breathe.

Kofi A. Annan

Secretary-General of the United Nations

Foreword by the Executive Secretary of the United Nations Economic Commission for Europe

For 25 years the UNECE Convention on Long-range Transboundary Air Pollution has been one of the main means of protecting public health and the environment from the harmful effects of air pollution across the UNECE region.

With its eight protocols, the Convention has developed comprehensive and strong commitments covering all major pollutants. It has thus significantly improved the air we breathe. For example, compared to 1980, sulphur emissions in Europe are down by 60 per cent while in Canada and the United States they are almost halved. However, we still have much to do, in particular to meet the goals set for the pollutants which migrate and affect millions of people living in cities throughout the world.

Over the past quarter of a century the politics of Europe has changed. These changes have not altered the political willingness of member States to work together under the Convention. On the contrary, the countries of the region increasingly share the conviction that further cooperation is needed to combat air pollution, as its impact on both human health and the future of the planet is a major preoccupation of public opinion.

The Convention and its protocols have set targets and defined legislative and other measures required for meeting them. A major challenge now is to implement these measures effectively, in particular in South-East Europe, Eastern Europe, the Caucasus and Central Asia, where countries need special support, as their industries develop and road traffic expands. I therefore welcome the Convention's increasing emphasis on protecting people and their environment in these subregions.

For its part, the UNECE secretariat will spare no effort in providing continued support for the work that the Parties to the Convention will undertake in the future.

I wish to congratulate all the stakeholders on the achievements of the past 25 years and look forward to further successes in meeting the challenges ahead, which, in many ways, are even more complex than those we have dealt with since the adoption of the Convention.

Brigita Schmögnerová

Executive Secretary of the
United Nations Economic Commission for Europe

List of Contributors

Altogether 58 persons worked to make this book a success as lead-authors, co-authors, reviewers or resource persons:

Roel van Aalst, Christer Ågren, Markus Amann, Helen Apsimon, Richard Ballaman, Lars Björkbom, Jim Bruce, Tom Brydges, Keith Bull, Mike Chadwick, Radovan Chrast, Harald Dovland, Wayne Draper, Martin Forsius, Oddmund Graham, Heinz Gregor, Peringe Grennfelt, Jean-Paul Hettelingh, Thomas Haußmann, Harry Harmens, Leen Hordijk, Helmut Hojeski, Andrzej Jagusiewicz, Dieter Jost, Willem Kakebeeke, Volkert Keizer, Endre Kovacs, Michal Krzyzanowski, Vladimir Kucera, Tuomas Kuokkanen, Berit Kvaeven, Lars Lindau, Martin Lorenz, Lars Lundin, Martin Lutz, Rob Maas, Hans Martin, Wojciech Mill, Gina Mills, Lars Nordberg, Max Posch, Peter Sand, Kaj Sanders, Toni Schneider, Jürgen Schneider, Brit Lisa Skjelkvåle, Johan Sliggers, Jaap Slootweg, Valentin Sokolovsky, Till Spranger, Patrick Széll, Jan Thompson, Johan Tidblad, Arne Tollan, Willemijn Tuinstra, Merete J. Ulstein, Les White, Henning Wuester.

A special thanks to Caroline Lambein and Keith Bull for editing the text and to Michel van Wassem for the design and lay out of this book.

Photo cover: www.renevanderhulst.nl

Preface

This book, like the Convention on Long-range Transboundary Air Pollution and its protocols, has been an international cooperative effort. The teams of authors have revisited the history of acid rain and air pollution in the UNECE region, an area that extends from the United States and Canada in the West to Central Asia in the East. But the Convention is not just history; the book also considers its future.

The memories, perceptions and reflections of the contributors have been brought together here to mark the 25th anniversary of the Convention. The contributors were or still are involved in the work of the Convention as government officials, members United Nations staff, national experts from institutes and universities or representatives of international NGOs.

Nearly 60 authors and other contributors have collaborated on this book, each with experience in one or more areas of the work under the Convention. They have contributed to the book in a private capacity so the views expressed are their own.

Without any exception, all who were asked were eager to contribute. We realize that no doubt others would have been equally willing; however, we hope that they will understand the limits to our ability to coordinate such a large number of contributors. Even so, the enthusiastic support given by the authors made it a pleasure for us as editors, assisted by the UNECE secretariat, to complete our task. It was hard work but enjoyable.

This book pays tribute to all our colleagues, past and present, who have helped to develop the Convention and its protocols and move from the 'Fruits of the Cold War' to 'Blue Skies Forever'.

Johan Sliggers and Willem Kakebeeke, editors

Table of contents

LRTAP 25th
Long-range Transboundary Air Pollution

Abbreviations

AOT40	Accumulated exposure over a threshold of 40 parts per billion
ASAM	Abatement Strategies Assessment Model
BAT	Best available technology/techniques
BATNEEC	Best available technology/techniques not entailing excessive costs
CAFE	Clean Air for Europe (programme)
CASM	Coordinated Abatement Strategy Model
CCC	Chemical Coordination Centre of EMEP
CCE	Coordination Center for Effects
CH_4	Methane
CIAM	Centre for Integrated Assessment Modelling
CO_2	Carbon dioxide
CORINAIR	Core Inventory of Air Emissions in Europe
CSCE	Conference on Security and Co-operation in Europe
DDT	1,1,1-trichloro-2,2-bis(4-chlorophenyl)ethane
EANET	Acid Deposition Monitoring Network for East Asia
ECOSOC	(United Nations) Economic and Social Council
EEA	European Environment Agency
EEC	European Economic Community
ELV	Emission limit value
EMEP	Cooperative programme for monitoring and evaluation of the long-range transmission of air pollutants in Europe
ENGO	Environmental non-governmental organization
ESP	Electrostatic precipitator
EU	European Union
FAO	Food and Agriculture Organization of the United Nations
FBC	Fluidized bed combustion
FGD	Flue gas desulphurization
GEMS	Global Environment Monitoring System
HAPRO	Finnish Acidification Research Programme
HELCOM	Baltic Sea Commission
ICP	International cooperative programme
IGCC	Integrated gasification combined cycle
IIASA	International Institute for Applied Systems Analysis
IPPC	Integrated Pollution Prevention and Control (Directive)
IUAPPA	International Union of Air Pollution Prevention and Environmental Protection Associations
LCP	Large combustion plant
MAGIC	Model of Acidification of Groundwater In Catchments
MARPOL	International Maritime Organization's International Convention for the Prevention of Pollution from Ships
MOI	Memorandum of intent

MSC-E	Meteorological synthesizing Centre East of EMEP
MSC-W	Meteorological synthesizing Centre West of EMEP
N_2O	Nitrous oxide
NAPAP	(United States) National Acid Precipitation Assessment Programme
NATO	North Atlantic Treaty Organisation
NEC	National emission ceilings
NFC	National focal centre
NGO	Non-governmental organization
NH_3	Ammonia
NILU	Norwegian Institute for Air Research
NITREX	NITRogen Experiments (project)
NIVA	Norwegian Institute for Water Research
NO_x	Nitrogen oxides
O_3	Ozone
OECD	Organisation for Economic Co-operation and Development
OSPARCOM	North-East Atlantic Commission
PAH	Polyaromatic hydrocarbon
PCB	Polychlorinated biphenyl
pH	Negative logarithm of hydrogen ion concentration (indicating the acidity of water)
PM	Particulate matter
POP	Persistent organic pollutant
QA/QC	Quality assurance/quality control
RAINS	Regional Acidification INformation and Simulation (model)
RAPIDC	Regional Air Pollution in Developing Countries (project)
RIVM	(Netherlands) National Institute of Public Health and the Environment
SAEP	Senior Advisors to UNECE Governments on Environmental Problems
SAFE	Soil Acidification in Forest Ecosystems (model)
SCR	Selective catalytic reduction
SEI	Stockholm Environment Institute
Sida	Swedish International Development Cooperation Agency
SMART	Simulation Model for Acidification Regional Trends
SO_2	Sulphur dioxide
UN	United Nations
UNECE	United Nations Economic Commission for Europe
UNEP	United Nations Environment Programme
USSR	Union of Soviet Socialist Republics
VOC	Volatile organic compound
WHO	World Health Organization
WMO	World Meteorological Organization

Introduction

Harald Dovland, Richard Ballaman and Jan Thompson

Since it was signed in 1979, the Convention on Long-range Transboundary Air Pollution has come to be regarded as a pioneering international instrument for the protection of the environment. It has paved the way for extensive and fruitful cooperation among up to now 49 Parties in the region of the United Nations Economic Commission for Europe (UNECE) to meet specific environmental targets. It has delivered legally binding protocols covering those air pollutants having the greatest impact on the environment and public health. Most importantly, it has brought about tangible results in reducing emissions and improving the environment. Its focus has been clearly regional, but the Convention nevertheless sets an example for other regions and for global action.

The Convention has provided a flexible framework under which 49 Parties have been able to cooperate in developing scientific understanding of the problems related to long-range transboundary air pollution; reports on national emissions and national policies; and exchange of knowledge about technologies to curb air pollution. A large number of cooperative programmes, task forces, expert groups and workshops, often reflecting national initiatives, have been put in place and formed the backbone of an extensive scientific and technical cooperation. Many scientists representing different subjects have been involved, contributing to a solid foundation on which policy makers have based their negotiations on emission reduction commitments.

The book

No wonder, then, that a number of the key persons involved in the Convention's development and operations, and contributing to its success, have volunteered to contribute to writing its history in celebration of its **25th anniversary**. This book will give insight into the life under the Convention and illustrate its tremendous achievements during its first 25 years of existence. Since its authors have been strongly involved in the Convention, the book may perhaps not be an impartial analysis, but it will certainly provide an interesting story told by the many enthusiastic contributors. All the way along, the Convention has benefited from the work of a large number of highly qualified and dedicated persons in undertaking its ambitious work programme. A factor conducive to the success of the Convention has also no doubt been a body of foresighted senior officials with shared perceptions of the challenges and a desire to find ways to overcome them, collaborating in an atmosphere of mutual respect and trust. Last, but not least, a key factor behind the achievements has been the broad political support that work under the Convention has enjoyed throughout the 25 years.

The early days

The starting point for transboundary air pollution on the political agenda was acid rain, linked initially to acidification of Scandinavian lakes and rivers, with focus on acidity and sulphur oxides. The cooperation under the Convention therefore started as a fight against emissions of sulphur oxides. As we gained more knowledge, the situation became more complex and new compounds had to be added to tackle other effects of air pollution (nitrogen oxides (NOx), volatile organic compounds (VOC), ammonia (NH_3), heavy metals and persistent organic pollutants (POPs)).

At the time of its adoption, the Convention was not generally considered a suitable platform for common abatement measures. There was political reluctance to enter into binding obligations to

ECONOMIC COMMISSION FOR EUROPE

1979 CONVENTION ON LONG-RANGE TRANSBOUNDA[RY] AIR POLLUTION

PROTOCOLS

1984 EMEP
1985 SULPHUR
1988 NITROGEN OXIDE[S]
1991 VOLATILE ORGAN[IC] COMPOUNDS
1994 SULPHUR

COMMISSION ÉCONOMIQUE POUR L' EUROPE

1979 CONVENTION SUR LA POLLUTION ATMOSPHÉRIQUE TRANSFRONTIÈRE À LONGUE DISTANCE

1998 PROTOCOLE RELATIF AUX POLLUANTS ORGANIQUES PERSISTANTS

1998 PROTOCOLE RELATIF AUX MÉTAUX LOURDS

NATIONS UNIES

ECONOMIC COMMISSION FOR EUROPE

Protocol concerning the Control of Emissions of Volatile Organic Compounds or their Transboundary Fluxes

COMMISSION ÉCONOMIQUE POUR L'EUROPE

Protocole relatif à la lutte contre les émissions des composés organiques volatils ou leurs flux transfrontières

ЕВРОПЕЙСКАЯ ЭКОНОМИЧЕСКАЯ КОМИССИЯ

Протокол об ограничении выбросов летучих органических соединений или их трансграничных потоков

UNITED NATIONS NATIONS UNIES

ОРГАНИЗАЦИЯ ОБЪЕДИНЕННЫХ НАЦИЙ

ECE/EB.AIR/61

UNITED NATIONS
ECONOMIC COMMISSION FOR EUROPE

PROTOCOL TO THE 1979 CONVENTION ON LONG-RANGE TRANSBOUNDARY AIR POLLUTION ON HEAVY METALS
and Executive Body decision 1998/1 on the Criteria and Procedures for Adding Heavy Metals and Products to the Protocol on Heavy Metals

NATIONS UNIES
COMMISSION ÉCONOMIQUE POUR L'EUROPE

PROTOCOLE À LA CONVENTION SUR LA POLLUTION ATMOSPHÉRIQUE TRANSFRONTIÈRE À LONGUE DISTANCE, DE 1979, RELATIF AUX MÉTAUX LOURDS
et décision 1998/1 de l'Organe exécutif concernant les critères à respecter et les procédures à suivre pour ajouter des métaux lourds et des produits au Protocole relatif aux métaux lourds

Организация Объединенных Наций
Европейская экономическая комиссия

ПРОТОКОЛ ПО ТЯЖЕЛЫМ МЕТАЛЛАМ К КОНВЕНЦИИ 1979 ГОДА О ТРАНСГРАНИЧНОМ ЗАГРЯЗНЕНИИ ВОЗДУХА НА БОЛЬШИЕ РАССТОЯНИЯ

UNITED NATIONS NATIONS UNIES

ОРГАНИЗАЦИЯ ОБЪЕДИНЕННЫХ НАЦИЙ

The texts of the Convention and its protocols have been the basis for air polution control in the UNECE region for 25 years reduce emissions. However, as the awareness of serious regional effects of air pollution grew and as it was realized that more or less all UNECE countries were affected, the political tide turned. The vehicles chosen to achieve emission reductions were protocols to the Convention. Each protocol constitutes an international agreement with signatories that vary from protocol to protocol.

The Convention has gone through stages with a different focus (see **chapter 2**). In the first phase it acted mainly as a vehicle for building trust between political blocs in need of non-contentious fields of cooperation. Subsequently, it was instrumental in creating awareness and shared perceptions as a basis for joint action. It was the first international legally binding instrument to deal with problems on a broad regional basis. And we should keep in mind that the region in question is truly vast, covering two continents and comprising most of the old industrialized world. The main driving forces have changed over time: from high politics via public concern over extensive environmental damage to - more lately - health concerns. Over the years, through the development of gradually more advanced protocols, it has broken new ground in environmental law-making and become an outstanding example of fruitful international cooperation.

The Convention has shown a remarkable ability to adapt to different circumstances and to shift operative focus. While the attention in the first years lay with building a sound scientific knowledge base, in the second phase lasting through the 1990s the focus shifted to development and negotiation of gradually more advanced and comprehensive protocols, while at the same time ensuring that the scientific knowledge was kept up to date. The present phase is marked by emphasis on implementation and compliance, and also of examination and review of protocols to ensure the adequacy of their provisions.

EMEP

An international study under the Organisation for Economic Co-operation and Development (OECD) in the early 1970s showed that air and precipitation quality in European countries were measurably affected by emissions in other European countries. It also illustrated that this was not an issue that could be addressed by West European countries alone; East European countries had to be included. The 1975 Helsinki Conference on Security and Cooperation in Europe paved the road directly for establishing the monitoring programme EMEP and later to negotiations leading to the Convention (see **chapter 3**). EMEP has during its existence demonstrated the contribution made by different countries to the deposition and air quality in other countries in the region. Early on we received information that told us that emission reductions were needed, but not by how much; we knew the direction, but the road map had to be developed.

Technology

In the cooperation and negotiations under the Convention, use of control technologies ("end-of-pipe solutions") has been an important issue. Without the development of control technologies that could be implemented while avoiding costs, the significant reductions that have been achieved would not have been possible. UNECE had initiated "desulphurization seminars" every five years as major events in sharing information on control technologies before the Convention was signed. These were continued and supplemented with other activities to define the “best available techniques” to be applied and to prescribe mandatory emission limit values under the Convention (see **chapter 4**).

Effects

As already noted, the political basis for legally binding commitments was laid only when it had become clear that virtually all UNECE countries were affected by transboundary air pollution. Increasing awareness of a growing number of different effects of air pollution was a decisive factor. In addition to damage to freshwater ecosystems, damage to forests, materials, crops and human health became increasingly evident. The need to know more about the effects of air pollutants formed the basis for important elements of the work under the Convention. Different countries emphasized different effects and extensive international cooperative programmes, as well as national programmes, were put in place to generate new knowledge (see **chapter 5**).

Integrated assessment

An instrumental factor in the development of the Convention has been the elaboration of the effects-based or critical loads approach, and the extensive use of integrated assessment models, as a basis for policy-making. Very briefly, this approach makes it possible to develop scenarios to achieve specified environmental goals in a cost-efficient way for Europe as a whole (see **chapter 6**). By making use of what we know about emission projections, the transfer of pollutants between European countries, the geographical variation of critical loads (or another "indicator" of effects of air pollution or an environmental goal) and control costs, modellers provide calculations for cost-efficient reduction scenarios that form a sound basis for policy makers' negotiations.

The Convention has provided an effective and flexible framework for joint action on common problems not least by fostering close contacts between the scientific experts and the policy makers involved. This has provided adaptability to new demands and circumstances and introduced an element of dynamism in policy development. But the high reliance on updated scientific knowledge has also added an element of vulnerability to work under the Convention because of the dependence on research budgets and countries' willingness to contribute to international cooperative efforts. It cannot be denied that some countries have had to bear a disproportionate share of the necessary funding. The issue of ensuring sufficient funds to keep up the good work under the Convention is a challenge that most likely will remain with us in the coming years.

While the Convention has never had an official logo, a number of "symbols" have been used in recent years in association with the Convention's publications, web site etc. to provide an image for the Convention. In 2004, the Bureau of the Executive Body selected a new symbol (left) and a special version of it for the 25th anniversary, both submitted by Canada, for use on the Convention's web site and elsewhere. Earlier versions (e.g. right) have often featured a globe showing the UNECE region, occasionally with the LRTAP abbreviation

The secretariat

Running the Convention "machinery" is not only a question of money but also of qualified and motivated individuals. Throughout the 25 years, ECE has provided the secretariat for the Convention, being responsible for preparing all formal meetings, including serving all negotiating processes.
An important task for the secretariat has also been to coordinate, support and manage a large number of various meetings held outside the formal meetings in Geneva. For this to happen, a good deal of creativity has been needed, given the limited resources available. But in this respect, credit should also be given to countries or groups of countries that have time and again generously sponsored workshops and scientific meetings. **Chapter 7** offers an insight into the challenges of the secretariat.

Compliance

At present, there are eight protocols to the Convention, covering the major air pollutants.
The protocols have developed from rather crude, flat-rate reduction obligations covering one substance only, into sophisticated and complex instruments both in terms of environmental and cost-effectiveness. To achieve the environmental goals, however, it is essential that countries actually live up to their commitments. In order to oversee the compliance with the various obligations, an Implementation Committee has been established as an important element of the cooperation. Since the Convention does not have recourse to any means to actually force a country to comply, the implementation mechanism is more supportive and persuasive in character. Some countries have not been able to comply with all commitments; some have problems with the reporting obligations, others have encountered problems in achieving the emission reductions they had signed up to. In our judgement, there is no reason to conclude that lack of strong consequences for non-compliance represents any serious drawback for the Convention as an effective legal instrument. Compliance issues, including a discussion of what type of pressure that can be put on Parties in non-compliance, are discussed in **chapter 8**.

Involvement of non-governmental organizations

Civil society has shown strong interest in "acid rain", both from environmental organizations and from industry (see **chapter 9**). The activities have perhaps been strongest at the national level, trying to influence the position of governments. The views of the different organizations most often followed the traditional pattern: industry fearing costly regulations and environmental groups calling for stronger action. Perhaps the most striking example of the impact of civil society was the growing public concern over extensive environmental damage like the German forest dieback in the early 1980s. This concern was voiced through an increasingly informed press and other media and paved the way for stronger political action at the international level. The pressure from non-governmental organizations (NGOs) has been less pronounced during later years, perhaps because of the increased focus on other environmental issues, such as climate change.

Environmental organizations have also played an important role in disseminating information about the long-range transport of air pollutants. An outstanding example of this is the newsletter "Acid News" from the Swedish NGO Secretariat on Acid Rain; its key people combine a deep understanding of the scientific facts as well as of the negotiating process with a rare ability to transmit this in a sober and easily accessible manner.

The future

The co-operation under the Convention will face new challenges in the future: several countries in the "far east" of Europe, in the Caucasus and in Central Asia have joined the Convention and more may follow suit. At the same time, the European Union (EU) is growing and issuing legislation on transboundary air pollution. As our knowledge advances, we realize that many of the pollutants are of a hemispheric and even a global character. For the Convention, therefore, it will be a challenge to improve cooperation between both sides of the Atlantic and to extend it to other countries in the Northern hemisphere - including sharing of experiences and establishing links with regional cooperative organizations in other regions. Furthermore, we have to acknowledge the linkages between the regional air pollution problems and global issues like climate change. Another question is whether new substances should be included in new or revised protocols. Particles represent an important issue because of their health effects. This will certainly play an important role on coming negotiations, but today it is premature to judge exactly how this issue will be handled in a legal context. Efforts to reduce particles were already launched under the protocols related to heavy metals and POPs, as well as by the cuts in sulphur dioxide (SO_2) and NOx, which form secondary particles in the atmosphere. Many challenges lie ahead of us (see **chapter 10**), but we believe the Convention, with its ability to adapt to new circumstances, its exceptional network of highly qualified specialists, and the broad support it enjoys, is well positioned to meet these challenges and to continue serving people and their environment for the next 25 years.

Fruits of the Cold War: The Convention and the First Sulphur Protocol

Willem Kakebeeke, Lars Björkbom, Dieter Jost, Hans Martin and Valentin Sokolovsky

Down memory lane

Acidification of the environment has been around for more than a hundred years. The massive increase in emissions of air pollutants after the Second World War, due to economic and industrial recovery and growth, made acidification an environmental problem of the first order in a large number of European countries and in North America. Scientific research on air pollutants and their deposition at the national and, to some extent, the international scale started to show the scope of damage that occurred, in particular in the Scandinavian countries. Fish loss in lakes, damage to vegetation and materials, and effects on human health became increasingly evident. The call for international action was heard more and more.

Against the background of the cold war, which divided Western and Eastern Europe, efforts were made to reduce air pollutants contributing to acidification. Countries of the UNECE region, emitting at that time more than half of the world's anthropogenic air pollutants, were first successful in 1979 by the adoption of the Convention on Long-range Transboundary Air Pollution. Concrete measures to decrease sulphur emissions in the form of the 1985 Sulphur Protocol had to wait another six years. This chapter deals with the birth of the Convention and the subsequent development of this first protocol.

Outline

In this chapter the reader will find the personal perceptions of five persons who, in the 1970s and 1980s, were involved in developing legally binding international agreements to reduce emissions of air pollutants at a pan-European scale and in North America. The contributions are written by:

- Mr. Valentin Sokolovsky: Fruits of a cold war;
- Mr. Dieter Jost: Waldsterben, a breakthrough;
- Mr. Hans Martin: The North American connection perceived by a Canadian;
- Mr. Lars Björkbom: Thoughts about the dynamics behind thr process: the role of externalities; and
- Mr. Willem Kakebeeke: The Fifth Perception.

The contributions address the geopolitical and the environmental implications as well as their interlinkages. A breakthrough, "Waldsterben" (forest die back), led to a successful instrument to combat sulphur emissions. The last part of this chapter summarizes, as a fifth perception, the history and reflects on the merits of the Convention and the 1985 Sulphur Protocol.

Fruits of a cold war

Valentin Sokolovsky

Preparatory movements

On 13 November 1979, the Convention on Long-range Transboundary Air Pollution was signed by governments of UNECE member States. At that time, this event attracted the close attention of the mass media and people in general because of several circumstances.

First and foremost, in the period of military and political confrontation between Western and Eastern blocs, the signing of the Convention by representatives of the countries separated by the cold war front was considered an extraordinary event. Besides, it was the first all-European environmental agreement signed by 34 governments of European countries, Canada and the United States of America, as well as by the European Economic Community (EEC). It is known that negotiations on the Convention were very arduous; politicians and environmental experts were far from unanimity. Nevertheless, they managed to compromise and the appropriate solutions were found. Finally, the signing of the Convention and the Declaration on Low- and Non-waste Technology and Reutilization and Recycling of Wastes took place during a high-level meeting on environmental problems organized on the initiative of the Union of Soviet Socialist Republics (USSR). It should be noted that the governments of several leading Western countries objected to this meeting for four years.

Now, 25 years later, the cold war has been consigned to the history books and the Soviet Union has been absent from the political map for 13 years, but specialists studying the preparation of international environmental agreements often ask: what were the reasons behind the decision of the USSR to initiate the negotiations, conduct them persistently, reach agreement and be the first country to ratify the Convention?

In order to clarify this, we need to characterize briefly the economic, ecological and socio-political situation in Europe at the beginning of the 1970s. It was a period when, owing to scientific and technical advances, there was a rapid growth in production. This growth was accompanied by an ever-increasing consumption of natural resources and an unprecedented increase in environmental pollution with various gaseous, liquid and solid industrial wastes and consumption residues exerting negative effects on the environment and human health. The hazardous smogs of 1952 and 1956 in London, which had taken the lives of more than 5000 people, was fresh in the memory; frequent smog in Los Angeles, Chicago, Tokyo and many other large cities caused great anxiety among the public.

Large-scale environmental problems, especially those related to air quality, became a matter of deep concern not only for scientists but also for the public in general, non-governmental ecological organizations and movements, as well as the Green parties. There was a growing demand for urgent government action.

The United Nations Conference on the Human Environment was held in Stockholm in 1972. During this Conference, representatives of Scandinavian countries tried to draw the attention of other delegates to the problem of acid rain. However, their European colleagues and the developing countries did not fully support this initiative. Representatives of the USSR and allied socialist States did not participate in this conference in solidarity with the German Democratic Republic, whose delegates were refused visas by the Swedish Government. However, while discussing the resolution of the General Assembly of the United Nations on the Stockholm Declaration, the Soviet Union supported it. In the same year, in 1972, environmental protection and the management of natural resources were discussed at the session of the Supreme Soviet of the USSR. On this basis, a governmental decree on environmental protection was adopted. In agreement with this document, the State system of environmental monitoring and control was organized in the USSR and the principles of the State policy in nature management and environmental conservation were clearly formulated.

Measures to control the pollution and degradation of the environment and to recover renewable natural resources were developed. State budget funds were regularly allocated for these purposes; corresponding work was included in current and future plans for the country's economic development. Intergovernmental agreements on environmental cooperation were concluded with the United States, France, Denmark and several other countries.

For several years, the Senior Advisers to UNECE Governments on Environmental Problems, established in 1972, were engaged in the preparation of relevant material for the Final Act of the Conference for Security and Co-operation in Europe signed in Helsinki in 1975. Part 5 of the Final Act was devoted to cooperation on environmental protection. The problem of acid rain was mentioned only briefly.

A USSR initiative

In 1976, the Government of the USSR suggested that a series of pan-European meetings and conferences aimed at putting into practice the provisions of the Helsinki Final Act should be organized within the UNECE framework at the highest ministerial level. A conference on environmental protection was included in this list. However, politicians of several Western countries, in connection with the violation of human rights in the USSR, declared this suggestion to be a propaganda manoeuvre and rejected it during the next session of UNECE. Under these circumstances the activity of the Senior Advisers was reduced to the exchange of information about national strategies and policies in various aspects of nature management and environmental protection.

Attempts by delegations of the USSR and other East European countries to initiate the adoption of decisions aimed at practical cooperation in the solution of particular ecological problems were not supported by delegations of the EEC countries. In order to avoid political discussions within the framework of the Senior Advisers, representatives of Western countries argued that practical cooperation should be organized only on ecological problems having the priority in all European countries. However, it was a challenge to determine these problems, especially taking into consideration the fact that all problems were considered by the participants from the viewpoint of their foreign policy priorities.

Searching for well-reasoned initiatives, Soviet experts turned their attention to the corresponding preparatory material for the United Nations Conference on the Human Environment in Stockholm and the Helsinki Final Act on Security and Co-operation in Europe. Their analysis showed that the problem of acid rain could be considered the most promising field for practical cooperation among the UNECE countries. In particular, all Scandinavian countries were deeply concerned about the problem of acid rain and its effect on the environment. The Institute of Applied Geophysics of the Hydro-meteorological Service of the USSR performed a preliminary study of this problem for the territory of the Soviet Union. This analysis proved that transboundary deposition of acid rain in the European part of the USSR was several times greater than the corresponding deposition from Soviet sources to the West of the State boundary. Annual damage from acid rain to the agriculture of regions now known as Belarus, Lithuania, Latvia, Estonia, the northern part of Ukraine and 11 administrative regions of European Russia was estimated to be more than $150 million.

The Norwegian-USSR connection

At the beginning of 1978, the Norwegian Minister of Environmental Protection, Ms. Gro Harlem Brundtland, was invited to the USSR. She confirmed that acid rain from sources in other countries caused serious damage to fisheries in the lakes of Norway and Sweden. She called for a convention on the reduction of sulphur dioxide emissions as a necessary measure to control acid rain. During Soviet-Norwegian consultations it was agreed that the two delegations should cooperate within the framework of the Senior Advisers and seek a decision on the drafting of a convention on the control of acid rain by the UNECE countries. It was assumed that the Norwegian delegation would persuade other Nordic countries to support this decision, whereas the USSR delegation would take care of the position of other socialist countries during the negotiations. Aware of the negative attitude of the EEC countries toward the proposals advanced by the USSR delegation, Norway took the initiative in advocating the need for a convention.

At the next session of the Senior Advisers, the Head of the Norwegian delegation, Mr. E. Lykke, announced this initiative, which was actively supported by delegations of Nordic and socialist countries and battered by delegations of the EEC countries, especially by France, the United Kingdom and the Federal Republic of Germany. In the course of the discussion, the United Kingdom's delegation expressed unequivocal doubt about the validity of the hypothesis of the transboundary character of acid rain. In response, delegations of Norway and Sweden presented their data from which it followed that the atmospheric deposition of sulphur dioxide over their territories exceeded national emissions of this substance by several times. It was also demonstrated that the United Kingdom and several other countries in Western and Central Europe should share responsibility for transboundary acid deposition originating in their territories. The delegation of the USSR drew attention to the fact that State boundaries could not be considered as barriers against flows of air carrying harmful mixtures to neighbouring and even distant countries. This fact was clearly proved by observations of global radioactive fallout after nuclear weapons' tests. On the basis of this reasoning it was argued that none of the countries could solve the problem of transboundary air pollution alone. For this purpose, coordinated efforts of many nations, as determined by international agreements should be made.

At the end of 1978, the arguments put forward by the delegations of the Nordic countries and the USSR were confirmed by the preliminary results of the Cooperative Programme for Monitoring and Evaluation of the Long-range Transmission of Air Pollutants in Europe (EMEP). Data had been collected since 1977 on the initiative of UNECE and financed within the framework of the United Nations Environment Programme (UNEP). These results clearly demonstrated the effect of transboundary air pollution, which put the United Kingdom's delegation in a corner. The delegations of the Federal Republic of Germany and France attempted to explain their objections against the preparation of a convention by the fact that cooperation in combating acid rain could not be considered an urgent task for all European countries. They argued that few countries were really interested in this problem. However, during the further discussions representatives of EEC were asked to pay attention to principle 21 of the Stockholm Declaration. As formulated in this principle in accordance with the Charter of the United Nations and the principles of international law, sovereign States have the responsibility to ensure that activities within their jurisdiction or control do not cause damage to the environment of other States or of areas beyond the limits of national jurisdiction. It followed from this principle that the solution to the problem of acid rain should be found not only by the countries subjected to their adverse effects but also by the

countries that were the sources of acid rain. The position of the Federal Republic of Germany at these negotiations was seriously undermined by the Green party, which criticized the Government in the Bundestag and pointed to the fact that about 50% of forests in the country suffered to various extents from acid rain. The unity of EEC countries was disrupted by Denmark, which supported Nordic countries in their efforts to develop and adopt a convention.

Thus, all the major arguments of the opponents to a convention were exhausted. As a result, the decision to prepare a convention was adopted during the next UNECE session. After a long discussion, a diplomatically amorphous formula suggested that the Senior Advisers should consider drafting a convention. In this way the political initiative of the USSR to convene a European conference on the environment at the highest governmental level got a real chance of success owing to a very favourable combination of national and international ecological interests.

Arduous negotiations

Negotiations on the main articles of the Convention were very acrimonious. To a certain extent, they were complicated by the political differences between the Western and Eastern blocs. During the negotiations, representatives of Western countries (whose number was three times as large as the number of eastern countries) while trying to avoid open disputes among themselves at plenary sessions, left thorny issues for discussions at closed meetings of their delegations. Open multilateral discussions of these problems at plenary sessions were resumed after compromise among Western countries had been achieved. However, such compromises were not always acceptable for countries of the Eastern bloc; delegations from both blocs had rigid instructions from their governments concerning the particular articles of the Convention. The whole procedure of finding mutually acceptable formulations and solving new problems required much time and effort.

In general, it was evident that the delegations of Norway, Sweden and Finland argued for the adoption of firm commitments, whereas those countries that had previously rejected the mere idea of a convention tried to weaken them and agreed to meet blunted commitments. The delegations of the United States and Canada did not want to quarrel with either the Nordic or the EEC countries and preferred the position of observers. At the same time, the Canadian delegation had certain grievances against the United States related to acid rain. From time to time, the two delegations had to conduct bilateral negotiations concerning this problem. It would be naive to think that countries of the Eastern bloc were unanimous in their attitude toward particular provisions of the Convention. For instance, representatives of the German Democratic Republic, Poland and Czechoslovakia argued against firm commitments to reduce their emissions of sulphur dioxide, as they were not aware of their ability to lower emissions of this top-priority air pollutant.

Disagreements between the Nordic and the EEC countries were discussed especially by the delegations of socialist countries. It was concluded that the problems facing the German Democratic Republic, Poland and Czechoslovakia were generally the same as the problems facing the EEC countries. It was evident that, eventually, some mutually acceptable decisions would be found. Therefore, considering the course of the negotiations and their political aspects, the delegations of the socialist bloc decided to support the Nordic countries in their dispute with the EEC countries.

Intense negotiations at the end of 1978 and the beginning of 1979 resulted in the final compromise concerning the character of the Convention. It was agreed that it should be a framework convention with clear statements of its final goal, urgent tasks, principles and fields of cooperation, mechanisms for the implementation of decisions and settlement of disputes etc. The particular measures aimed at reducing transboundary air pollution had to be determined later, after special scientific studies and economic assessments. It was assumed that these measures should be fixed in separate protocols. However, it was evident that at least some aspects of cooperation had to be clearly stated in the Convention. In particular, it was suggested that estimates of transboundary air pollution by substance regulated by the Convention should be obtained within the framework of EMEP.

Data on emissions from grid cells or data on transboundary fluxes of pollutants?

For the USSR, it was not a problem to submit information on total national emissions. However, model calculations according to EMEP could be done only if data on emissions from agreed grid unit of the EMEP region had been submitted. At the time, this obligation was unacceptable to the USSR, and probably to the United States. The submission of data revealing the distribution of industrial potential in the USSR to EMEP was impossible because of the secrecy conditioned by not only politica but also military opposition between eastern and western blocs. In fact, the positions of the USSR an the United States on this issue had much in common. This was indirectly proved later, after the signing and ratification of the Convention by the United States, when this country did not enter into commitments to finance EMEP on a long-term basis and to submit data on the distribution of emissions of agreed air pollutants in the United States to EMEP. Nevertheless, the United States started to pay towards the EMEP budget voluntarily.

Before the adoption of the Convention, the Norwegian Meteorological Synthesizing Centre performed model calculations using EMEP. However, the USSR also had highly qualified specialists and a specia mathematical model to calculate the transfer of pollutants with air fluxes. The validity of this model had already been tested and confirmed by calculations on the transfer of radioactive pollutants during nuclear weapons' tests. To ensure the participation of the USSR in the Convention without violation o secrecy demands, Soviet specialists declared their readiness to submit data on total national emissions and on the fluxes of air pollutants from Soviet sources crossing western borders of the country along the segments of an agreed length.

The acceptability of this proposal was specifically discussed during the meeting of Soviet, Norwegian and American experts in Oslo. They concluded that it was possible to compare model data obtained i the Western and Eastern centres. The formulation of a corresponding article regulating the exchange of information and submission of national data was suggested. After the USSR agreed to exchange modelling data on transboundary fluxes, this article was included into the Convention and, later, into the first three emission reduction protocols. Before 1991, the Moscow Meteorological Synthesizing Centre performed calculations of transboundary fluxes not only for the USSR but also for its allies. Th need for this approach disappeared only after the end of the cold war and the establishment of an atmosphere of confidence and close cooperation throughout Europe.

Though the problem of acid rain gave the initial impetus to the development of the Convention, it wa agreed in the course of negotiations that the Convention should not be restricted to the regulation of

the emissions of sulphur dioxide, sulphuric and sulphurous acids and nitrogen oxides, i.e. substances causing acidification of the environment. Other harmful substances in transboundary air fluxes - lead, mercury, other heavy metals, dioxins and persistent organic pollutants - were also mentioned at the early stages of preparation of the Convention.

Declaration in addition to the Convention

As the work on the Convention shaped into a real document, there was an important prerequisite for the organization of a European summit devoted to environmental protection. The signing of the Convention would be the culmination of such a meeting. However, for Western politicians, this would have meant that the USSR had succeeded in the realization of its political initiative despite all the obstacles. Therefore, during disputes among the UNECE countries, political opponents of the USSR rejected the idea of a European meeting on environmental problems at the highest governmental level with the only outcome as the Convention on Long-Range Transboundary Air Pollution.

In response to this position, representatives of the USSR suggested that a declaration on low-waste and non-waste technology could also be developed and signed during the meeting. It was stressed that such a declaration would be a useful tool in the practical realization of the purposes of the Convention and would also foster environmental conservation policy and promote the prevention of environmental pollution by liquid and solid industrial and municipal wastes. Hoping that it would be impossible to realize this suggestion in practice in 1979, the representatives of Western countries agreed to give the Senior Advisers a chance to develop this declaration. Professor G.A. Yagodin from the USSR successfully chaired the working group for the preparation of the declaration. The declaration was prepared simultaneously with the Convention. Considered together, these two documents formed a solid base for the organization of the European meeting on environmental problems initiated by the USSR. However, Western countries rejected the idea of a summit, and the meeting was organized at the highest ministerial level.

The Soviet Union was the first country to ratify the Convention on 22 May 1980. Three years later, the Convention entered into force. The development and signing of the Convention on Long-range Transboundary Air Pollution in 1979, despite the disputes and political obstacles, was largely due to the fact that scientists, specialists and the general public in Europe and North America were fully aware of the need for the joint cooperative efforts of all countries in Europe to solve urgent ecological problems. Governments of the countries from the two opposing blocs could not fail to take this into consideration. For the first time, the priority of common ecological interests was acknowledged; it proved to be superior to the political disagreements.. In essence, the Convention on Long-range Transboundary Air Pollution served as a bridge across the invisible cold-war front; this was a bridge with two-way traffic. It was destined to serve faithfully the common interests of all European nations seeking cooperation, favourable and sustainable environment, peace and harmony. This became evident when steps were undertaken to agree on targets to achieve concrete emission reductions of sulphur dioxide some years later.

A protocol on sulphur dioxide emission reduction

In the UNECE context the renewed search for the reduction of sulphur emissions into the air dates back to the time of the first session of the Executive Body for the Convention on Long-range

Transboundary Air Pollution (7-10 June 1983), where it received primary consideration. Discussing the strategies and policies concerning the reduction of air contamination with sulphur compounds Norway, Finland and Sweden submitted a proposal for a concerted programme to reduce sulphur emissions. In this document it was suggested that the Parties to the Convention should reduce, not later than by 1993, sulphur emissions by at least 30% as compared with the emission levels of 1980. By that time in the USSR the limit values of reducing sulphur dioxide emissions had been determined on the basis of realistic capabilities to fulfil assumed obligations. To solve the problems in terms of technology it was suggested to install flue gas desulphurization devices at thermal electric power plants but this did not produce good results. The project to equip large power generating units of the Ryazan power plant with desulphurization devices proved to be very expensive and was rejected. At the same time it became evident that the changes in the fuel balance of the country (replacement of coal and fuel oil by natural gas) implemented on a routine basis produced both economic and ecological benefits. Therefore, bearing in mind the further plans for converting the European USSR's heat power industry to gas the appropriate assessments of the sulphur dioxide emission reductions were made. What remained was to identify the deadlines for different options of the emission reduction and to determine the option acceptable for the USSR.

Third session of the Executive Body (8 July 1985, Helsinki) with UNECE Executive Secretary, Mr. K. Sahlgren (left) and Chairman of the Executive Body, Mr. Valentin Sokolovsky (right)

The 30% reduction by 1993 at the latest, proposed by Scandinavian countries, appeared to be acceptable for the USSR. There were plans for 1980-1993 to reduce sulphur dioxide emissions on the European territory of the country by at least 43%, therefore the Soviet Union supported the Scandinavian proposal implicitly (the plans were fully implemented, in 1993 sulphur emissions in European Russia were 50.3% less than in 1980). There was a tempestuous debate in the working group on the sulphur draft protocol chaired by Mr. Jim Bruce (Canada). The USSR, Ukraine SSR and Belarus SSR supported the proposal of the Scandinavian countries, some delegations stated that time was not ripe for any target figures concerning reducing sulphur dioxide emission, others stressed the importance of acid rain and proposed to address the problems of sulphur emissions together with those of nitrogen oxides.

The United Kingdom attempted to present an alternative document but this was opposed by the Soviet Union. The USSR urged the countries not able to meet the 30% reduction not to interfere with the finalization of the draft protocol, emphasizing that it should be signed on a voluntary and sovereign basis. The United Kingdom and some other countries, including socialist countries, did not sign the protocol and experts from the Soviet Union concluded that plans to develop identical obligations for all countries were not productive. Therefore, when the Protocol on Nitrogen Oxides was under preparation in 1984, the USSR delegation insisted that decisions should be scientifically grounded on the basis of the critical loads concept. In 1988, the Soviet Union initiated the decision to establish the Working Group on Abatement Strategies, and Mr V. Sokolovsky was elected Chairman. The Working Group aimed at developing strategies based upon the critical loads concept. Such a strategy was formulated and implemented in the preparations for the second Sulphur Protocol (Oslo, 1994) and for the 1999 Gothenburg Protocol.

Waldsterben, a breakthrough

Dieter Jost

The 1985 Sulphur Protocol

The 1985 Sulphur Protocol, also known as the 30% Protocol, was the first air pollution abatement protocol to the 1979 Convention on Long-range Transboundary Air Pollution and it opened the way for further measures to reduce emissions from the whole UNECE region.

After the adoption and signing of the Convention in 1979 it still took some time before a large number of signatories were really convinced of the need to take costly measures to abate long-range transboundary air pollution. There had been strong indications that acid deposition from transboundary air pollution was causing harm to freshwater lakes. But the suffering lakes were situated in Scandinavia “only”. Central, West and East European countries brushed international air pollution policy aside. South European countries were not interested and North America stressed the non-existence of transboundary air pollution besides that already discussed in its region bilaterally. In fact, acid deposition and long-range transboundary air pollution had been the focus of scientific studies and cooperation, e.g. by the Air Management Policy Group of the Organisation for Economic Co-operation and Development (OECD); but environmental policy-making in European countries did not take note of the problem. Saving Scandinavian fish in Scandinavian freshwaters had been deemed too costly, and frequently high chimneys had been the choice for solving local air pollution problems.

From 1982 the forest damage in Germany linked to air pollution changed the attitude of the German Government towards long-range air pollution. Forest damage became a major policy concern in Germany; the German verb for forest damage “Waldschäden” found its way into other languages. Articless in German news magazines contributed more to public awareness of environmental problems than the many scientific publications on forest damage at that time could achieve. Those magazines could base their articles on a long series of scientific publications on acid deposition problems of many years before. But scientific publications themselves could not manage to raise public awareness.

At that time environmental policy-making in the Federal Republic of Germany became an increasing priority. The "Green" movement, in spite of not yet being represented by a Green party at the federal level, influenced environmental thinking in all parties in Germany.

Political pressure for action to combat air pollution increased not only in Germany but in several European countries and in North America too, since forest damage was also detected in those countries. In addition to the "Green pressure", technologies that had been developed to decrease sulphur dioxide (SO_2) emissions from large coal-fired power plants, supported the understanding of requirements for abatement of long-range transboundary air pollution among policy makers. Whereas in some countries environmental policy may have been influenced by the 1982 Stockholm Conference on Acidification of the Environment. In Germany the policy changed in favour of environmental protection just before the Stockholm Conference due to the forest damage problem. The German Government could take the opportunity of the Stockholm Conference to present its new view to the public.

Against that background, Germany invited UNECE member States to a multilateral environment conference (Munich, June 1984). Perhaps it was not forest damage alone which led Germany to take an active role in the abatement of long-range air pollution, but also the knowledge on technical solutions to the problem: flue gas desulphurization, a new technique developed in Germany, improved and applied in Japan and imported to Germany. Similar developments took place to purify car emissions with catalysts developed in Japan and the development of flue gas denitrification. Both techniques became a basis for the later Protocol on Nitrogen Oxides.

From today's point of view it is difficult to judge whether there was a scientific evaluation or more a political assessment leading to an obligation to reduce national SO_2 emissions by 30%. In any event, it was a very simple calculation at that time which convinced policy people at their meeting during one afternoon and evening in Munich in 1984 that:

- Flue gas desulphurization yielded 80 to 95% SO_2 emission reduction at power plants fired by coal or by SO_2 rich oil;
- Flue gas desulphurization applied to all new and existing power plants would decrease national sulphur emissions by 30% in most countries; and
- Continuing fuel switching would further decrease national emissions.

This Munich Conference opened the way for a quick development of the first emission reduction protocol within the framework of the 1979 Convention. In the end the Sulphur Protocol (Helsinki, 1985) received 19 signatures. It was the first substantive protocol with obligations to reduce national emissions and to abate long-range transboundary air pollution. Up to now this Protocol and the 1988 Protocol on Nitrogen Oxides are the only ones whose obligations have been met without delay by all Parties.

The merits of the 1985 Sulphur Protocol were the following:

- The 30% approach provided a clear basis for political negotiations;
- The Protocol was easy to verify. Later on the Protocol proved to be clearly met by all Parties. Most Parties did even more than meet their 30% SO_2 national emission reduction; and
- The 30% reduction was seen as a first step in a direction leading to further protocols. These further protocols should then be based on more scientifically evaluated goals.

There were, however, shortcomings too. From the beginning, the lack of a direct relation between obligations and ecological goals received critical comment with respect to the pragmatic 30% approach. The economic consequences for some countries were still unknown at the time of negotiations and even at ratification. And finally, there was only a poor scientific basis for the 30% approach. Subsequent protocols to the 1979 Convention overcame these shortcomings and built upon its achievements.

Mr. Dieter Jost started his "work for the Convention" in 1974, when he was a delegate of the Federal Republic of Germany during the early deliberations on a regional agreement. He was subsequently involved in the preparation and negotiation of all the Convention's protocols. Mr Jost currently chairs the Expert Group on Heavy Metals that is preparing for the review of the Protocol on Heavy Metals. The photograph shows Mr. Jost (second from the left) at the second meeting of the Expert Group meeting held in April 2004 in Brussels.

The North American connection perceived by a Canadian

Hans Martin

Throughout the history of the Convention on Long-range Transboundary air Pollution, Canada has welcomed the opportunities to play an active part in the work of the Convention. From the start, during the UNECE negotiations as a response to the Conference on Security and Cooperation in Europe, Canada supported the Scandinavian countries in their insistence that the environmental response be an international convention on transboundary air pollution. Its results could be of value in the bilateral context as well. In this way the Convention also had an indirect impact on North American bilateral relations.

In the late 1970s, acid rain moved from being a concern of a few environmental scientists to a political issue in Canada. Studies by environmental ministries and agencies and many universities had shown that sources in the United States and in eastern Canada were significantly contributing to acid deposition on the sensitive Canadian Shield, and in parts of the north-eastern United Sates. Acid rain damage was being observed in the Muskoka and Haliburton lakes areas of Ontario, in southern Quebec, in much of northern New York State and New England, and as far east as Nova Scotia. On the domestic front, an intense debate was evolving among the federal Government, provincial governments and large industrial emitters. The issues included the level of risk, accountability and responsibility. The focus was primarily on eastern Canada.

In 1978, the United States passed legislation authorizing negotiation of a bilateral acid rain control agreement. Negotiations were to be conducted under a memorandum of intent (MOI) on transboundary air pollution, signed in August 1980. The MOI noted that one of the justifications for such action was the fact that both countries had signed the UNECE Convention on Long-range Transboundary Air Pollution. The technical reports of the MOI were released in February 1983 and confirmed the seriousness of the problem.

Hans Martin became involved in science and policy aspects of acid rain in 1979. He worked for the Canadian Government as a senior scientific adviser and then as director of the Federal air-quality research laboratory until 1995. He participated in many Convention meetings.

In the 1980-82 period, Canadian Ministers and scientists lobbied extensively in the United States for the implementation of a control programme based largely on the agreed bilateral MOI reports. Unfortunately, the time was not yet ripe for an agreement on emission reductions. Both countries faced a significant uphill challenge to confirm the science and convince policy makers of the need to take action and ensure that any adopted control programme would have the desired effect. The United States undertook a 10-year research programme, the National Acid Precipitation Assessment Program (NAPAP), to confirm and elaborate upon the scientific findings. Meanwhile in Canada, since the provinces have the main responsibility for pollution control, two senior-level federal-provincial committees were established, one to continue scientific exchanges and the other to negotiate a domestic emission-control programme.

As progress on negotiating a bilateral acid rain agreement lagged, Canada took the lead - in the context of the Convention – in creating the so-called "30% Club" with the aim of seeking commitments for initial sulphur emission reductions of this magnitude from as many UNECE countries as possible. It was hoped that the United States would join as well. Subsequently, in Ottawa in March 1984, Canada hosted a meeting of nine West European and Canadian Ministers to commit their countries as members of the 30% Club. This 30% emission reduction target was consistent with an earlier Nordic proposal on sulphur emissions reductions in the UNECE context.

The 30% sulphur emission reduction received even broader support at the Munich Multilateral Environment Conference (June 1984), where East European Ministers, in particular from the Soviet Union, gave general support to a 30% reduction of emissions or their transboundary fluxes.

By this time, the Executive Body had established a working group under the Convention to negotiate a formal agreement on sulphur emissions reductions. Negotiations under the chairmanship of Mr. Jim Bruce (Canada) were somewhat difficult until Mr. Sokolovsky (USSR) and his Eastern bloc colleagues agreed, at the last minute, to an emission reduction programme. This paved the way for the Helsinki Sulphur Protocol of July 1985, which contained the initial 30% reduction targets. Canada and 18 other Parties to the Convention signed the Protocol while others, including the United Kingdom, Poland and the United States, did not. At home Canada's emission reduction plan was being put in place with federal-provincial negotiations.

In the autumn of 1985, Canada hosted a major international acid rain conference in Muskoka, attended by nearly 700 scientists. The proceedings of that conference, published in the scientific literature, were a benchmark in the scientific understanding of acid rain. Also in 1985, President Reagan met with Prime Minister Mulroney at a summit in Quebec City. While not the prime focus of discussion, the meeting did re-emphasize the need to address acid rain.

In 1985-1987 federal-provincial agreements were signed to cut eastern Canadian sulphur dioxide (SO_2) emissions in half by 1994, using 1980 levels as the starting point. This programme targeted major smelting facilities and coal-burning power plants in the seven eastern-most provinces.

For its part, the United States decided to act on the acid rain issue with the Clean Air Act Amendment of 1990. It set a target 40% below 1980 emissions, or an annual 10 million ton reduction with a mandatory cap on emissions from major point source emissions of SO_2 and established an innovative emissions trading programme. In 1991, Canada and the United States signed the Air Quality Agreement. This bilateral Agreement focused on acid rain and commitments to reduce SO_2 and nitrogen oxides (NO_x), the primary precursors of acid rain. The two countries also signed and ratified the 1988 NO_x Protocol, which also contributed to reducing acid rain.

Throughout this period, the Canadian scientific community participated, and in some areas provided leadership, in the technical and scientific work of the Convention's working groups, the International Cooperative Programmes and EMEP. Collaboration in atmospheric research and monitoring was particularly beneficial given the transboundary nature of the work of the Convention. In addition, the aquatic and terrestrial ecosystems in the two regions have many similarities. Collaboration was, and still is, an efficient and economical strategy to address environmental issues of regional, national and international dimensions.

However, it was not always "plain sailing" regarding Canada's participation in the Convention, which was essentially a pan-European body. Difficulties could have been anticipated in the critical area of common interest, the development of control protocols. The cause of the difficulty derives from geography, demographics and political boundaries. Aside from Canada, the Russian Federation and the United States, the UNECE region consists of smaller, high-population countries. In the late 1980s this difficulty became apparent. Consequently, during negotiations of the 1991 VOC Protocol, Canada proposed an approach that took into account the differences between the North American and the pan-European regions. This initiative was a significant policy development.

Earlier protocols routinely required emissions reductions on a national basis. However, nationwide, emission-reduction measures for air issues that are regional in nature may be inappropriate, particularly for geographically large countries. To overcome this Canada proposed that, in such situations, emission controls should be limited to those emission source areas found to be contributing to transboundary pollution. Provisions of this nature were adopted in relevant protocols thereafter. They even found their way in the 2000 Ozone Annex to the 1991 Canada/United States Air Quality Agreement.

During the preparation of this text, Messrs. Jim Bruce, Tom Brydges and Wayne Draper provided valuable assistance.

Thoughts about the dynamics behind the process: the role of externalities

Lars Björkbom

Externalities behind international treaties

International intergovernmental institutions are, indeed, special creatures. They have very little in common except that they all need to arrive at consensus solutions to achieve results that are instrumental to their purposes. Thus each institution has to be studied on its own merits and shortcomings. In comparison with most other international agreements to protect the environment, the

Convention on Long-range Transboundary Air Pollution has had a positive and observable impact on the state of the environment in the geographical area it covers.

There is today a relatively large literature analysing the reasons leading to this indisputable success, if measured by the large number of binding protocols negotiated and adopted under the Convention and the relatively good implementation performance of the obligations that Parties have bound themselves to achieve. Much of this literature has been mainly descriptive, but when problem-oriented approaches have been essayed, focus has in particular been on the interesting and successful interplay between science and policy-making, the organizational set up under the Convention, strategies and tactics used by different Parties or groups of Parties in the negotiating processes leading to the Convention and its protocols. Few reflections in this literature have been given to the impact of external, non-environmental, policy areas that may have guided Parties' behaviour under the Convention. But to what extent did security, trade, economic and perhaps even cultural and political considerations of Parties affected the process?

For a long time the importance of externalities has been underestimated or even disregarded, when authors have analysed the political dynamics of the process. It is understandable why these aspects have been belittled or neglected. For those involved directly in negotiations and competent to consider such aspects it has been a sensitive issue to enlarge upon at least before the process has been fully concluded (and that may take a rather long time) in order not to disturb the expected results or risk their own careers or the sensitivities of their political peers. For those studying the process from outside there will be difficulties to get access to relevant documentation. They mostly lack personal experiences that could throw light on the evasive interplay between different policy areas as assessed by different Parties over different times, when brought to action under the Convention.

Externalities behind the Convention

It is not possible to understand the politics leading to the Convention by considering environmental policy goals alone. It only makes sense if the elements and logic of the cold war are brought in. During most of the 1970s a policy of détente characterized the relationship between the two superpowers, the United States and the USSR, and their respective allies in the North Atlantic Treaty Organization (NATO) and the Warsaw Pact. The major symbol of this détente was the Conference for Security and Co-operation in Europe (CSCE) agreement in Helsinki in summer 1975, which could be seen as a belated peace treaty after the Second World War and a recognition of the geopolitical changes that took place in its aftermath. The countries involved agreed in the Final Act to cooperate in three areas ("baskets" as they were called during the negotiations), namely in armament control, human rights and economic affairs. In the last basket there was a sub-basket about cooperation on environmental issues, reflecting the growing concern among some of the signatories about the ongoing environmental degradation.

The implementation of the Final Act was, in spite of the superficial détente, a sluggish process and came almost to a standstill as détente turned into confrontational policies between East and West for reasons that are not considered here. Arms control negotiations were not considered worthwhile from either side. The Soviet side did not favour developments in human rights, and economic cooperation was also a non-starter. Both sides, however, were aware of the dangers of non-communication. When the Soviet Union in late 1975 proposed cooperation on the environment in UNECE (besides transport and energy) it was hardly because of its strong environmental views. And when Western and non-aligned governments responded favourably to the proposal, few of them were guided by urgent environmental objectives. Most likely, it was considered to be an area of cooperation that would pose little danger to the overall balance between the two power blocs and at the same time it could serve as the needed bridge or communication link between them. When Norway and Sweden proposed their priority, long-range transboundary air pollution, as a suitable subject matter for a convention, there was no major alternative proposal and it was therefore accepted. But a large majority of UNECE member States on both sides of the Iron Curtain saw to it that the negotiation would result in undemanding obligations.

Even efforts by the two proposing States to include a provision for possibilities to negotiate future protocols on reductions of air pollutants were defeated. Still, the required linkage between the two power blocs was established and some opportunities for future cooperative action were at least saved when the Convention was adopted. And that, as we all know, was used to an extent never imagined by its "founding fathers".

The 1985 Sulphur Protocol

The next phase which should be highlighted is the one that led to the surprising signing of the first substantive protocol, that on sulphur emissions reductions, by 21 Parties to the Convention in Helsinki in 1985. This process has been commented upon by many writers, who note that the 30% club and its successive enlargement from 1989 in Geneva via Ottawa and Münich (both in 1984) was a major promoter for the final Protocol.

There are, however, other developments which assisted in the process. In Geneva at the first meeting of the Executive Body in spring 1983, when the Convention came into force, the Nordic countries proposed that the Parties should negotiate an agreement on a 30% reduction of sulphur dioxide (SO2) emissions (or their transboundary fluxes) based on the emission values of 1980. Their intention was primarily to set the ball rolling. Support came hesitatingly from the Federal Republic of Germany (after a volte-face in its air pollution policy in 1982), the Netherlands, Switzerland, Austria and Canada. The Soviet bloc countries were initially against. How to declare their change in attitude soon thetreafter?

Consideration should be given to the overall political spectrum of the NATO/Warsaw Pact relationship at that time. This was the time of the first Reagan administration's very confrontational policy of trying to get the upper hand in the balance of power between West and East. Without going into the "raison d´être" of this policy and of that of the Soviet response, it resulted in the breakdown of the intermediate-range nuclear forces negotiations and the United States, with reluctant support from the United Kingdom, was pressing for the deployment of Pershing II missiles inter alia in the Federal Republic of Germany to counter the SS-20 missiles on the other side of the Iron Curtain. This met with fierce but understandable political reaction in the Federal Republic of Germany and elsewhere in Western Europe and of course in the Warsaw Pact countries, particularly among left wing and "green" political groups, which were also, in general, in favour of environmental protection policies.

When the United States and the United Kingdom reacted very negatively to the Nordic proposal, arguing (correctly) that there was no scientific justification for this reduction target, the Chairman of the Executive Body, Mr. Valentin Sokolovsky, then Vice-Minister of the Soviet Union's Ministry of the Environment, adjourned the meeting temporarily to consult other members of the Warsaw Pact countries. This happened when all or most delegations were still in the room and could overhear what was going on. The outcome of the consultations, with one exception, was to positively reserve their countries' positions for the time being. Why? Was this because of changed attitudes to the environmental objective in the Nordic proposal? It seems unlikely.

Most likely the Chairman and the countries which were allied to his country saw an opportunity to sow division in the NATO stand on the nuclear issue by appealing to the anti-deployment public opinion and its political spokesmen through a changed though moderate stand on anti-air pollution measures in Europe. A political settlement was reached in Munich in summer 1984, after a late evening consultation between the major powers from both sides of the Iron Curtain. How the arguments then ran has not been revealed, but it is difficult to believe that the 30% SO_2 reduction had suddenly convinced those who were involved in the consultations. The Nordic countries and some others rejoiced. The Norwegian delegate, Mr. Erik Lykke, concluded that this was the end of the tall stack policy.

Thereafter the negotiations on a sulphur protocol under Mr. Jim Bruce proceeded in Geneva without too many obstructions and in July 1985 the Protocol was signed, also by the Soviet Union. The United States and the United Kingdom, as well as some other countries did not sign. The Pershing II missiles were later deployed inter alia in the Federal Republic of Germany. Did the fact that the Soviet Union had by then got a new Secretary-General as head of the Communist Party, Mr. Gorbachov, play a role? In retrospect, his entering on the political scene was the beginning of change in East-West relations that later led to major upheavals in European geopolitics.

Mr. Lars Björkbom (left), Chairman of the Working Group on Strategies 1991-1999, with Mr. Henning Wuester and Mr. Lars Nordberg of the secretriat

The 1985 Helsinki Protocol came into force reasonably quickly and was well implemented by all Parties and also by some non-Parties by the 1993 deadline. To what extent the obligations in the Protocol propelled the implementation results is an intriguing matter to reflect on. Many countries could implement their obligations by switching to nuclear power and natural gas electricity generation based on planning and decisions long before the Convention. Also, the Protocol was negotiated after the effects of the major oil crises in the 1970s and thus without extra costs for the fulfilment of the obligations in the Protocol, although there were some exceptions. Others were "helped" by the downturn in economic activity and the industrial structural changes following the dissolution of the communist countries Council for Mutual Economic Assistance. The United Kingdom's ferocious resistance to the Protocol is an interesting case in point. Based on scientific and economic arguments, the UK turned later to support further reductions of sulphur emissions (the 1994 Oslo Protocol). Its resistance evaporated after the Government's showdown against the coal miners' union in 1986 and the decisions which could then be taken for deregulating the nationalized energy industry. This does not take away from the importance of the efforts to negotiate and adopt this and other international legally binding agreements in order to come to grips with common environmental problems, in this case to curb acid rain. Such processes are of immense educational and political value. But we have to remind ourselves that such a process does not take place in isolation from the overall pattern of international relations and that these relations often strongly influence the process, for better or for worse.

A Nordic reflection

Considering the Convention's history from a Nordic perspective, it is clear that the Nordic countries, at least those on the Fenno-Scandinavian peninsula, have been very favourably treated by the outcome of the 1985 Helsinki Protocol as well as other protocols, in particular those related to the abatement of acidification, eutrophication and tropospheric ozone. The countries' geographical positions downwind from densely populated and highly industrialized countries together with the poor buffering capacity of most of their soils, easily explains why these countries have pushed for far-reaching emission reductions and requested other countries to act.

The sparsely populated Nordic countries, although highly industrialized, are relatively well-endowed with water power (except Denmark) and a large part of their electricity demand is met by nuclear power generation (in Sweden and Finland). They have had relatively small emission reductions to offer the Convention's other Parties in their neighbourhood or further away in return. What they have been able to offer has been active and constructive inputs to make the negotiation processes effective and based on sound scientific developments by providing intellectual, financial and other support. One can well understand those delegations which have at times questioned the Nordic countries' dominating role in the processes, but it is surprising as well that this role has been so indulgently accepted by most delegations. Still, it has to be remembered that the Nordic countries, singly or as a group, have had little, overall political clout to push their interests towards, for them, the satisfactory or acceptable solutions; this has proved to be the case for all those countries in most of the protocols. That is why it has been necessary to highlight some of the external political forces which have helped to provide and sustain the dynamics of the Convention's process.

The Fifth Perception

Willem Kakebeeke

A common denominator, nothing more

On 16 March 1983 the Convention on Long-range Transboundary Air Pollution entered into force. The Convention contains a number of elements which have been developed at the international level during the 1960s and 1970s as a basis for international legally binding policy instruments.

Its preamble refers to principle 21 of the 1972 Stockholm Declaration of the United Nations Conference on the Human Environment. This principle expresses the common conviction that States have "the responsibility to ensure that activities within their jurisdiction or control do not cause damage to the environment of other States or of areas beyond the limits of national jurisdiction." The East European countries, which for political reasons did not attend the Conference, accepted its results at the United Nations General Assembly of that year.

Furthermore, the preamble refers to the Final Act of 1975 Helsinki Conference on Security and Co-operation in Europe. The Final Act includes a chapter on "Environment". It calls inter alia for cooperation to control air pollution and its effects, including long-range transport of air pollutants. It was at the instigation of Norway in particular that this notion was incorporated.

Less successful was the outcome of the negotiations on the Convention in respect of its "Fundamental Principles" (arts. 2-5). During the negotiations on the obligations to be undertaken by Parties to the Convention, which took place in the context of the Senior Advisers, the Nordic countries proposed concrete emission reductions. These proposals received some support from the USSR, but they were not acceptable to most of the Western countries. They did not believe that the Eastern side would fulfil concrete emission reduction obligations. A framework convention was therefore born. It included the general obligation that countries "shall endeavour to limit and, as far as possible, gradually reduce and prevent air pollution including long-range transboundary air pollution". To the regret of the Nordic countries, the Convention had no teeth. It could not be foreseen at that time that within a couple of years the situation would change completely.

For a time the emphasis of the Convention was mainly on scientific cooperation and information exchange. The Convention had incorporated EMEP, which had already made a start, in 1977, in the context of the Senior Advisers to UNECE Governments on Environmental Problems. On this issue earlier experience had been gained by West European countries under inter alia the OECD Programme on Long-range Transboundary Air Pollution (1972-1977). It was felt that there was a need to extend such a programme to the whole of Europe. Quite deliberately the Convention did not include an article on future protocols as a number of Western countries did not want to consider a possible extension to the scope of the Convention at that time.

Mr. L. Ginjaar, Minister of Environment, signs the Convention on behalf of the Netherlands. Mr. Kakebeeke, with moustache, stands behind the Minister

Thirty per cent sulphur emission reduction: it's a deal

Already at the time of the negotiations on the Convention damage to the environment became more and more evident. In particular the "discovery" of Waldsterben (forest dieback) in the Federal Republic of Germany brought about a complete turn about of that country and some other West European countries, with respect to their attitude towards the Convention. The entry into force of the Convention formed a useful basis for addressing acidification in that context. This momentum was maintained by holding a number of meetings at the level of environment ministers and of conferences of scientists and policy makers:

- Before the entry into force of the Convention, at the Stockholm Ministerial Conference on Acidification of the Environment (1982), the mainly Western Environment Ministers attending stated their interest in emission reduction measures for air pollutants, in particular sulphur dioxide. Large stacks used to achieve emission dispersion, which often led to long-distance transport, were considered an obsolete solution;
- Following the entry into force of the Convention, its independent managing organ, the Executive Body, was convened in June 1983. At the first meeting, chaired by Mr. V. Sokolovsky, there was a large measure of agreement on the need to reduce sulphur emissions. Proposals by Finland, Norway and Sweden (overall goal: 30 per cent reduction of sulphur emissions) and Austria, the Federal Republic of Germany and Switzerland on a "Common Strategy for the Implementation of the Convention" were presented. It was, however, not possible for the Executive Body to agree on a quantitative target for sulphur emission reductions or its transboundary fluxes. The need for a breakthrough was felt;
- The international symposium on "Acid Deposition, a Challenge for Europe" (Karlsruhe (Germany), September 1983) brought together scientists and policy makers from Europe and North America. The Chairman of the symposium Mr. L. Ginjaar, a former Environment Minister of the Netherlands, in his conclusions suggested developing a harmonized policy to define national emission levels over time e.g. 30 per cent in five years. This was in line with the proposals made by Finland, Norway and Sweden at the first meeting of Executive Body; and
- It was the Environment Ministers who pushed the issue to a political decision. This occurred in two stages. At the invitation of the Canadian Minister of Environment, nine West European countries (Austria, Denmark, United Kingdom, Federal Republic of Germany,

France, Netherlands, Norway, Sweden and Switzerland) were represented at the International Conference of Ministers on Acid Rain held in March 1984 in Ottawa. The Ministers agreed to reduce national annual sulphur emissions by at least 30 per cent as soon as possible and at the latest by 1993, using 1980 emission levels as a basis for the calculation of reductions. The so-called "30% Club" was born.

Before being invited to Ottawa the Netherlands had to prove that it could fulfil the 30% reduction commitment. In the past it had often insisted that its sulphur emission reduction achieved before 1980 should be counted as well.

It must have been satisfying for the three Nordic countries to see their long-time efforts rewarded. There was however a need to extend the support for a 30 per cent reduction, in particular to Eastern Europe. Therefore, the Federal Republic of Germany, becoming more and more aware of environmental damage by acidification, decided to hold the Multilateral Conference on the Environment at the ministerial level (Munich, June 1984). The outcome of the Ottawa Conference stimulated the results of the Munich Conference. In fact the USSR complained that it had not been invited to Canada. It claimed that already at that time it was in a position to subscribe to a 30 per cent reduction target, however not of sulphur emissions themselves but of their transboudary fluxes.

Transboundary Fluxes

The USSR could not accept reductions of sulphur emissions to be measured on the basis of the agreed EMEP grid. As Mr. Sokolovsky explains in his contribution to this book such emissions data could reveal the distribution of its industrial potential. Furthermore, secrecy conditioned by political and military considerations was at stake. For these reasons the concept of transboundary fluxes was introduced as an alternative.

Not all East European countries were inclined to follow the USSR in its preparedness to accept a reduction target. This became evident only later during the negotiations on a sulphur protocol. The timing of the Conference in Munich and the grave environmental situation were such that there was a political breakthrough in the attitude of most governments attending the Conference (all Parties and Signatories to the Convention had been invited). As a result the Executive Body of the Convention was invited to give priority in its activities to work on a specific agreement to reduce national sulphur emissions or their transboundary fluxes by 1993, taking into account that many countries had agreed to such reductions. It took a working group, mandated by the Executive Body (September 1984) and chaired by Mr. Jim Bruce (Canada) only half a year to prepare a specific agreement: the Sulphur Protocol to the Convention. This would become the second Protocol to the Convention, the first being the Protocol on the Long-term Financing of the Cooperative Programme for Monitoring and Evaluation of Long-range Transmission of Air Pollutants in Europe (EMEP) adopted in September 1984.

The Protocol on the Reduction of Sulphur Emissions or their Transboundary Fluxes by at least 30 per cent was adopted and signed by 21 countries, Parties to the Convention, in Helsinki in July 1985.

It entered into force on 2 September 1987. A number of important sulphur emission exporting countries like Czechoslovakia, Poland, the United Kingdom and the United States of America stayed outside the Protocol.

Did the Protocol matter?

Analysing the levels of sulphur emissions in Europe in 1993 the question arises to what extent the reductions achieved by that year can be attributed to the implementation of the obligations under the Sulphur Protocol by the Parties. The "Major Review of Strategies and Policies for Air Pollution Abatement" (ECE/EB.AIR/65, page 85, table 2) shows that all Parties to the Sulphur Protocol had achieved a 30% reduction or (much) more. All Parties together reduced their emissions by more than 50%. The reductions have been achieved on the one hand by national policies to implement the obligations under the Convention and the Protocol, and on the other by the application of cleaner technologies. Economic and industrial decline, inter alia due to the geopolitical changes in Europe at the end of the 1980s and 1990s, have in Eastern Europe acted additionally to achieve emission reductions. These developments have affected many countries, both Party and non-Party to the Protocol. This might explain how some non-Parties achieved emission reduction results comparable to those of the Parties. There is no doubt however that the wake-up call by Waldsterben in the beginning of the 1980s influenced government policies and stimulated industry to introduce cleaner technologies to reduce emissions of air pollutants throughout the UNECE region. More protocols on other pollutants were to follow.

The Convention and Sulphur Protocol: what made the difference?

To understand why it was not possible to agree on concrete reductions of sulphur emissions in the 1970s while six years later the Sulphur Protocol was adopted, one can apply the following criteria. These may be considered as prerequisites for successful completion of negotiations on international environmental agreements:

1. Is the relevant environmental issue addressed at the appropriate geographical level?
2. Does the international community recognize the environmental issue as warranting international action?
3. Is there a high level of international scientific consensus?
4. Is sufficient and accepted leadership available?
5. Compared to national measures, does international action add value?
6. Are measures to address the problem available and affordable?

Obviously, the Convention and the Protocol both address sulphur emissions at the continental scale. In the light of the possible transboundary impact of such emissions this seems fully appropriate. Also, there was strong evidence of environmental damage due to air pollution and the transboundary contribution to it. Nevertheless, quite a number of governments in the 1970s were not convinced that action was needed. This attitude changed considerably on the one hand through increased and internationally recognized scientific knowledge on the basis of research and monitoring in the 1980s and on the other through public and political pressure that was created by large-scale media attention.

Furthermore, the character of leadership changed considerably. In the 1970s there were two kinds of leadership, environmental (Nordic countries) and political (USSR) that proved to be a hurdle. It was met

with suspicion by most West European countries and the United States. At a later stage, environmental considerations came to the forefront when a number of West European countries joined the Nordic interest to combat air pollution. In the 1980s an increasing number of countries became aware that a purely national approach to combating acidification was not efficient or even possible. Transboundary air pollution contributes more than significantly to acidification of the environment and could even counter national measures in this field. This made international action profitable. And last, but not least, it was demonstrated that emissions of sulphur dioxide could be reduced to a large extent, and at reasonable cost, by flue gas desulphurization and fuel shifts.

A final remark

Reviewing the perceptions two major conclusions could be drawn. The first is that the Convention is really a fruit of the cold war. The Eastern and the Western blocs were clearly in need for some sort of détente and the only subject they could agree on was environment. Acidification as a transboundary problem became the subject of agreement although the same cold war problems prevented the Convention itself setting emission reductions. The second conclusion is that, despite better information on effects, science, measures and costs, it was the momentum created by the media on large-scale forest dieback that led to the first firm emission reductions in the first Sulphur Protocol.

EMEP - Backbone of the Convention

Toni Schneider and Jürgen Schneider

The Cooperative Programme for Monitoring and Evaluation of the Long-range Transmission of Air Pollutants in Europe (EMEP) is an essential part of the Convention on Long-range Transboundary Air Pollution (see box EMEP objectives). As the source of information on the emission, transport and deposition of air pollution, it has a major role to play in the establishment of air pollution protocols to the Convention.

EMEP objectives

The main objective of the programme is to provide Governments with information on the deposition and concentration of air pollutants, as well as on the quantity and significance of the long-range transmission of air pollutants and fluxes across boundaries.
Information on the relative importance of local and distant sources resulting from the programme will guide national authorities in setting appropriate local and regional permissible emission levels, taking into account the international implications of these levels. The information on the deposition and concentrations of air pollutants will be a basis for abatement strategies in the regions affected.

Outline

The first section of this chapter describes the conception and birth of EMEP. This is followed by an overview of its further development. The next section deals with the activities of the EMEP centres and task forces, including some results of recent EMEP activities. Finally, there is a brief look into the future.

Conception and birth of EMEP

In the early 1970s many bilateral and multilateral programmes on air pollution were started, e.g. Federal Republic of Germany/Netherlands, Nordic countries, Benelux countries, Organisation for Economic Co-operation and Development (OECD), United States/Canada. The development of modern air pollution monitors and the formulation of several types of transport models promoted the creation of many international expert meetings, working groups and measurement campaigns to obtain "comparable" monitoring and modelling results. Also ideas about large-scale monitoring networks with central data analysis were born. A large international exchange of expertise, experience and background information was started; that improved cooperation between research institutes and government policy groups.

Birth of the EMEP Steering Body

It is difficult to really pinpoint the beginning of the Steering Body of EMEP, but important meetings in this context were the expert meeting in Oslo, 3-5 December,1974, and even more important the two meetings of a task force in May and November 1976 (Chairman, Mr. Leslie Reed). This task force was established by the Working Party on Air Pollution Problems of the Senior Advisers to UNECE Governments on Environmental Problems. The task force had to develop a programme for monitoring and evaluation of the long-range transmission of air pollutants in the UNECE region. After approval of the mandate by the Senior Advisers, Mr. J. Stanovik, Executive Secretary of UNECE, opened the first session of the Steering Body on 31 August 1977.

Of course many informal discussions preceded the official first meeting of the Steering Body. A few difficult items were: the selection of the coordination centres; cooperation with the World Meteorological Organization (WMO) and the United Nations Environment Programme (UNEP); the status of Canada and the United States vs. participating European member countries; and last but not least the number of vice-chairmen in the Bureau of the Steering Body. Among several important items that were discussed at the first meeting was, as usual, the financing of the international activities. The national efforts of participating countries were covered nationally. UNEP financed (in part) the expenses of the Western coordinating centres, with separate funding for the Eastern meteorological centre. The first phase of EMEP was planned to cover 1978-1980. The number of bureau members was also solved: Mr. T. Schneider (Netherlands) was elected Chairman, Mr. D.J. Szepesi (Hungary), Mr. G. Persson (Sweden), Mr. A. Pressman (Union of Soviet Socialist Republics (USSR)) and Mr. L. Reed (United Kingdom) were elected Vice-Chairmen. Over the years a number of changes have taken place.

Major steps in the development of East-West cooperation were taken at an informal meeting in Oslo on 23-24 November 1978 at the invitation of the Minister of the Environment, Ms. Gro Harlem Brundtland. Nevertheless modelling exercises remained difficult, as is shown by one of the final statements:
"It was stated by the delegate of the USSR that according to present plans, the dispersion of pollutants within the USSR will be calculated by the Meteorological Synthesising Centre-East (MSC-E). MSC-E is planning to provide the Meteorological Synthesising Centre-West (MSC-W) with transboundary flux data towards the west across the USSR border. The flux data will be given as vertically integrated quantities for line segments of 150 km along the border. Time resolution will be 6 hours or better. Calculated fluxes will be broken down into those due to indigenous emissions in the USSR and those due to emissions in other specified countries. Flux data on both sulphur dioxide and particulate sulphate will be provided. Similar data of pollutants from Western Europe towards the East will be provided by the MSC-W. Appropriate ways for exchanging the flux data would be through the WMO telecommunication network."
Luckily, the mechanism was made simpler in later years.

Further development of EMEP

The reports of the Chemical Coordination Centre (CCC), MSC-W and MSC-E certainly had some teething troubles. This was not so much due to insufficient work in the centres, but was caused by late or incomplete reports of the coordinating laboratories in the participating countries. A major improvement followed after rigorous round-robin exercises that produced more comparable measurement results. This improvement in measurements and technical know-how was also enhanced by the visits to the monitoring sites in the participating countries by experts from CCC, although in the early days it was difficult to get permission from some (former) Eastern-bloc countries to visit their sites. Some of the monitoring sites were located in remote areas (figure 3.1).

Figure 3.1. An EMEP monitoring site in Finland

Modelling

Of course not only the physical measurements also the modelling activities met with some problems. In the MSC reports over the years, hundreds of different graphs and tables presented the results from modelling activities. Although proof of transboundary air pollution was available, e.g. the undeniable transport of oxidized sulphur from the Ruhr area in Germany towards the Netherlands if the wind blew in that direction, the actual separation of local (national) deposition and imported deposition on such a large scale (Europe) was calculated for the first time within the EMEP structure. These results were made available in different forms, but the most impressive one was, and still is, the source-receptor matrices.

In the early days of EMEP many countries (their political/policy authorities) had reservations. After many discussions and explanations however, this approach was accepted and is now widely used.

Using such data it is possible to show how much of country's own emissions fall with its territory (table 3.1). It is also possible to show the transboundary fluxes from a selected country, in this illustrative case for Austrian emissions of NOx in 2002, to other regions (e.g. figure 3.2); corresponding figures are available for all countries in the EMEP region.

Table 3.1. Source-receptor relationships for sulphur (in 100 tonnes of S) for 2000
Source: EMEP Status Report 2003.

	Albania	Armenia	Austria	Bosnia and Herc.	Belgium	Bulgaria	Belarus	Stitzerland	Cyprus	Czech Republic	Germany	Denmark	Estonia	Spain	Finland	France	UK	Georgia	Greece	Croatia	Hungary	Ireland	Iceland	Italy
Albania	68	0	0	14	0	36	0	0	0	1	2	0	0	5	0	3	1	0	40	1	5	0	0	28
Armenia	0	12	0	1	0	2	0	0	1	0	0	0	0	0	0	0	0	1	1	0	0	0	0	1
Austria	1	0	60	16	6	11	0	5	0	28	105	0	0	28	0	27	13	0	3	13	35	1	0	102
Bosnia and Herc.	4	0	2	373	1	21	0	0	0	7	9	0	0	18	0	10	2	0	9	18	23	0	0	63
Belgium	0	0	0	0	139	0	0	0	0	1	30	0	0	25	0	79	41	0	0	0	1	2	0	3
Bulgaria	13	0	1	42	1	861	1	0	0	7	10	0	0	11	0	6	3	0	57	5	33	0	0	36
Belarus	2	0	2	31	5	58	247	1	1	31	47	2	7	17	4	16	21	0	10	6	61	1	0	24
Switzerland	0	0	1	1	4	1	0	27	0	1	19	0	0	42	0	46	10	0	1	1	1	1	0	57
Cyprus	0	0	0	0	0	1	0	0	10	0	0	0	0	0	0	0	0	0	1	0	0	0	0	1
Czech Republic	0	0	15	12	8	3	0	2	0	244	139	1	0	18	0	25	20	0	2	6	57	1	0	28
Germany	1	0	11	13	167	7	1	19	0	114	1620	5	0	156	0	333	249	0	3	6	23	12	0	75
Denmark	0	0	0	1	12	1	1	0	0	6	49	14	0	18	1	19	53	0	0	0	3	4	2	2
Estonia	1	0	1	6	3	4	5	0	0	5	14	1	30	5	4	6	7	0	1	1	9	1	0	5
Spain	0	0	0	3	3	3	0	0	0	1	5	0	0	1842	0	39	21	0	2	1	2	2	0	20
Finland	1	0	1	18	9	14	12	1	0	18	46	3	56	17	117	18	41	0	4	3	26	2	0	14
France	0	0	1	11	54	7	0	7	0	7	101	0	0	922	0	1075	163	0	3	4	6	16	0	112
UK	0	0	0	1	18	1	0	0	0	2	20	1	0	72	0	70	1310	0	0	0	2	65	0	4
Georgia	0	3	0	2	0	6	0	0	1	0	0	0	0	1	0	0	0	8	2	0	1	0	0	2
Greece	30	0	1	30	1	283	1	0	0	4	7	0	0	12	0	6	2	0	428	3	18	0	0	46
Croatia	2	0	3	100	1	18	0	0	0	7	11	0	0	19	0	11	3	0	5	66	25	0	0	74
Hungary	2	0	9	95	2	28	1	1	0	24	28	0	0	17	0	14	7	0	9	32	248	0	0	59
Ireland	0	0	0	0	2	0	0	0	0	0	3	0	0	12	0	5	58	0	0	0	0	154	0	0
Iceland	0	0	0	0	0	0	0	0	0	0	1	0	0	5	0	1	8	0	0	0	0	1	15	0
Italy	9	0	5	74	5	47	1	5	0	10	31	0	0	139	0	95	16	0	41	29	22	2	0	1125
Kazakhstan	2	1	1	17	2	44	8	0	1	7	11	0	3	8	2	6	6	2	9	3	20	0	0	14
Lithuania	0	0	1	9	3	9	13	0	0	12	23	1	2	7	1	7	13	0	2	2	15	1	0	7
Luxembourg	0	0	0	0	4	0	0	0	0	0	4	0	0	3	0	8	2	0	0	0	0	0	0	1
Latvia	0	0	1	8	3	8	12	0	0	8	19	2	6	6	2	6	11	0	2	2	13	1	0	6
Republic of Moldova	1	0	0	12	0	38	1	0	0	3	5	0	0	4	0	2	2	0	7	1	13	0	0	7
The FYR of Macedonia	23	0	0	11	0	51	0	0	0	1	2	0	0	4	0	2	1	0	33	1	6	0	0	13
Netherlands	0	0	0	1	76	0	0	0	0	2	41	0	0	20	0	45	72	0	0	0	1	2	0	3
Norway	0	0	0	4	17	4	2	0	0	11	64	7	4	32	4	30	133	0	1	1	11	6	0	5
Poland	4	0	11	64	24	34	13	3	0	201	283	8	2	40	2	58	83	0	13	17	192	5	0	55
Portugal	0	0	0	0	0	0	0	0	0	0	0	0	0	79	0	3	3	0	0	0	0	0	0	0
Romania	11	0	4	159	3	306	3	1	0	26	37	0	0	32	0	19	11	0	47	17	180	0	0	83
Russian Federation	16	6	14	193	33	414	233	4	5	138	245	9	224	113	105	108	153	17	87	32	317	9	1	158
Sweden	3	0	3	24	23	27	10	2	0	35	130	22	13	40	24	47	107	0	8	5	50	5	1	22
Slovenia	1	0	4	12	1	9	0	0	0	2	8	0	0	9	0	5	1	0	2	21	8	0	0	53
Slovakia	1	0	7	33	2	13	0	1	0	35	24	0	0	9	0	8	6	0	5	11	254	0	0	26
Turkey	10	6	2	36	2	285	7	1	37	9	15	1	1	21	1	11	7	5	148	5	32	1	0	63
Ukraine	10	1	6	139	9	359	64	2	2	66	87	2	6	50	4	35	36	1	61	21	255	2	0	98
Yugoslavia	21	0	2	206	1	79	1	0	0	11	14	0	0	17	0	10	4	0	22	12	62	0	0	64
Baltic Sea	2	0	4	39	32	36	16	1	0	61	217	26	45	47	33	62	113	0	10	9	76	5	0	38
North Sea	0	0	2	7	132	6	2	1	0	29	262	17	1	209	1	288	1638	0	3	2	13	60	2	26
Remaining N.E. Atlantic	1	0	2	30	62	25	14	1	0	39	185	9	35	1467	43	233	1116	0	7	7	55	269	104	42
Mediterranean Sea	74	1	15	315	14	705	5	7	80	45	85	2	2	784	1	296	56	1	836	66	125	4	1	1346
Black Sea	10	1	3	65	3	392	12	1	3	17	30	1	2	18	1	13	11	3	68	9	61	1	0	52
Other	48	11	9	172	17	653	28	3	109	47	67	3	38	1255	17	90	191	5	662	14	67	21	8	552
Tot. emissions	372	42	204	2400	904	4910	714	96	250	1323	4155	137	477	7675	367	3296	5825	43	2655	453	2427	657	134	4615

	Kazakhstan	Lithuania	Luxembourg	Latvia	Republic of Mold.	The FYR of Mac.	Netherlands	Norway	Poland	Portugal	Romania	Russian Fed.	Sweden	Slovenia	Slovakia	Turkey	Ukraine	Yugoslavia	Baltic Sea	North Sea	Rem. N.E. Atl.	Med. Sea	Black Sea	Other	Tot. depositon
Albania	0	0	0	0	0	21	0	0	5	1	13	1	0	1	1	6	3	17	0	0	1	22	0	28	324
Armenia	1	0	0	0	0	0	0	0	1	0	1	2	0	0	0	104	2	0	0	0	0	2	0	54	186
Austria	0	0	0	0	0	1	3	0	29	3	14	2	0	65	7	3	2	15	1	6	4	20	0	35	664
Bosnia and Herc.	0	0	0	0	5	0	0	17	2	14	2	0	6	3	3	3	61	0	1	2	30	0	38	747	
Belgium	0	0	1	0	0	0	16	0	4	3	0	0	0	0	0	0	0	0	1	34	5	2	0	9	396
Bulgaria	0	0	0	0	1	47	0	0	36	1	265	6	0	4	7	28	33	69	1	1	1	23	5	69	1684
Belarus	1	18	0	5	2	5	2	1	384	2	88	49	3	7	18	20	115	31	15	8	3	11	3	69	1454
Switzerland	0	0	0	0	0	0	1	0	2	4	0	0	0	1	0	0	0	1	0	4	4	15	0	23	268
Cyprus	0	0	0	0	0	0	0	0	0	0	0	0	0	0	0	20	0	0	0	0	0	4	0	6	43
Czech Republic	0	0	0	0	0	1	3	0	157	2	12	1	0	15	17	2	2	11	2	8	3	8	0	20	845
Germany	0	1	6	0	0	1	82	1	174	16	11	3	2	10	6	2	3	10	36	135	30	31	0	87	3462
Denmark	0	0	0	0	0	0	8	1	23	2	1	7	1	0	0	0	0	1	31	36	6	1	0	383	687
Estonia	0	5	0	4	0	1	1	1	42	1	9	14	2	1	2	2	8	5	19	4	1	2	0	15	248
Spain	0	0	0	0	0	0	1	0	2	221	1	0	0	1	0	0	0	2	0	6	109	105	0	131	2523
Finland	1	10	0	6	1	2	5	4	131	2	26	173	19	4	7	5	27	17	69	15	5	5	0	77	1032
France	0	0	2	0	0	1	14	0	18	75	2	0	0	4	1	0	1	5	2	121	120	120	0	188	3163
UK	0	0	0	0	0	0	8	0	10	10	1	1	1	0	0	0	0	1	2	143	74	5	0	95	1917
Georgia	1	0	0	0	0	0	0	0	3	0	5	8	0	0	0	155	10	1	0	0	0	3	2	62	276
Greece	0	0	0	0	0	42	0	0	21	1	81	6	0	2	4	41	22	32	1	1	1	72	3	88	1290
Croatia	0	0	0	0	0	2	0	0	13	2	11	1	0	16	3	3	2	39	0	1	1	32	0	23	494
Hungary	0	0	0	0	0	4	1	0	65	2	59	2	0	23	32	3	6	86	1	2	2	21	0	33	918
Ireland	0	0	0	0	0	0	1	0	2	2	0	0	0	0	0	0	0	0	0	7	22	1	0	38	307
Iceland	0	0	0	0	0	0	0	0	1	0	0	1	0	0	0	0	0	0	0	1	4	0	0	40	78
Italy	0	0	0	0	0	8	2	0	26	15	25	2	0	27	4	11	6	35	1	6	11	237	1	318	2391
Kazakhstan	108	2	0	0	1	3	1	0	50	1	51	222	1	3	5	120	146	16	2	2	1	8	3	226	1139
Lithuania	0	36	0	2	0	1	1	0	147	1	16	17	2	2	4	2	12	9	14	5	1	3	0	19	422
Luxembourg	0	0	2	0	0	0	0	0	1	0	0	0	0	0	0	0	0	0	0	1	0	0	0	1	27
Latvia	0	20	0	17	0	1	1	1	86	1	14	13	2	2	3	3	11	7	17	5	1	3	0	18	342
Republic of Mol.	0	0	0	0	9	2	0	0	23	1	82	4	0	1	3	9	30	12	1	1	1	6	2	12	295
The FYR of Mac.	0	0	0	0	61	0	0	5	0	15	1	0	0	1	4	4	19	0	0	0	8	0	22	288	
Netherlands	0	0	0	0	0	0	84	0	5	2	0	0	0	0	0	0	0	0	1	63	5	1	0	13	437
Norway	0	2	0	1	0	0	10	37	62	3	8	59	12	1	2	1	5	4	26	58	17	3	0	96	743
Poland	0	5	0	1	1	6	11	2	2269	5	75	20	6	25	59	5	50	57	49	33	8	20	1	78	3898
Portugal	0	0	0	0	0	0	0	0	0	329	0	0	0	0	0	0	0	0	0	1	45	7	0	21	488
Romania	0	1	0	0	4	24	1	0	154	5	1209	15	0	13	31	26	92	218	2	4	3	44	6	122	2913
Russian Fed.	147	60	0	28	10	31	16	8	1126	13	577	4899	34	36	83	763	1682	186	128	53	26	84	29	1410	14063
Sweden	2	10	1	4	1	4	15	15	276	5	42	68	112	7	13	9	36	22	149	57	13	9	2	97	1570
Slovenia	0	0	0	0	0	1	0	0	4	1	5	1	0	47	1	2	1	9	0	1	1	12	0	9	231
Slovakia	0	0	0	0	0	2	1	0	116	1	33	1	0	13	96	2	5	32	1	2	1	8	0	22	771
Turkey	3	2	0	1	2	16	1	1	55	2	135	55	1	5	7	4136	140	38	3	3	2	156	32	773	6275
Ukraine	7	9	0	2	17	22	4	1	612	7	549	153	4	19	74	187	1449	143	17	12	6	57	25	237	4929
Yugoslavia	0	0	0	0	0	137	0	0	40	2	77	3	0	6	9	7	10	348	1	1	2	31	1	66	1167
Baltic Sea	0	21	0	11	0	3	16	3	500	5	51	59	40	10	17	10	37	32	419	59	11	14	1	96	2287
North Sea	0	1	1	0	0	1	86	17	106	24	5	5	9	3	2	0	2	5	42	1058	117	17	0	287	4489
Rem. N.E. Atl	2	6	0	3	0	3	33	36	227	441	40	916	26	9	13	6	48	27	56	237	2861	69	0	7416	16221
Mediterranean Sea	2	2	0	1	2	74	6	1	144	73	284	31	2	47	26	1063	99	176	7	20	69	3121	20	1206	11342
Black Sea	4	3	0	1	5	22	1	0	123	2	364	110	1	9	14	486	382	72	5	4	2	47	127	135	2696
Other	434	2	2	3	5	71	20	1	258	584	289	3053	8	35	25	3309	524	64	20	48	901	1444	21		
Tot. emissions	713	216	15	90	61	526	456	131	7555	1875	4560	9986	288	480	600	10558	5010	1935	1142	2268	4503	5944	284		

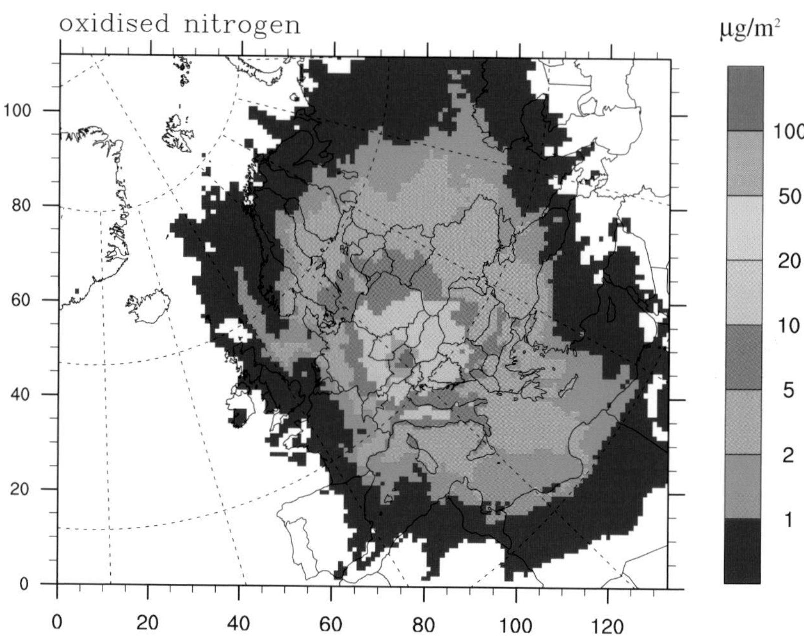

FIGURE 3.2. CONTRIBUTION OF AUSTRIAN NOx EMISSIONS TO THE DEPOSITION OF OXIDISED NITROGEN IN EUROPE, CALCULATED FOR 2002
SOURCE: MSC-W

Language problems

Next to the physical visits to the sites that caused some problems, the centres had to cope with language translation problems. UNECE "protocol" required translation of reports into the three official languages: English, French and Russian. In the meetings of the Steering Body the official representatives of participating countries were mostly accompanied by the official representatives of embassies or consulates that took care of official political notes. The Steering Body succeeded in convincing the higher official levels that this was, as far as technical reports were concerned, counterproductive. As a result it was agreed that technical reports would be in English only.

Exit of the Permanent Representatives

It was not only the content of the reports of the coordinating centres that caused problems in the early days of the Steering Body. The approval of the reports of the Steering Body's meetings themselves also caused difficulties. It is standard practice that reports of UNECE meetings are translated into English, French and Russian before discussion and approval. The majority of the expert-oriented members of the Steering Body, including the Bureau, found this a "waste of time" and were willing to accept final conclusions and recommendations in English only. After a series of formal confrontations with the Permanent Representatives of several participating countries, the argument was won that in this case expert content was more relevant than diplomatic/political nicities. Looking back one can conclude that this new procedure (for UNECE) did not harm the results obtained within EMEP, nor the use made of them within the framework of the Convention.

Meetings of the Bureau of the Steering Body

Official Bureau meetings started a fruitful cooperation between the coordination centres, away from the more diplomatic and politically correct discussions and presentations that were staged in the early days of the Steering Body. After a number of meetings the discussions in the Bureau became solution-finding exchanges among experts, who became "old friends". Undoubtedly, this was also encouraged by unofficial meetings of the Bureau.

Unofficial Bureau meetings

Once the initial political hesitation was left behind, the members of the Bureau met with the experts of the coordination centres on a regular basis at the time of the Geneva meetings but outside the UN buildings. This was mostly in the hotel frequented by the Soviet MSC-E members. Using the spiritual enhancement of a first-class vodka, open and friendly discussions found solutions to overcome the political difficulties raised in the official circuit. A close friendly network developed over the years, acknowledging each other's expertise and demonstrating a willingness to reach a joint successful result.

Currently, the EMEP Steering Body meets once a year to critically assess the implementation of the current activities and discuss the future work-plan and financial issues. The extended Bureau (consisting of the chairperson of the EMEP Steering Body, the vice-chairpersons, representatives from the EMEP centres and the chairpersons of the task forces) meets twice a year and provides guidance to the work of the centres and prepares the sessions of the Steering Body.

Financial Matters

In its early days, apart from nationally funded activities, the international coordination work needed financial support for the coordinating centres. This was provided by the Nordic countries and USSR. Voluntary contributions from several participating countries also sustained the EMEP activities. UNEP contributions supported EMEP in the first and second phase. In the later phases of EMEP a fairer financing scheme was adopted through the first protocol to the Convention, adopted in September 1984. After many intensive discussions in special ad hoc groups with unrelenting diplomatic activity a contribution scheme was accepted based on the UN scale of assessment. This scale has been updated at regular intervals and provides the basis for sharing contributions to the budget of the centres (see table 3.3).

Table 3.3. Mandatory EMEP contributions for 2004 calculated on the basis of the 2003 United Nations scale of assessment (updated annex referred to in article 4 of the 1984 EMEP Protocol).

Parties	UN 2003 assessment rate (in %)	EMEP share (%)	EMEP scale of contributions (%)	2004 contribution (US $)
Belarus	0.019	0.0441	0.0442	950
Bosnia and Herzegovina	0.004	0.0093	0.0093	200
Bulgaria	0.013	0.0302	0.0303	650
Canada	2.558	voluntary	voluntary	voluntary
Croatia	0.039	0.0906	0.0908	1,950
Cyprus	0.038	0.0883	0.0885	1,900
Czech Republic	0.203	0.4716	0.4727	10,130
Estonia	0.01	0.0232	0.0233	500
Hungary	0.12	0.2788	0.2794	5,990
Latvia	0.01	0.0232	0.0233	500
Liechtenstein	0.006	0.0139	0.014	300
Malta	0.015	0.0348	0.0349	750
Monaco	0.004	0.0093	0.0093	200
Norway	0.646	1.5007	1.5041	32,240
Poland	0.378	0.8781	0.8801	18,860
Romania	0.058	0.135	0.135	2,890
Russian Federation	1.2	2.7877	2.794	59,890
Serbia and Montenegro	0.02	0.0465	0.0466	1,000
Slovakia	0.043	0.0999	0.1001	2,150
Slovenia	0.081	0.1882	0.1886	4,040
Switzerland	1.274	2.9596	2.9663	63,580
Turkey	0.44	1.0221	1.0245	21,960
Ukraine	0.053	0.1231	0.1234	2,640
United States	22	voluntary	voluntary	voluntary
Austria	0.947	2.1999	2.205	47,260
Belgium	1.129	2.6227	2.6287	56,340
Denmark	0.749	1.74	1.7439	37,380
Finland	0.522	1.2126	1.2154	26,050
France	6.466	15.0209	15.0552	322,680
Germany	9.769	22.694	22.7457	487,520
Greece	0.539	1.2521	1.255	26,900
Ireland	0.294	0.683	0.6845	14,670
Italy	5.06475	11.7657	11.7926	252,760
Luxembourg	0.08	0.1858	0.1863	3,990
Netherlands	1.738	4.0375	4.0467	86,730
Portugal	0.462	1.0733	1.0757	23,060
Spain	2.51875	5.8512	5.8646	125,700
Sweden	1.02675	2.3852	2.3906	51,240
United Kingdom	5.536	12.8604	12.8898	276,270
European Community		3.33	3.3376	71,540
Total		**99.7723**	**100**	**2,143,350**
Parties to the Convention not Party to the EMEP Protocol				
Armenia	0.002	0.005	n/a	n/a
Azerbaijan	0.004	0.009	n/a	n/a
Georgia	0.005	0.012	n/a	n/a
Iceland	0.033	0.077	n/a	n/a
Kazakhstan	0.028	0.065	n/a	n/a
Kyrgyzstan	0.001	0.002	n/a	n/a
Lithuania	0.017	0.039	n/a	n/a
Republic of Moldova	0.002	0.005	n/a	n/a
The FYR of Macedonia	0.006	0.014	n/a	n/a
Total (excl. Canada and USA)	**41.61325**	**100**		

The computer that travelled from West to East

Detailed transport models use up a lot of calculation power. In the early days of EMEP, MSC-E did not have sufficient hardware available. The bureau asked for international support to obtain some convertible currency in the budget of MSC-E. After some quiet and some not so quiet diplomacy, a relatively small part in the budget was changed from non-convertible into convertible currency. At that time it seemed that the exchange of model calculations results would be obtained by the purchase of a modern portable computer in the West. No direct solution was available however, due to the export restrictions of the United States. It seems unbelievable nowadays, but after some serious multilateral diplomatic discussions and negotiations a solution was found, and finally a modern computer travelled from West to East.

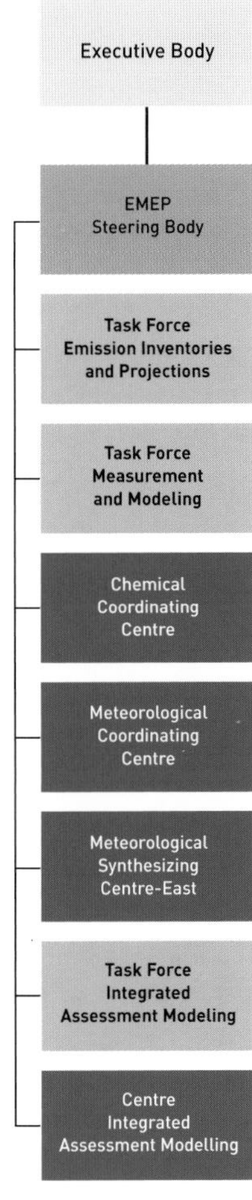

Figure 3.3. EMEP structure in 2004

Coordinating centres in EMEP

The operation of the programme at the international level was designed to be carried out in two parts; one dealing with the chemical activities (monitoring) and the other with the meteorological activities (modelling). CCC at the Norwegian Institute for Air Research (NILU) is responsible for the coordination of the chemical measurement and analysis part of the programme. Two Meteorological Synthesizing Centres in different parts of Europe, one Western centre (MSC-W) at the Norwegian Meteorological Institute and one Eastern centre (MSC-E) at the Hydrometeorological Service in Moscow, are responsible for the final evaluation of the meteorological data, both working in close cooperation with CCC. Recently, the Centre for Integrated Assessment Modelling (CIAM) at the International Institute for Applied Systems Analysis (IIASA) was also incorporated into EMEP (see chapter 6). Currently EMEP has four centres and three task forces (figure 3.3). The centres and task forces report annually to the Steering Body, which in turn reports each year to the Executive Body of the Convention.

Chemical Coordinating Centre

Most of the work to coordinate the monitoring of air pollution concentrations and depositions is carried out at CCC. The programme also relies strongly on the active participation of the Parties that are running the monitoring sites. In EMEP, concentrating on regional-scale concentrations and depositions, data quality and comparability have always been of the utmost importance. The cornerstones of the quality assurance work in EMEP are, for example: providing written guidance on sampling and analysis and quality assurance; carefully verifying data submitted by the Parties; laboratory intercomparisons and field intercomparison campaigns, where participating institutes perform measurements at one place over one time period. An example of EMEP monitoring data is shown in figure 3.4. All observational data submitted to CCC are assessed, published, stored in a database and made freely available for national and international applications, including those outside EMEP.

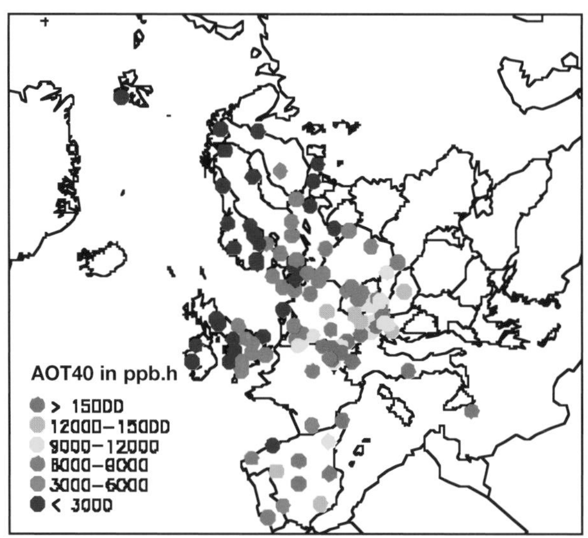

Figure 3.4. Ozone AOT40 (this is an indicator for effects of ozone on crops) in 2001

Source: CCC

Meteorological Synthesizing Centre-East

MSC-E is currently responsible for the atmospheric modelling of heavy metals and persistent organic pollutants (POPs). This is a challenging tasks. For example, POPs comprise a large number of different compounds, with different chemical and physical properties. However, they all have a high toxicity, they are transported over large distances, they may accumulate in different environmental media like soils, the marine environment etc. and they can be found almost everywhere on the globe, including in regions like the Arctic far away from sources. Consequently, the model must not only cover the atmospheric transport of POPs adequately, but also needs to simulate the behaviour of those substances in other media for example in soil and seawater. POPs are modelled separately by MSC-E (e.g. figure 3.5).

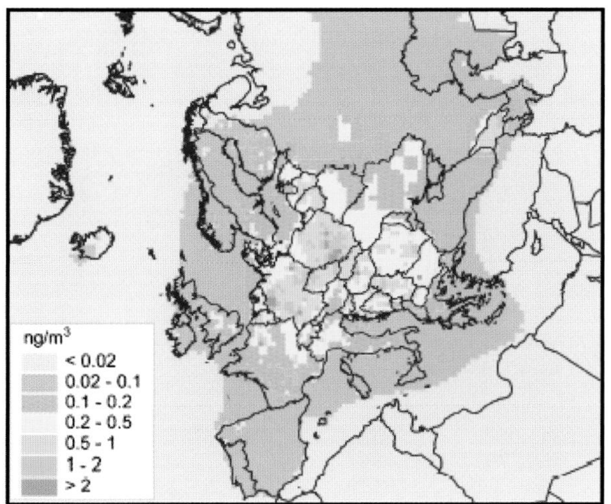

Figure 3.5. Air concentrations of benzo[a]pyrene, a carcinogenic substance, in 2000

Source: MSC-E

Meteorological Synthesizing Centre-West

MSC-W has two main responsibilities. The first is modelling acidifying and eutrophying pollutants, ozone and particulate matter. In addition, MSC-W maintains a database of the emissions data that are reported by Parties to the UNECE secretariat. For many years,

MSC-W relied on its Lagrangian model to simulate air pollution transport over Europe. Recently, this model was replaced by a Eulerian model, which is currently running with a spatial resolution of 50 km * 50 km. A review of this new model in 2003 confirmed the high quality of the work done within EMEP; the review concluded that there was currently no better regional European dispersion model. As an example of the model output work, total deposition of (acidifying) sulphur is shown in figure 3.6 for two years: 1980 and 2000.

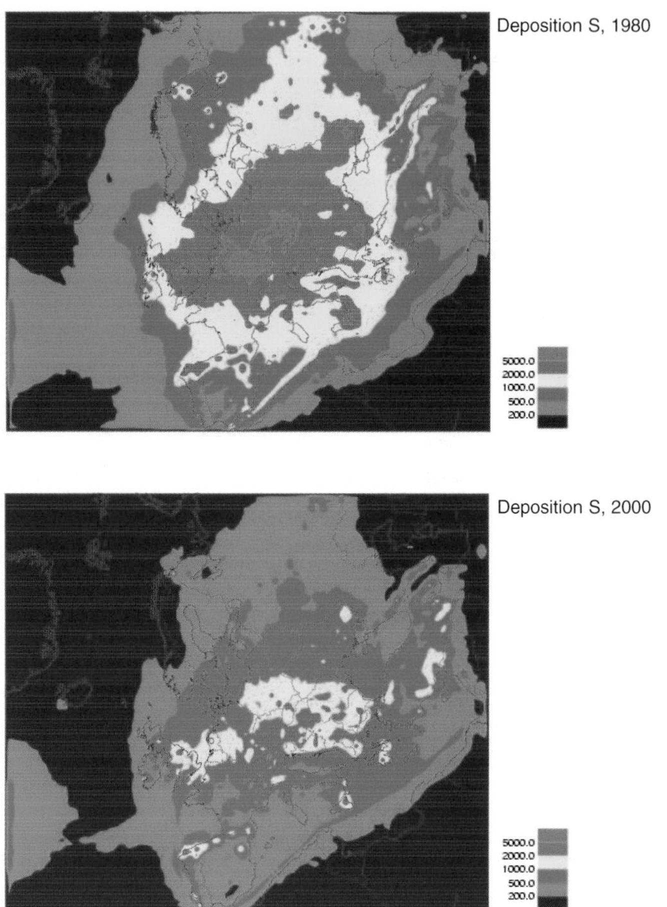

FIGURE 3.6. TOTAL DEPOSITION OF SULPHUR IN 1980 AND 2000.

SOURCE: MSC-W

EMEP task forces

The tasks of EMEP have increased steadily to match the increasing demands of the Convention. The EMEP Steering Body is now supported by three task forces (see box), which each provide a forum for technical discussions and close exchange and coordination of activities between experts from Parties to the Convention and the four EMEP centres. The task forces are led by designated Parties and chaired by experts nominated by the lead country. Representatives of international organizations with allied interests may be invited to nominate a co-chair. Task Forces meet regularly and report to the Steering Body. They are essential to maintain the close network of country experts, representatives from the centres and the scientific community at large.

Current EMEP task forces

- Task Force on Measurement and Modelling (co-chaired by the United Kingdom and WMO). This Task Force supports the EMEP Steering Body (and its Bureau) by reviewing and assessing the scientific and operational activities of EMEP related to monitoring and modelling, e.g. in developing the EMEP monitoring strategy, EMEP monitoring manual and the review of the new Eulerian transport model. It also provides for closer collaboration of Parties to the Convention, the EMEP centres, other bodies under the Convention, other international bodies and the scientific community in strengthening scientific communication and cooperation in air pollution monitoring and modelling.
- Task Force on Emission Inventories and Projections (co-chaired by Norway and the European Environment Agency). The objectives of the Task Force include providing a technical forum to discuss, exchange information and harmonize emission inventories including emission factors, methodologies and guidelines. An important output of this Task Force is the regular updating of the EMEP/CORINAIR Emission Inventory Guidebook, which is an important basis for establishing national emissions inventories. The Task Force also conducts in-depth evaluations of emission factors and methodologies.
- Task Force on Integrated Assessment Modelling (chaired by Netherlands). Chapter 6 provides detailed information on integrated assessment modelling activities, including the work of the Task Force.

Future of EMEP

The scope of EMEP has widened over recent years and will continue to do so in the coming decade(s). In preparation for these tasks, EMEP developed and published a strategy for the period of 2000-2009 (see box). It marked the continuation of a development from a scientific monitoring and modelling community exclusively serving particular needs of the Convention to a much more open organization, where science is still the leading principle, but the results are discussed and evaluated from a policy perspective. The increasing cooperation with institutions of the European Community, including the European Commission, the European Environment Agency and the Joint Research Centre, has been a major sign of this change. It is fair to say that for example the European Commission's Clean Air for Europe programme relies largely on the expertise developed within and provided by EMEP experts. EMEP itself puts more emphasis on the support of policy pressures, primarily in the Convention, but is aware of the needs of other frameworks as well. This development is expected to continue.
There are a number of challenges ahead for EMEP which it will master only if it remains flexible and gets strong input not only from the centres, but also from experts from all Parties to the Convention. These challenges include:

- Expansion of the pollutants covered: EMEP started with acidifying and eutrophying pollutants, but now also covers ground-level ozone, particulate matter, heavy metals and a number of POPs;
- Expansion of the EMEP modelling scale (a) to a hemispheric scale, not only because some of the species considered in EMEP, such as ozone, mercury or POPs, require modelling at this scale, but also because the countries in Central Asia, also part of the UNECE region, are becoming Parties to the Convention and have a strong interest in being involved in EMEP activities; (b) the inclusion of health effects in the work of the Convention has made it necessary to cover also the urban scale, in particular in integrated assessment modelling;

- Extension of the monitoring efforts to include the application of state-of-the-art methods and to cover regions where monitoring is sparse;
- Extension of the work on emissions from providing guidance and maintaining a database of emission data to validation and verification of those data;
- Exploring links and synergies with other relevant fields, in particular to climate change. There are for example links concerning the sources of pollution, possible abatement measures and the atmospheric processes;
- Better integration of modelling and monitoring, e.g. by data assimilation;
- Enhanced collaboration with experts and institutions outside of EMEP, without duplicating work.

Vision for an EMEP strategy 2000-2009 as presented to the Executive Body in 2000

EMEP will continue to be the main science-based and policy-driven instrument for international cooperation in atmospheric monitoring and modelling, emission inventories and projections, and integrated assessment to help solve transboundary air pollution problems.
To this end it seeks to develop:

- **Science** - EMEP establishes sound scientific evidence and provides guidance to underpin, develop and evaluate environmental problems;
- **Partnership** - EMEP fosters international partnership to find solutions to environmental problems;
- **Openness** - EMEP encourages the open use of intellectual resources and products;
- **Sharing** - EMEP is transparent and shares information and expertise with research programmes, expert institutions, national and international organizations, and environmental agreements;
- **Organization** - EMEP is organized to integrate information on emissions, environmental quality, effect and abatement options, and to provide the basis for solutions.

Acknowledgements

We would like to thank Roel van Aalst for contributing to the text and for the photo of the Finnish monitoring site.

Software and hardware, no protocols without technologies

Chapter 4

Lars Lindau, Andrzej Jagusiewicz and Endre Kovacs

There has been a rapid development of technologies and techniques to reduce emissions of air pollutants in a wide range of sectors - energy, traffic, agriculture, industry and domestic - since the adoption of the Convention in 1979. But, while these new techniques and also non-technical measures, such as energy conservation and traffic management, have played an important role in decreasing pollution, industrial production, transport activity and energy demand have increased significantly. However, the emission ratio or unit emission per activity has been considerably lowered.

Information gathered about the technical issues have played an important role and contributed substantively to the success of the Convention and its protocols. The organizational setting in which this was done has changed over the years, as shown in the box.

Abatement techniques, organizational setting
Around 1965 the first expert group on air pollution, the Working Party on Air Pollution Problems, was established by UNECE. Its first chairman was Mr. Leslie Reed from the United Kingdom. In the 1960s and 1970s, the major concern was air pollution related problems and the inventory of available measures, their effectiveness and costs. For quite some time, this was done by specific task forces and in governmentally designated expert groups, operating under the Working Party. In 1991, at its 9th session, the Executive Body for the Convention established a special group to deal with technical issues. It existed until 2000 as the Working Group on Abatement Techniques and focused on technical solutions in support of policy development under the Convention. After the signing of the Gothenburg Protocol and as part of the restructuring of work under the Convention, it was decided at the 17th session of the Executive Body in 1999 to continue the work on techniques and their cost calculations via ad hoc expert groups under the Working Group on Strategies and Review.

At present, new groups are involved with abatement techniques, the Expert Group on Techno-economic Issues and the Expert Group on Ammonia Abatement.

In addition to this work on abatement techniques, the Task Force on Economic Aspects of Abatement Strategies dealt with, among other things, (inter)national economic instruments to control emissions. A few years ago this Task Force was replaced by the Network of Experts on Benefits and Economic Instruments.

Emission abatement requires technologies and techniques. This means applying process changes and installations such as flue gas desulphurization, selective catalytic reduction and electrostatic precipitators - real "hardware". Without technologies (the hardware) to abate emissions, one cannot make meaningful international agreements (protocols) which carry obligations to reduce pollution. This chapter deals with the development and use of technology within the Convention and its protocols.

Outline

The following sections briefly outline some developments of abatement technology in major economic sectors (energy, traffic, industry and agriculture) in relation to emission reductions in Europe. This followed by descriptions of the impact that various types of provisions in the protocols, i.e. those concerning technical annexes, emission ceilings, exchange of technology and economic instruments, have had, or could have had, on the application of technologies. This second section ends with a shor reflection on costs. The chapter concludes with an overview of possible future developments with respect to abatement techniques in the context of the Convention.

Technologies and reduction of emissions

The technical development

Whether emission reductions are caused by autonomous developments in industry, by political and economic changes, by national policies or by the policies of the Convention on Long-range Transboundary Air Pollution and its protocols, it is beyond dispute that "hardware" - in the literal sense of the word - has to do the job and reduce emissions.

Impressive reductions of the emissions caused by combustion processes have taken place over the past 25 years - mainly of sulphur oxides, nitrogen oxides and some heavy metals, although in many countries nitrogen oxides (NOx) cuts were only taken seriously in the early 1990s. Also, emissions of volatile organic compounds (VOCs) show a promising decrease. The protocols to the Convention and their annexes have played a major role in achieving these reductions.

From 1980 to 2000 sulphur emissions decreased considerably in most parts of Europe. The overall reduction in the EMEP area was nearly 70%, but there were large differences between countries and regions. The decreases so far in nitrogen oxides and VOCs are not as large as in sulphur, around 25 - 30% between 1990 and 2000, and the differences between regions are again noteworthy. In southern Europe the nitrogen oxide emissions have not changed. National studies of particulates and heavy metals show a substantial decrease of emissions from 1990 till 2000, e.g. for lead 60-70% and for mercury 50%.To a lesser extent, the emissions of ammonia and persistent organic pollutants (POPs) decreased as well during this period. For example, ammonia emissions decreased around 20% by technical means, mainly in agriculture.

In East European countries, the political changes around 1990 resulted in major structural changes. Production of heavy industry fell, energy efficiency and energy saving became important and a considerable shift occurred in the fuel mix of the energy sector (coal _ fuel oil _ natural gas). Due to these changes and the general economic collapse, emissions fell drastically in most of these countries.

Many task forces and expert groups under the Working Group on Abatement Techniques and its predecessors have been established to collect and review information on abatement techniques suitable for the main economic sectors. The work of these bodies has been associated with the development of nearly all protocols to the Convention (table 4.1).

Table 4.1 Convention bodies dealing with technologies and techniques

Task force/expert group (reporting year)	Associated protocol
Task Force on Technologies for Controlling NOx Emissions from Stationary Sources (1986)	1988 Nitrogen Oxides Protocol
Task Force on Cost Calculations (1988)	
Task Force on Emissions of VOCs from Stationary Sources Task Force on VOCs from On-road Vehicles	1991 VOC Protocol
Task Force on Exchange of Technology (1991); Working Group on Technology	1994 Sulphur Protocol
Task Force and Preparatory Working Group on POPs	1998 Protocol on POPs
Task Force and Preparatory Working Group on Heavy Metal Emissions	1998 Protocol on Heavy Metal
Task Forces s on Assessment of Abatement Options/Techniques for VOCs and for nitrogen oxides (1999)	1999 Gothenburg Protocol
Expert Group on Control Techniques for Emissions of VOC and NOx from Selected Mobile Sources (1999)	

An important input was also provided by the Task Force on By-products Utilization and Waste Management from Fuel Treatment and Combustion succeeded by the Task Force on By-product Utilization from Stationary Installations chaired by Austria. Since 1998 the Task Force further changed its name to Management of By-products and Residues Containing Heavy Metals or POPs. Its aim was to help Parties comply with the requirements of the Aarhus Protocols on Heavy Metals and on POPs. In particular, it was meant to assist them in the use and management of wastes containing these pollutants from different industrial sectors, including waste incineration. The close contacts with the European Union (EU) Integrated Pollution Prevention and Control (IPPC) bureau in Sevilla, Spain, and with the International Institute for Applied Systems Analysis (IIASA) in Laxenburg, Austria, have also been very useful. It has also opened the way to harmonize approaches between the EU and the Convention.

Although transboundary air pollution in Europe and in North American differs considerably, and in a number of cases the obligations under protocols are not the same, there is sufficient similarity in the use of air pollution control technologies for fruitful cooperation. Close contacts between the subregions exist within the Convention as well as contacts with business partners and scientific and technical groups.

Energy

The reduction of nearly 70% in the emissions of sulphur oxides between 1980 and 2000 is, to a large extent, due to the achievements in the energy sector. Since 1980, two parallel, equally important, developments can be observed. First, structural changes and energy management, for example, energy-saving and energy-efficiency measures, the use of wind and solar energy and the switch to natural gas and low-sulphur fuels. Second, the use of primary measures, for example, advanced combustion and combustion modifications (e.g. low-NOx burners and fluidized-bed combustion), or secondary measures, for example, flue gas desulphurization (FGD), denitrification (selective catalytic reduction (SCR)) and precipitators (e.g. electrostatic precipitator (ESP)), baghouses and catalytic/thermal oxidation.

Energy management has resulted in a significant reduction in emissions of sulphur oxides but also of nitrogen oxides. The potential for these measures in the near future is impressive, particularly in countries with economies in transition. However, the single most successful measure for the reduction of sulphur oxides has been the introduction and implementation of FGD on medium-size and large combustion installations in power plants and district heating. Also, the use of catalytic reduction of flue gases has had major effects on nitrogen oxides emissions. It is clear that system changes often take a long time, while technical measures can give quick results.

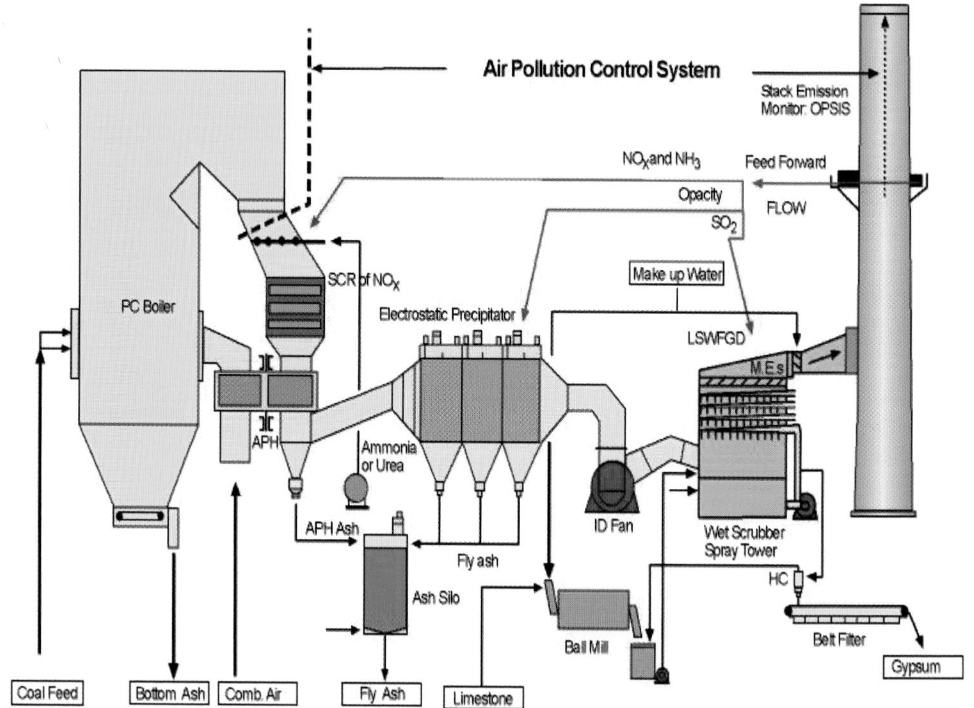

Figure 4.1. A diagram of a pulverized coal boiler with SCR, ESP and FGD

Source: ALSTOM

Traffic

The decrease in nitrogen oxides emissions by about 25% was mainly accomplished in the traffic sector. Again there have been two parallel developments: changes in traffic infrastructure and traffic management; and engine modifications and exhaust treatment. Measures for non-road vehicles are also important. Traffic has a tendency to increase, with the highest rates in road transport and aviation, accompanied by a steady increase in fuel use. But the emissions of air pollutants have

decreased, owing to control of evaporative VOC emissions and the successful introduction of engine modifications and implementation of advanced catalytic exhaust treatment on petrol-fuelled passenger cars. For heavy-duty vehicles, engine modifications have been most important. The ratio of emissions per distance driven has been significantly reduced for all vehicle types.

The quality of the fuel has a major influence on the level of emissions from both petrol-fuelled and diesel-fuelled vehicles. Fuel with low sulphur content is especially important in this respect, since, apart from causing sulphur dioxide emissions, sulphur impairs the efficiency of catalytic converters and leads to the formation of small particles. Lead in petrol also impairs catalytic converters. This was one of the reasons for the introduction of unleaded petrol, though the main reason was the serious health effects associated with lead emissions. In a more general way the Gothenburg Protocol integrated environmental requirements for motor fuels, though separately for petrol and diesel, in a similar fashion to those of the EU.

Industry

Industry emits not only combustion-related pollutants but also a variety of process-related pollutants like VOCs, POPs and heavy metals. Measures taken in industry have certainly helped to reduce VOC emissions. There are different possibilities for reducing emissions. In general, improvements have been achieved with cleaner fuels, by use of combustion modifications, with alternative cleaner processes or raw materials, by process modifications, by closed-circuit processes and using internal recycling. Product control measures, product management, energy management and good housekeeping have also been important. Obviously, with respect to particulates, heavy metals and POPs, flue gas treatment has been a basic measure.

Agricultural

The Protocol on POPs, the Gothenburg Protocol and to some extent the VOC Protocol, are among the first international agreements to deal with the environmental effects of agricultural practices. The agricultural sector is responsible for more than 90% of the ammonia emissions in Europe. If farmyard manure is handled in the wrong way, more than half the ammonia content can evaporate before the manure reaches the soil. It is very important that the manure is spread at the right time and in the right weather conditions and that it is injected in the soil or quickly ploughed down. Measures applied to cut ammonia emissions are alternative livestock feeding strategies, low-emission manure spreading and storage, low-emission animal housing systems and measures connected to the use of mineral fertilizers, including their restriction.

Protocols and technologies

The impact of the annexes

Apart from the 1985 Sulphur Protocol, all pollutant-related protocols agreed upon so far have technical annexes. They have contributed considerably to achieving the main target, to decreasing emissions and thus reducing deposition and harmful effects. The preparation of annexes has also contributed to the development of consensus on what is considered as best available technology (BAT) for both stationary and mobile sources. The discussions among designated experts helped to put aside

possible national prejudices about cost or efficiency and applicability of certain technologies. Exchange of information on operating experience on specific technologies (e.g. fluidized-bed combustion (FBC), integrated gasification combined cycle (IGCC)) stimulated the understanding and application of certain "new" technologies.

Historically, the 1988 NOx Protocol, although still based on a flat-rate reduction (stabilization), introduced the application of national standards based on BAT as mandatory for new sources. It provided in its technical annex guidance to the Parties on identifying BAT for NOx control options and techniques for major new and existing stationary sources as well as for new mobile sources.

This annex is the only one, so far, that has been updated (at the 12th session of the Executive Body in 1994). The NOx Protocol further required its Parties to make unleaded petrol available to facilitate the use of cars with catalytic converters. The next Protocol, that on VOCs signed in 1991, provided Parties with guidance not only on BAT, but also on managing VOC-containing products, including recycling.

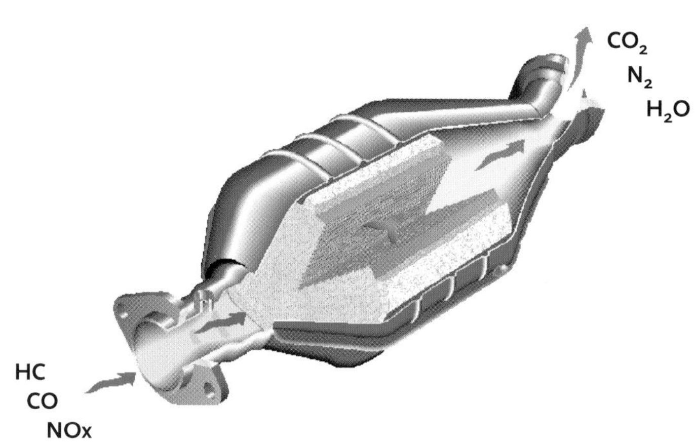

Figure 4.2. A diagram of a catalytic converter

Source: Association for Emissions Control by Catalyst

In the early 1980s, FGD was demonstrated in practice as BAT and an important discussion took place under the Convention in Geneva. In Germany, FGD was introduced in national legislation, taking effect in 1983, and it was used as a basis for the 1988 EU Large Combustion Plant (LCP) Directive. This technical development was a major step forward and was later reflected not only, indirectly, in the target of the 1985 Sulphur Protocol, but also in the 1994 Sulphur Protocol, which had the standard from the LCP Directive in its annex. For nitrogen oxides comparable technical developments, e.g. broad-scale flue gas denitrification through SCR, took place in the early 1990s.

A milestone in the development of annexes was the 1994 Sulphur Protocol, which, apart from a general BAT obligation, imposed emission limit values (ELVs) on new and existing large stationary combustion sources, and made energy management measures and fuel standards, e.g. sulphur content in oils, obligatory.

In 1996, the Executive Body, revising the NOx and VOC Protocols, extended the technical guidance on BAT to mobile sources other than road vehicles, i.e. off-road vehicles and machines, ships and aircraft. The extension of the NOx annex came into force shortly after its adoption. For VOC, the revision to the annex became operational in September 1997, when the VOC Protocol itself came into force.

The 1998 Protocol on Heavy Metals and the 1998 Protocol on POPs added new features to the technical compliance regime. They require Parties to apply BAT and ELVs to cadmium, lead and mercury and certain POPs (especially PAHs, and dioxins/furans) and product control and management measures to 13 other POPs, like DDT, PCB, etc. This means bans or restrictions on their production and use.

Finally, the 1999 Gothenburg Protocol to Abate Acidification, Eutrophication and Ground-level Ozone set emission ceilings for NOx, SOx, VOCs and ammonia and required Parties to control them following the so-called multi-pollutant and multi-effect strategy. The latter has been based not only on traditional tools like BAT and limit values for emissions from all potential source categories. It has also, as was done before in the 1994 Sulphur Protocol, a wider range of measures, including structural changes in the most polluting sectors, i.e. energy, traffic and agriculture.

Ammonia is emitted mainly from agriculture and the mandatory and recommendatory packages of the Gothenburg Protocol and its guidance documents, complete with a target-oriented advisory code of good agricultural practice, are very important for the reduction of emissions in UNECE countries.

Figure 4.3. A manure injector (Photo: J. van Reeken Studio/P. Schutte)

Since the mid-1990s the annexes have had strong connections to the corresponding directives of the European Union. In many cases the EU directives and the requirements in the annexes are similar. The process of gathering information on available technologies, cost data etc. has for the greater part been well integrated. For example, for car exhaust and the sulphur content of gas oil, the Executive Body has simply agreed to include, as far as possible, the directives in force in the EU. This has had the beneficial effect of harmonizing the EU and the UNECE regions.

There are also cases where the Convention has taken the lead and where the EU has, later on, taken on board the knowledge gathered. Apart from FGD, already mentioned above, an interesting example is the 1999 EU Directive on Solvent Use in Industry, which refers to the VOC Protocol, although the European Community is not a Party to it. Also, the Protocols on Heavy Metals and on POPs and their annexes have been the driving force for the implementation of measures, including the guidance for a global approach within the Stockholm Convention on POPs. Other examples are ammonia abatement measures developed under the Convention on Long-range Transboundary Air Pollution.

For the ten countries that became member States of the EU in May 2004 the fulfilment of the requirements stipulated in the various protocols proved to be an important promoting factor in the accession process. Acceptance and implementation of the EU directives became much easier; for instance, the annex to the 1994 Sulphur Protocol helped to comply with the 1988 LCP Directive.

The impact of emission ceilings

In the 1994 Sulphur Protocol and in the Gothenburg Protocol, individual national emission ceilings for each Party are established for sulphur oxides, NOx, VOCs and ammonia to be met by 2010. The ceilings are based on calculations with integrated assessment models leading to cost-efficient solutions (see chapter 6). They are, in most countries, strong driving forces for the further development of (mainly) energy and traffic policies and abatement programmes based on a wide choice of possible techniques. However, the use of such ceilings alone would result in not using the state-of-the-art control technology and possible distortion of international competition in countries where, as a consequence of favourable environmental circumstances, national ceilings are easily reached. For this reason, the overall reduction on the basis of national ceilings is, in both protocols, combined with mandatory application of BAT and emission limit values.

The Gothenburg Protocol has not yet entered into force and there are still six years to go to meet the final requirements. However, the reporting under the corresponding EU National Emission Ceiling (NEC) Directive indicates that the prognosis for sulphur oxide abatement is encouraging, with several countries doing much better than their targets. For nitrogen oxides especially, but also for VOCs and ammonia, there is a possibility that some countries will not achieve their targets. It will be interesting to see which initiatives countries will take to apply additional technical measures to comply with their ceilings. Major difficulties are the increased emissions of heavy-duty traffic and the need for further product management measures. EU member States face an extra problem because they are not allowed to solve these product-related problems by simply applying stricter emission standards, as they are considered to be barriers to the free circulation of goods within the European Community. Changing these standards is the exclusive competence of the European Commission.

Exchange of technology

There has been a strong need for transfer of technology from West to East and Central European countries since the adoption on the Convention in 1979. The exchange process only started when the required political conditions were met and then focused mainly on software or knowledge rather than on hardware or physical support.

Numerous examples of measures taken to facilitate the exchange of technologies can be given, varying from the convening of workshops or seminars to capacity-building, and from establishing business partnerships and international financing facilities and to making information accessible on the Internet.

An activity of major importance has been the exchange of information on technology and operational experience, including costs. This was initiated under UNECE in the 1970s and later continued under the Convention. Six seminars and a number of workshops were organized to review available efficient control technologies for reducing air pollution from stationary sources and to present recent developments, including information on investments and operation costs in the field (table 4.2).

Table 4.2. Exchange of technology seminars

Place	Date	Seminar/workshops	Report
Geneva	1970	Seminar on desulphurization of fuels and combustion gases	
Washington,D.C.	1975	Seminar on desulphurization of fuels and combustion gases	
Salzburg, Austria	18-22 May 1981	Seminar on desulphurization of fuels and combustion gases	ENV/SEM.1/3 of the UNECE Working Party on Air Pollution Problems
Graz, Austria	12-16 May 1986	Seminar on control of sulphur and nitrogen oxides from stationary sources	EB.AIR/SEM.1/3
Nuremberg, Germany	10-14 June 1991	Seminar on emission control technology for stationary sources	EB.AIR/SEM.2/3
Budapest	14-17 Oct 1996	Seminar on control technologies for emissions from stationary sources; gas engines in co-generation plants; control options for use of solvents	EB.AIR/SEM.3/3; Air Pollution Studies series
Warsaw	5-7 Dec 2001	Workshop on control technologies for emissions from stationary sources	EB.AIR/WG.5/2002/5

The agenda of each seminar followed the need to integrate technical knowledge into the protocols' annexes starting with FGD, then with SCR, catalytic and thermal oxidation for VOCs and finally all measures together, including facilitation of exchange of technology and databases. In addition to the seminars, target-oriented and subject-specific workshops were organized to solve problems identified by the countries with economies in transition. A particular role was played by the Task Force on Exchange of Technology, led by Finland, which, over the two and a half years of its work, drew up a series of recommendations on good practice.

Most of the technical task forces and expert groups were organized by lead countries from the West but had active participation from the East. The technical task forces were supported for many years mainly by Germany, United Kingdom and the Netherlands as lead countries. Valuable information was gathered relating to technical details, cost data, performance of installations etc. The development of a database for technologies, performance and costs has also been of great value. The University in Karlsruhe, Germany, started this work, developed it and recently passed it to France's Agence de l'environnement et de la maîtrise de l'énergie and Centre interprofessionnel technique d'études de la pollution atmosphérique which have been the driving force behind the current Expert Group on Techno-economic Issues.

A number of authoritative reports on the current state of development of techniques for the reduction of emissions of sulphur oxides, NOx and VOCs at stationary sources, have been produced, circulated to the Parties and made available on the Internet. Special emphasis has been put upon information on operational experience and costs.

The impact of economic instruments

Nationally, demonstration projects, subsidies and financial support schemes strongly promoted the introduction of new control technologies. Demonstration projects helped gain experience with complex technologies such as combustion modifications, IGCC, FGD and SCR in specific national settings. Fiscal incentives and financial support schemes speeded up the introduction of "clean" cars and of control equipment and techniques in industry and in agriculture. Starting with the VOC Protocol, the use of economic instruments is explicitly addressed in the protocols.

Schemes for international economic optimization were exhaustively discussed when preparing the 1994 Sulphur Protocol. In connection with the decision to aim at maximum environmental protection in each European country, at the lowest overall costs, the possibility of "burden sharing", as proposed by the Netherlands, was discussed. For this the need for and possibility of allocating these costs, in a way justifiable to the economic capacity and previous abatement efforts of each country, was studied. However, in the end burden sharing was not introduced because neither the majority of potential donors nor the potential receivers in Central and Eastern Europe seemed to support the idea. The latter most likely because their dramatic economic changes had made it possible to comply with the protocol obligations without much use of expensive technology.

The other instrument explored for international economic optimization of sulphur reduction was "joint implementation" . This principle was introduced in the 1994 Sulphur Protocol but it did not prove possible to develop operational rules, nor has any potential case of joint implementation been put forward. The instrument did not recur in the Gothenburg Protocol.

Joint implementation means cooperation between two parties to jointly implement their reduction obligations in such a way that one party (for which emission reduction is expensive) reduces less and another (for which reduction is cheap) reduces more than required under its national ceiling.

When negotiating the Oslo Protocol, Norway put much effort into convincing other delegations of the merits of joint implementation as an instrument for cost-effective emission reductions. Many countries were willing to explore the possibilities of such an approach, others opposed it on principle or on practical grounds. In contrast to the effects of CO_2 on climate, the acidifying effects of SO_2 depend on the places where it is emitted. Atmospheric transport (its duration and route) and the specific vulnerability of receptors in the deposition area, determine the place and extent of the damage (table 4.3).

TABLE 4.3. EXAMPLES OF THE DEPOSITION CHANGES IN THE NETHERLANDS, GERMANY AND POLAND RESULTING FROM IDENTICAL SO_2 REDUCTIONS IN THE NETHERLANDS AND POLAND (BASED ON 1995 EMEP DATA)

1 kton emission reduction in	Deposition Netherlands	Deposition Germany	Deposition Poland
Netherlands	- 151 tons	- 116 tons	- 24 tons
Poland	- <1 ton	- 25 tons	- 330 tons

The fact that the national emission reduction obligations are already based on cost-effect optimization, limits the chances for improvement through joint implementation. However, a paragraph was introduced in the 1994 Sulphur Protocol allowing for joint implementation though rules and conditions needed to be developed separately. As illustrated by the table, changes in emission reduction patterns influence the deposition on the territories of joint implementation partners and also on that of neighbouring countries. Therefore, possibly affected third parties should have a say in any joint implementation agreement.

Rules for joint implementation were agreed upon at the 15th session of the Executive Body in 1998. They allow for a certain increase in the deposition in third-party countries, but the actual percentages for acceptable increases were left open till experience had been gained with real cases. However, up to now no potential joint implementation agreement has been brought before the Executive Body.

Costs

Air pollution abatement entails costs, and for some measures substantial costs. It is rather problematic to reach consensus about of the costs for different control options since there are differences in interpretation of costs, the basis for comparison, accountancy practices and because the estimates of experts may partly be inspired by national policy. Over the years, however, consensus has grown due to increased practical experience with technology. Costs have shown a declining trend, especially with respect to new sources. For example, the costs of FGD are half the first estimates of the early 1980s. Moreover, very cost-effective solutions related to structural changes are possible. For these reasons the calculations with the RAINS integrated assessment model (see chapter 6) when preparing for the Gothenburg Protocol overestimated the costs of reducing emissions. Only technical emission abatement measures, very often end-of-pipe solutions, were considered with no account taken of structural changes such as switching from coal to gas, increasing energy efficiency, greater use of alternative energy sources and changes in transport and agriculture.

Cost-benefit analyses based on the abatement measures needed to comply with the Gothenburg Protocol show clearly that preventing and controlling air pollution pays. The calculated benefits exceeded the costs quite substantially, in spite of the fact that a number of benefits, such as protection of nature and prevention of damage to historical monuments, were not included. In addition to such calculations, it is also evident that there are synergies and trade-offs between the control of greenhouse gases and air pollution, which have further economic benefits.

What's next on technologies?

The protocols to the Convention are based on both environmental targets - critical loads and critical levels and air quality limit values - and also the application of BAT. The annexes with requirements for the emission performance of specific sources and/or release of chemicals will also be important in the future and should therefore be updated regularly. A further developed database for technology performance and costs will be very valuable in this respect, as well as further work on national abatement programmes and the further development of integrated assessment modelling.

There is a good possibility that we can improve the environmental situation significantly and come closer to the critical loads and levels in most of Europe in the not too distant future. The most crucial challenges will be to decrease emissions of nitrogen oxide, particulates and ammonia sufficiently.

A notable problem within the Convention's system is the very long time between the adoption of a protocol and its entry into force. This has sometimes led to more than six years going by between the negotiation phase and the starting point for implementation, a time that is too long in practice. Often there are more cost-efficient technologies available at the time the protocol takes effect. This problem can be solved by updating the annexes or guidance documents decided by the Executive Body without reviewing the whole protocol. So far, only the annex to the NOx Protocol has been updated in this way (in 1994).

The most recent protocols to the Convention, the 1999 Gothenburg Protocol, the 1998 Protocol on Heavy Metals and the 1998 Protocol on POPs, are now being reviewed, or the preparations for their review has started. Probably the new target year for a revised Gothenburg Protocol will be 2020. The same time horizon is targeted by the European Commission's Clean Air for Europe (CAFE) programme using the same approach. That means that the technical developments will be very important. A strong driving force for such developments in the energy and transport sectors will be climate change policy but the wish to decrease the health effects of particulates and ozone will also put pressure on technical developments. It is obvious that a combined approach towards greenhouse gas mitigation and air pollution control provides a necessary synergy and gives significant environmental and health benefits. Thus low-carbon paths will turn out to be highly cost-effective for protecting the environment from both air pollution and climate change.

There are some emerging technologies/techniques which will most probably be implemented in the

near future. They are already available and will eventually be used on a large scale. Examples are particulate filters on diesel engines for light- and heavy-duty vehicles, fuel cells for heavy-duty cars/buses, more advanced energy-saving systems in industrial processes and buildings and advanced techniques in the transport sector. This again highlights the need for a timely update of technical annexes to protocols.

The future of the transport sector requires a consistent and balanced package of measures focusing on technology of vehicles. Consideration should also be given to fuels and infrastructure and changes in transport activity. Heavy vehicles with diesel engines are of particular concern. Their emissions of volatile hydrocarbons and particles can be decreased with oxidative converters, particle filters and clean fuels. For nitrogen oxides emissions from these heavy vehicles, using SCR is a solution. Maritime transport is also of particular concern since shipping is an important source of sulphur and nitrogen oxide emissions. However, there is considerable potential in this sector for further measures such as the use of clean fuels and/or end-of-pipe techniques. For nitrogen oxides emission from ships the relevant solution is SCR, which can cut emissions by 90%.

In recent years the Convention and the EU have developed a kind of symbiotic relationship, which has stimulated the establishment of increasingly ambitious obligations, thus further reducing emissions. On 1 May 2004 the EU extended its number of member States to 25 countries, embracing 10 additional countries, all Parties to the Convention. However, behind the new Eastern border of the EU are 20 more countries, which are also Parties to the Convention. The 10 new EU members are now obliged to comply with the EU directives, which generally set stricter rules than the Convention and its protocols. All Parties to the Convention, the 25 EU members, the other European and Central Asian countries and the North American Parties, share the unique network of scientific expertise and all the experience gathered on technical solutions, their costs and implementation. In this context the Convention can continue to play a vital role in future.

Acknowledgement
The authors owe much gratitude to Mr. Volkert Keizer for his assistance in finalizing the chapter.

Air pollution effects drive abatement strategies

Jean-Paul Hettelingh, Keith Bull, Radovan Chrast, Heinz-Detlef Gregor, Peringe Grennfelt, Wojciech Mill.

Over the past 25 years, the activities of the Convention's Working Group on Effects evolved from developing "effects-supported" approaches, in the first decade of the Convention, to the "effects-based" approaches used at present.

Twenty-five years ago the Convention invited its Contracting Parties, inter alia, to "initiate and cooperate in the conduct of research into and/or development of the effects of sulphur compounds and other major air pollutants on human health and the environment, ... with a view to establishing a scientific basis for dose/effect relationships designed to protect the environment" (art. 7). The main objective was to establish knowledge on important dose-response relationships and the extent of estimated damage to materials, including historic and cultural monuments, aquatic ecosystems and to soil, groundwater and vegetation. This work developed into well-defined international cooperative programmes (ICPs), which have extended their work to include also the modelling of cause-effect relationships. This modelling progressed to contribute to effect-based approaches in support of the development of the Convention's protocols and their review.

The Working Group on Effects

Early in the discussions on the Convention it was recognized that a good understanding of the harmful effects of air pollution was a prerequisite for reaching agreement on effective pollution control. To develop the necessary international cooperation in the research on, and the monitoring of, pollutant effects, the Working Group on Effects was established under the Convention. The Working Group provides information on the degree and geographic extent of the impacts of major air pollutants, such as sulphur and nitrogen oxides, ozone and heavy metals, on human health and the environment. Its six international cooperative programmes (ICPs) identify the most endangered areas, ecosystems and other receptors by considering damage to terrestrial and aquatic ecosystems, human health, and materials. An important part of this work is long-term monitoring. The work is underpinned by scientific research on dose-response relationships, critical loads and levels and damage evaluation. The Working Group meets annually to discuss the results of the international programmes and the current and future needs of the Convention. It considers its future work and that of the programmes and prepares a work-plan for the coming year for consideration by the Executive Body for the Convention. Important results are brought to the attention of the Executive Body; they are also published in the scientific literature and disseminated to the public through the publication of reports and through UNECE press releases. The Working Group also publishes substantive reports summarizing and assessing the most important results of the activities of the international programmes.

The effects programme provides a structure that is essential for the development, accumulation and use of scientific knowledge. It has ensured the support of effect-based policies which have increased in complexity from single-pollutant-single-effect approaches to multi-pollutant-multi-effect ones.

Currently the emphasis of the Working Group is on the benefits of the integration of both effect-supported and effect-based approaches. This is important for the advancement of multi-pollutant-multi-effect approaches so that they may include more information on synergies with other triggers of adverse effects on public health and the environment. This could also be important for other environmental action programmes such as those of the European Commission.

Outline

This chapter first outlines the development of scientific knowledge specific to the Convention. This is followed by an overview of the history of the most important policy requirements for this knowledge. The context of European policies addressing air pollution effects is broadened to highlight the role of the Convention before and after 1989. Then the historical development of the current structure of the Working Group on Effects is described. Next, the use of critical thresholds in integrated assessments for supporting the two effect-based protocols is summarized. Finally, there are conclusions and remarks on challenges.

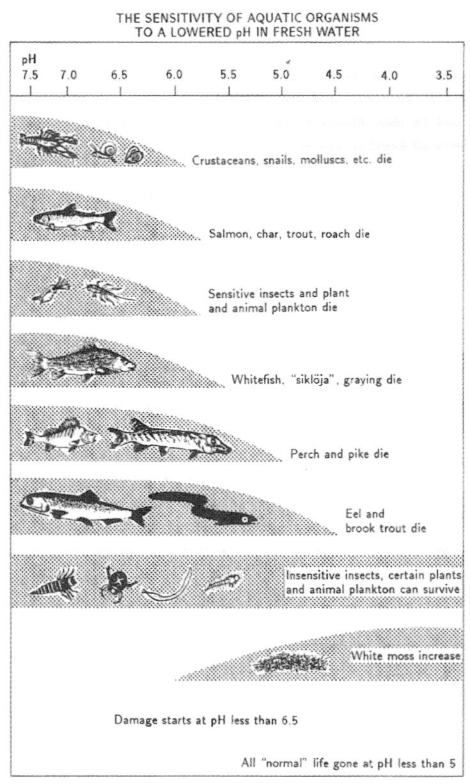

Figure 5.1. The sensitivity of aquatic organisms to lowered pH in fresh waters

Source: Swedish Ministry of Agriculture, 1982

Development of scientific knowledge for the Convention

Acidification

The first observations on ecosystem effects from acid deposition were made at the beginning of the 20th century. In Norway a decrease in the occurrence and catch of salmon and trout in rivers was noticed about 100 years ago and this was soon linked to the acidity of the rivers.

In figure 5.1 we see how increasing acidity (indicated by a decreasing pH) first affects the population of crustaceans, eventually leads to the extinction of salmon at a pH of about 5.5 and finally leads to a watershed where only white moss increases and where all "normal" life is no longer possible, i.e at a pH below about 4.5. It was also demonstrated very early on that acid deposition led to a decrease in base saturation (the availability of elements such as calcium and magnesium, the base cations, which are essential for plant growth) in forest soils.

Several observations during the following decades were able to further elaborate the problem of acidification, but a coherent picture of an ongoing European acidification problem that received public and policy attention was not available until 1968, when Mr. Svante Odén published his observations on ongoing acidification of rain and surface waters. He linked these observations to sources and effects and drew attention to possible future developments. He attributed the acidification to the increased coal and oil burning in Europe and he saw acid deposition as the cause of the observed fish extinction in Scandinavian lakes. He also foresaw several other consequences such as acidification of forest soils, a depletion of base cations in soils and a risk of damage to forests. Mr. Odén based his assumptions on measurements within the European Air Chemistry Network, a precipitation chemistry network set up in the mid-1950s. His observations and reports became a starting point not only for policy interest but also for scientific research on the effects of sulphur and nitrogen deposition and for international scientific collaboration.

International Cooperative Programme on Assessment and Monitoring of Acidification of Rivers and Lakes (ICP Waters)
Lead countries: Canada (1985-1986) and Norway (from 1986)

Acidification of freshwater systems provided some of the earliest evidence of the damage caused by sulphur emissions. The sensitivity of these systems meant that they were ideal for studying the effects of, and response to changes in, pollution deposition. The objectives of ICP Waters are to assess, on a regional basis, the degree and geographical extent of acidification of surface waters. The data collected should provide information on dose/response relationships under different conditions and correlate changes in acidic deposition with the physical, chemical and biological status of lakes and streams. Chemical and site data from more than 200 catchments in 17 countries in Europe and North America are available in the database of the Programme Centre at the Norwegian Institute for Water Research (NIVA), Oslo.

Further information: www.niva.no/ICP-waters/ICP_index.htm

Much of our present understanding of how acid deposition affects aquatic ecosystems originates from investigations during the 1970s. Several investigations showed how acid deposition had affected fish populations not only in Scandinavia but also in Scotland, Northern England and North America. The understanding of the ecological effects and the underlying mechanisms increased rapidly. Among results of importance for our understanding, we should note the importance of inorganic aluminium for the extinction of fish, the importance of snowmelt acidification episodes and the invasion of sphagnum (peat moss) in acid lakes. It is also worth mentioning that liming already at that time was a successful way of combating acidification and ensuring the survival of threatened fish populations.

Around 1980 interest in the effects of regional air pollution turned from water to terrestrial ecosystems. The main reason was the observed forest damage in Germany and later in other parts of Europe and North America. The observed damage was immediately attributed to air pollution, even if it was, in most cases, difficult to find simple cause-effect relationships. The effects on forests were front-page news for several years and in many countries it was the main reason for action against emissions of sulphur and nitrogen oxides.

Forest damage increased the interest in studies of the changes in soils caused by air pollution. Several hypotheses were put forward and tested, most of them with little evidence of the main cause for the forest damage. There were, however, some results of particular interest for our understanding of how forest soils and forests were affected by acid deposition. The responses in soils to acid deposition could be explained as a sequence starting with leaching of base cations leading to decreased base saturation and increased soil acidity followed by the release of inorganic aluminium ions into the soil solution. Long-term experiments such as that at Solling in Germany and revisiting sites where soil chemistry had been measured decades ago showed clear evidence of long-term soil acidification.

International Cooperative Programme on Assessment and Monitoring of Air Pollution Effects on Forests
(ICP Forests)
Lead country: Germany

ICP Forests was set up to monitor the effects of air pollution on forests in the UNECE region. The mandate of ICP Forests is: to monitor effects of air pollution as well as other anthropogenic and natural stress factors on the condition and development of forests and to contribute to a better understanding of cause-effect relationships in forest ecosystem functioning. Since 1986, ICP Forests has been surveying large-scale forest condition on a transnational grid of about 6,000 sample plots (level I). This transnational survey comprises annual surveys of crown condition on all plots (about 130,000 trees) as well as single surveys of soil condition and foliage chemistry on part of the plots. Cause-effect relationships are studied on about 860 intensive monitoring plots (level II). On all plots the intensive monitoring comprises surveys of crown condition, soil condition, foliar chemistry, tree growth and ground vegetation. Atmospheric deposition, ambient air quality, meteorology and tree phenology are assessed on part of the plots. Thirty-nine countries participate in the programme. The monitoring is conducted in close cooperation with the European Commission. The European Union (EU) countries participate through an EU directive that has recently been revised (Forest Focus) to encompass biodiversity, the effects of climate change and carbon sequestration.

Further information: www.icp-forests.org

Nitrogen

Much of the early interest in acid rain was focused on sulphur, although it was recognized that nitrogen compounds were oxidized in the atmosphere to nitric acid and thus contributed to the acidification in precipitation. The interest in nitrogen increased after 1980, in particular since several observations indicated a large nitrate leaching from some soils in Europe. It was however recognized that soils in general were able to immobilize large amounts of nitrogen deposition and that nitrate leaching occurred only in situations where nitrogen deposition was above a certain level. The concept of nitrogen saturation was therefore developed. It also became obvious that ammonia, which was, in terms of nitrogen, emitted in quantities comparable to nitrogen oxides, could, after nitrification in soils, contribute to acidification in a similar way as nitrogen oxides.

Nitrogen eutrophication also became an important issue at this time. Nitrogen deposition had caused large ecosystem changes, in particular on heathlands with poor soils where the traditional vegetation dominated by heather had turned into grasslands.

Critical loads and critical levels

The Swedish Conference 'Acidification Today and Tomorrow' (Stockholm, 1982) was one of the first which aimed to set limits for atmospheric deposition of acidifying substances to protect ecosystems.

The idea of setting quantitative values on what could be seen as an acceptable level of pollution load to ecosystems then slowly matured over the following years. Scandinavian scientists and policy makers, in particular Mr. Jan Nilsson at the Swedish Environment Protection Agency, were the main promoters of the idea. A first attempt to develop the concept was made at a Nordic workshop on critical loads for nitrogen and sulphur[1]. It was followed by a Convention workshop on critical loads for sulphur and nitrogen, held in Skokloster (Sweden)[2] early in 1988. The output from this meeting stimulated an interest in the concept which went through the Convention's organization, first through the Working Group on Effects and then through the Executive Body in late 1988. Such was the interest that the idea of developing critical loads was written as an obligation in the Protocol on Nitrogen Oxides, which was adopted in October 1988.

The role of nitrogen in the acidification of soils and surface waters received more attention in a collaboration between the Nordic Council of Ministers and the United States Environmental Protection Agency[3]. Meanwhile, in parallel with the development of the critical loads concept, a critical levels concept was developed for gaseous exposure of vegetation and materials to air pollution. The first scientific workshop was held under the Convention in Bad Harzburg (Germany) in 1988 at about the same time as the Skokloster workshop. At Bad Harzburg the critical levels concept was agreed upon for forests, crops and materials.

The development of critical loads and levels modelling and mapping methodologies have since that time regularly been submitted for review under the Convention and updated in a "Mapping Manual" (see www.icpmapping.org).

Modelling acidification

Theoretical models have not only been important for understanding acidification processes but also to predict responses to deposition changes and to generalize results to large areas. The first lake acidification models were already developed in the 1970s. In Norway a simple compartmental model was developed. Later, more advanced models were developed such as the Model of Acidification of Groundwater In Catchments (MAGIC), which has been widely used for assessing lake acidification all over the world. In parallel soil models were also developed, e.g. the Swedish Soil Acidification in Forest Ecosystems (SAFE) model and the Netherlands Simulation Model for Acidification Regional Trends (SMART), through which the chemical processes in soils could be modelled over long time periods.

Photochemical oxidants

Even though critical levels were set for several gases and for effects on materials as well as on vegetation, it has been the effects of ozone to vegetation that have attracted the greatest attention.

The effects of photochemical oxidants on vegetation were first observed in the Netherlands in connection with local ozone formation close to Rotterdam. When the regional ozone episodes were discovered in the early 1970s, studies on effects using indicator plants became common in many European countries. Many studies used open-top field experiments, primarily on agricultural crops but also on forest trees, to investigate ozone effects. Through these experiments it was possible to establish dose-response relationships for ozone effects, and it was on these that critical levels were based. The interest in establishing critical levels has been an important factor for stimulating international collaboration. Much progress has been made and recent developments have enabled the replacement of the early simple critical levels for forests, crops and natural vegetation by more process-oriented methods.

International Cooperative Programme on Effects of Air Pollution on Natural Vegetation and Crops (ICP Vegetation)
Lead country: United Kingdom

The programme was established in 1987 as ICP Crops to consider the underlying science for quantifying the effects of ozone pollution on crops. In 1999, the programme was renamed ICP Vegetation to reflect the incorporation of the effects of ozone on (semi-)natural vegetation (28 sites). In 2001, the programme expanded considerably by the inclusion of an ongoing pan-European study assessing the heavy metal concentrations in mosses (6000 sites). The programme's objectives are to provide realistic ozone dose-response relationships, develop concentration- and flux-based critical levels of ozone for crops and (semi-)natural vegetation, facilitate the production of European ozone exceedance maps, and produce European maps of the heavy metal concentrations in mosses. The programme includes 32 Parties to the Convention.

Further information: http://icpvegetation.ceh.ac.uk/

International collaboration and conferences

International collaboration on effects of transboundary air pollution was in the early years before the Convention mainly a scientific activity. An international conference held in the United States

(Columbus, Ohio, 1975) was the first large meeting where acidification effects were a major topic. This conference set the scene for international collaboration and has been followed by a series of similar conferences every five years: Sandefjord, Norway (1980); Muskoka, Canada (1985); Glasgow, United Kingdom (1990); Gothenburg, Sweden (1995); and Tsukuba, Japan (2000). The seventh conference is scheduled for Prague in 2005. These conferences have, together with a few others, brought the global scientific community together. One of the main objectives of the conference in Sandefjord was to present the main results from the first large-scale integrated project on acidification – the Norwegian interdisciplinary research programme Acid precipitation – effects on forests and fish. This was at a time when the Convention had been adopted, but specific action on pollution control was lacking.

In Germany, the political attitude towards the effects of air pollution changed in 1982, immediately before the Stockholm Ministerial Conference on Acidification of the Environment. The German Interior Minister, who was responsible for environmental affairs at that time, had been shown a number of photographs of extreme forest damage on the Czech side of the Ore Mountains. “This will never happen to German forests” he said. At the Conference the European public was for the first time confronted with a German Environment Minister who pushed for strong abatement measures, especially against sulphur dioxide. At that time a monitoring scheme that routinely assessed forest condition (first report 1982) was also installed in the Federal Republic of Germany.

From about 1980 a number of large-scale national projects were set up, e.g. the United States National Acid Precipitation Assessment Program (NAPAP), which was a 10-year programme; the Finnish Acidification Research Programme (HAPRO), the Swedish Gårdsjön Project and the Netherlands National Acidification Programme. These were all national programmes and projects, although some of them, for example the Lake Gårdsjön project, attracted scientists internationally. One of the first truly international projects on acid rain was the Surface Water Acidification Project, set up as a collaborative effort between the academies in United Kingdom, Norway and Sweden. The project was supported by the British coal and power industries, and although it was originally seen by some as a project aimed at delaying control measures by the British power industry, it was remarkably successful in linking together scientists from the different countries to collaborate on the effects of air pollution.

Progress in effect-related knowledge was also ensured through a series of Convention workshops, continuing up to the present day, dedicated to particular subjects such as empirical critical loads for nitrogen[4], critical levels for ozone[5], health effects of ozone and nitrogen oxides[6] and critical loads for heavy metals (Potsdam, Germany 4-5 March 2004). Collaboration between the Convention and the World Health Organization (WHO) has been instrumental in the further development of knowledge of the effects on human health including those of widely dispersing compounds such as persistent organic pollutants[7]. Finally, regular workshops held by the Coordination Center for Effects (www.rivm.nl/cce) and the programme centres of the other ICPs have contributed to the application of knowledge on a UNECE-wide scale by bringing together scientists, representatives of national focal centres (NFCs) of the ICPs and experts from the ICP Centres.

The European Union has also contributed to developing the scientific knowledge on regional air pollution effects, in particular under the 4th and 5th Framework Programmes. Several projects which

have had a large influence both scientifically and with respect to policy were set up. One such example was the NITREX (NITRogen EXperiments) project, which aimed to better understand responses in soils to increased and decreased nitrogen deposition. Some important aspects of nitrogen saturation were explored.

International Cooperative Programme on Modelling and Mapping of Critical Loads and Levels and their Air Pollution Effects, Risks and Trends (ICP Modelling and Mapping)
Lead country: Germany
Programme Centre (CCE): Netherlands

The objectives of ICP Modelling and Mapping are to: (a) determine receptor-specific critical loads for indirect effects of the (long-term) deposition of various air pollutants, and critical levels for direct effects of gaseous air pollutants; (b) map pollutant depositions and concentrations which exceed critical thresholds; and (c) establish appropriate methods as a basis for assessing potential damage, e.g. via dynamic modelling. The work is supported by the Coordination Center for Effects (CCE) in the Netherlands at the National Institute of Public Health and the Environment (RIVM), whose mandate includes the development of modelling and mapping methodologies for the assessment of critical loads and exceedances on a European scale. At present 25 Parties participate in the programme's activities and contribute national data to produce European critical load maps. These are used for integrated assessment modelling by the Convention's Task Force on Integrated Assessment Modelling. A recently revised Mapping Manual, produced in collaboration with other ICPs, describes the methods to be used by the programme's NFCs.

Further information: www.icpmapping.org www.rivm.nl/cce

Policy developments driving the effects programme

Alarming reports

In the 1960s and, in particular, in the 1970s there was growing environmental concern and the problems of air pollution received wide public and governmental attention in most countries of the UNECE region. The alarming reports on the acidification of lakes and streams in Norway and Sweden emphasized the magnitude of the problem in Scandinavia and indicated the priority that these countries attached to concerted measures to reduce the effects of acid rain. Considerable damage to forests was observed in Northern and Central Europe as well as in North America and it was believed that, at least in Central Europe, the damage was mainly due to air pollutants. Substantial damage to materials, including historic buildings and cultural monuments, was also reported.

It was widely agreed that the acidity of the soil in many parts of Europe and North America was increasing. The acidity of rainfall in the north-eastern part of the United States and southern Quebec and Ontario even appeared to exceed Scandinavian values.

The need for international cooperation

With air pollution growing and its effects becoming more severe, the need for effective practical action was urgent. As a political goal environmental protection was almost unanimously approved and the need for increased international cooperation in related areas was recognized. The signing of the Convention in 1979 confirmed that the time was ripe for the mobilization of broader political support for internationally agreed control measures. While some countries, especially those most severely affected, pressed for harmonized international remedial measures without waiting for final proof concerning the precise mechanism of the air pollution effects, some others felt that any recommendations for remedial action needed to be based on more complete knowledge.

Already at its first session, in 1980, the Interim Executive Body for the Convention established the Working Group on Effects of Sulphur Compounds on the Environment. The Working Group was to facilitate the decision-making process with respect to air pollution effects. The Executive Body requested it to collect and assess available information on dose-effect relationships, the extent of estimated damage caused by sulphur compounds and estimated benefits of emission reductions. The benefits included economic benefits regarding materials, including historic and cultural monuments, aquatic ecosystems and soils, groundwater and vegetation. The work of the Working Group (and its groups of designated experts and later ICPs and task forces) not only strengthened the sense of scientific objectivity of information used for political decisions, but also facilitated a broad dissemination of available knowledge.

International Cooperative Programme on Effects of Air Pollution on Materials, Including Historic and Cultural Monuments (ICP Materials)
Lead country: Sweden

Extensive damage has been observed to buildings and constructions and to historic and cultural monuments. One objective of ICP Materials is to perform a quantitative evaluation of the effect of sulphur and nitrogen compounds and other major pollutants, and climatic parameters, on the atmospheric corrosion of important materials. The other main objective is to describe and evaluate long-term corrosion trends attributable to atmospheric pollution. Fifteen Parties participated in the original eight-year exposure programme (1987-1995) performed at 39 sites. Currently 18 Parties participate in the multi-pollutant exposure programme performed at 29 test sites, which started in 1997. The quantitative evaluation aims at determining dose/response relationships as a basis for assessing critical and/or target levels and calculating costs due to material damage. Structural metals, stone materials, paint coatings, electric contact materials, samples representative of medieval stained-glass windows and polymer materials have been studied in the programme.

Further information: www.corr-institute.se/ICP-Materials/

Eastern Europe and the Convention before and after 1989

Before 1989

Up to the end of the 1970s, despite the occasional distressing reports about possible serious environmental and health risks of growing air pollution and even with first-hand evidence of serious consequences, e.g. in the "black triangle", environmental problems were not among the official priorities of the East European countries. Unfortunately, mainly due to a lack of credible information, the general public perceived these problems more as annoying than alarming. Surprisingly, even the mention of environmental problems in the Final Act of the Conference for Security and Co-operation in Europe (Helsinki, 1975), calling for cooperation to control air pollution and its effects, did not attract too much attention. In fact, even during the process of preparing for the High-level Ministerial Meeting on the Protection of the Environment (Geneva, November 1979) a number of East Europe countries objected to the proposed internationally binding instrument to control transboundary air pollution and suggested other topics (e.g. protection of fauna and flora).

Nevertheless, in the "post-Helsinki" atmosphere of political détente, the signing of the Convention became inevitable for the majority of East European countries. Already the provisions of the Convention, not to speak of its subsequent protocols, put the Governments under strong moral pressure and their respective action or inaction under continuing critical review. After a period of initial obstruction, these countries gradually engaged in ongoing international cooperation, e.g. by submitting official air pollution data, sharing new knowledge and information and participating in the activities of task forces or international cooperative programmes. As a result of a need to meet the obligations of the Convention and its protocols and the requirements of agreed international cooperation, several new environmental institutes/institutions were created and some new research programmes were launched.

The beginning of the 1990s

Dramatic changes in East European countries in the beginning of the 1990s had a profound positive effect on the attitude of their Governments as well as the general public with respect to environmental problems. The quality of the environment became an important factor determining the quality of life and deserving continuing attention. However, in the early 1990s it was not easy for representatives from countries in Eastern Europe to participate actively in various bodies and expert groups under the Convention. Many years of isolation resulted in a low level or even a lack of institutional or personal contacts with international communities not least caused by a language barrier. These obstacles were gradually overcome. Better understanding of effect-based concepts and, in particular, appreciation of their importance for developing effective national pollution control policies resulted in increasing policy support for, and deeper involvement of, relevant governmental agencies in national effect-related activities coordinated by the ICPs and the Working Group on Effects. The progress achieved since 1990 by East European countries in capacity-building, development of effect-related scientific and monitoring activities and in gathering, assessing and sharing data, new knowledge and information has been remarkable. The positive results of this broader international cooperation were duly reflected, for example, in the link-up of national environmental monitoring systems with the unified EMEP monitoring network and in the successful preparation of maps of critical loads of acidity, nitrogen eutrophication and critical levels of ground-level ozone, which provided the scientific basis for the Gothenburg Protocol.

Improvement of air quality in Eastern Europe

The considerable decrease in the emissions of atmospheric pollutants observed since the early 1990s in most East European countries was caused mainly by the transition from a centrally planned to a free-market economy. This was generally accompanied by a significant decrease in economic activity, including energy production, and to a lesser extent by the implementation of effective environmental protection programmes. Since the mid-1990s the converse occurred, and air quality was improved further mainly due to the implementation of emission reduction strategies. This was another benefit of being a Party to the Convention that provided valuable guidelines for the development of efficient national air pollution control strategies, which fully respected and properly balanced ecological, economic and technological considerations.

Becoming EU members

The experience with the implementation of the Convention's protocols and the ability to prepare and implement national effect-based abatement strategies in particular, will facilitate the effective integration of the East European countries that are now becoming members of the European Union into its environmental protection programmes. Such a very specific benefit of being Party to the Convention could not have been predicted 25 years ago, when it was signed.

The current structure of the Working Group on Effects

Before the Convention entered into force (1980-1983), three groups of designated experts operated under Working Group on Effects of Sulphur Compounds on the Environment. They worked to collect and assess available knowledge on important dose-effect relationships and the extent of estimated damage to materials, including historic and cultural monuments, aquatic ecosystems and to soil, groundwater and vegetation.

Following the Convention's entry into force in 1983, the Executive Body set about developing its work for more specific action on pollution control. To provide information on the effects of pollution, it established ICP Forests, ICP Waters and ICP Materials in 1985. Later, in 1987, it agreed to establish ICP Crops (later to become ICP Vegetation) and also in that year the Pilot Programme on Integrated Monitoring, later ICP Integrated Monitoring, was created. The Task Force on Mapping was established in 1988 and this has continued as the Task Force for ICP Modelling and Mapping. The work of the programmes is guided by the mandate of the Working Group on Effects, drawn up by the Executive Body in 1999. For this, the Working Group collects, assesses and further develops knowledge and information on:

(a) The present status and long-term trends in the degree and geographical extent of the impact of air pollution, in particular its long-range transboundary impact;
(b) Dose-response relationships for agreed air pollutants;
(c) Critical loads, levels and limits for agreed air pollutants;
(d) Damage and benefits, as a basis for the further development of air pollution abatement strategies.

International Cooperative Programme on Integrated Monitoring of Air Pollution Effects on Ecosystems (ICP Integrated Monitoring)
Lead country: Sweden
Programme Centre: Finland

The objective of ICP Integrated Monitoring is to determine and predict the state of ecosystems (catchment approach) and the changes from a long-term perspective with respect to the regional variation and impact of air pollutants, especially nitrogen, sulphur, ozone and metals and including effects on biota. Investigations of air pollutants acting on particular receptors have shown that an integrated approach is needed to understand the mechanisms of damage and the resulting effects (also in relation to climate conditions). Thus, the impacts of acidic deposition may take place in the soil, but effects are more likely to be seen in the vegetation or in the water leaching from the system. Nineteen Parties contribute to the programme, which consists of 50 sites. The detailed databases and the long time series from the sites have been used to assess critical thresholds and trends in damage/recovery and for the application/testing of complex mathematical models. These models have been used to assess the consequences of future impact scenarios and their uncertainties.

Further information: www.environment.fi and click on "Research"

All programmes have addressed the scientific, research and monitoring issues within a wide regional framework providing data and information which could not have been produced by any single institution or country. They have also promoted the development and dissemination of multidisciplinary expert knowledge on the effects of air pollutants both nationally and internationally. Their results have facilitated:

- Assessment of the impacts and effectiveness of the implementation of existing protocols to the Convention; and
- Identification of the most endangered areas, ecosystems and receptors and the extent of the effects, as a basis for setting priorities in the further development of air pollution abatement strategies.

Up to 1997 health aspects of air pollution were addressed within the framework of the Convention on an ad hoc basis in cooperation with the World Health Organization's Regional Office for Europe. However, the further development and practical application of effect-based approaches required a more systematic assessment of possible health effects of major air pollutants subject to long-range transport. Hence, in 1997 the Executive Body and the World Health Organization (represented by its European Centre for Environment and Health) established the Joint Task Force on the Health Aspects of Long-range Transboundary Air Pollution with the aim of quantifying the contribution of transboundary air pollution to human health risks and to help define priorities for future monitoring and abatement strategies.

The Joint Task Force on the Health Aspects of Long-range Transboundary Air Pollution Task Force on Health
Led by the World Health Organization/European Centre for Environment and Health

The Executive Body and the World Health Organization established the Task Force in 1997. Its aim is to provide the Convention with a state-of-the-art assessment of the health effects of long-range transboundary air pollution and with guidance on priorities for monitoring and abatement strategies. Between 1999 and 2003, the Task Force prepared and published assessments of the contribution of long-range transboundary air pollution to the health risk from particulate matter, heavy metals and persistent organic pollutants.

The Task Force brings together experts delegated by Parties to the Convention, and its work is based on estimates of air pollution concentrations, in particular those derived by EMEP, and on the results of hazard assessment performed by WHO.

Further information: www.unece.org/env/wge/who.htm

In 1999, at its 17th session, the Executive Body (ECE/EB.AIR/68, annex III), following the adoption of the Gothenburg Protocol, decided that the Working Group on Effects would continue to provide the scientific basis for the review of air pollution effects, including the recovery of the environment and human health following emission reductions in line with protocols, and carry out damage and benefit evaluations. It would also alert the Executive Body to any perceived additional, or changed, threats caused by air pollution that might require policy response. The Executive Body also stressed the importance of monitoring and dynamic modelling of recovery. The aims and scope of the effect-oriented activities had developed substantially over the years. The effect-related origin of the work focused on the evaluation of the magnitude and geographical extent of damage and on assessing its cause. While this remains relevant, moving to a more effect-based approach required critical loads and levels to be estimated. Now after some years of pollution control it is important to assess long-term trends, including through the use of dynamic models, to assess time delays of recovery or damage.

Currently, the effect-oriented activities are coordinated by six ICPs, each supported by programme centres, and by the Joint Task Force on the Health Aspects of Air Pollution (see figure 5.2).

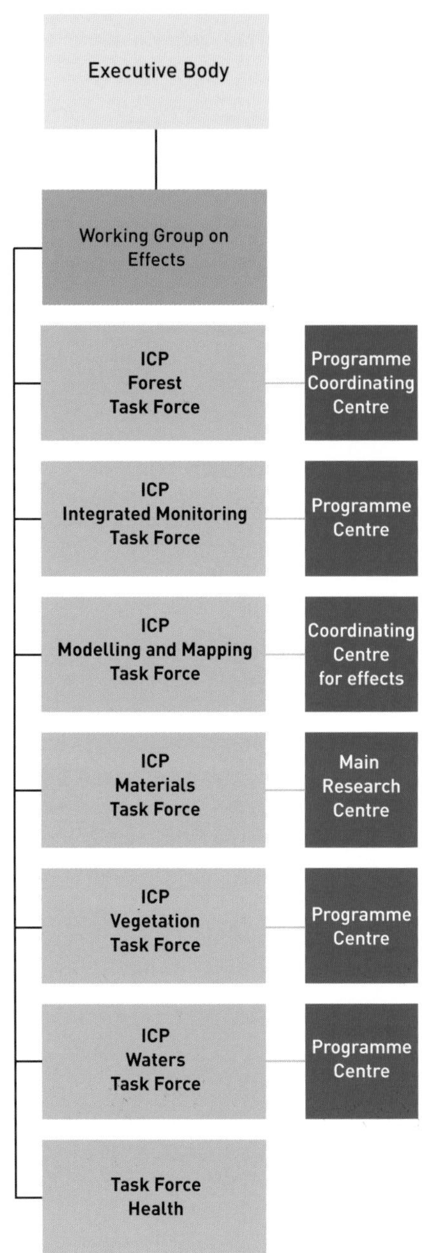

Figure 5.2. The current organization of the Working Group on Effects

The number of Parties to the Convention actively participating in the effect-oriented activities has been growing continuously, but this positive development inevitably makes coordination of the work more demanding and costly. There are also demands for the effect-related work to effectively collaborate with other bodies and groups under the Convention, especially with the Steering Body of EMEP and its centres and task forces, as well as with relevant bodies and programmes outside the Convention.

The cost of the coordination activities of the international centres has generally been borne by the lead countries or countries hosting the programme centres, though some voluntary contributions from Parties have been made available through a trust fund. In recent years there have been discussions among the Parties on a funding mechanism to share the costs of those centres. While a mandatory arrangement, a protocol, has not proved acceptable to some countries, the Executive Body has agreed a formal decision (decision 2002/1) that has provided a mechanism for making voluntary contributions to support the work according to a scale based upon the UN scale of assessment. In 2005 the Executive Body will, in the light of the effectiveness of decision 2002/1, review the need for adopting a protocol on the financing of core activities to achieve long-term stable funding.

Modelling and mapping of critical loads and levels for use in integrated assessment

In 1990 the Working Group on Abatement Strategies defined the critical load approach as "a procedure for developing optimized abatement strategies by which differentiated emission reductions are arrived at on the basis of scientifically derived critical values" (EB.AIR/R.53, para. 4). In the beginning of the 1990s, policy negotiators grew interested in the possibilities of using integrated assessment modelling to develop abatement strategies. Integrated assessment became increasingly recognized as a means to make computerized comparisons between alternatives for cost-effective pollution cuts.

> Very few believed in the critical load concept when it was first brought up at the Working Group on Effects in 1987. But following the meetings in Bad Harzburg and Skokloster in 1988 the concept became a major force in the negotiation process. Even though at that time "fast had to be better than good," the concept worked successfully and today, while "good has become better than fast," it is being applied to a wide range of problems. In bridging the gap between researchers and policy makers, the critical load concept has developed from "the vision of a few" to a European strategy for agreed policy. At the Executive Body's session in Sofia in November 1988, when the Protocol on Nitrogen Oxides was signed, a working group on critical loads was also proposed. Some delegations expressed the opinion that the application of a critical load approach to Western Europe was "unrealistic" and abatement strategies other than critical loads, such as BAT, should be used instead. Therefore, the new body was named the Working Group on Abatement Strategies.

While information on effects generated by the various ICPs did not include sufficient data to assess ecosystem damage and protection across the UNECE region, the Task Force on Mapping started in 1989 to focus on the development of European maps of critical loads. In 1988 in Sofia, the Executive

Body noted with appreciation the offer of the Netherlands Government for a coordinating centre for the activities on effects and invited the Netherlands to elaborate further its proposal for consideration by the Working Group on Effects taking into account the suggestion that the centre could provide technical and scientific input to the activities on critical loads. The Executive Body established the Coordination Center for Effects (CCE) in 1990 at the Netherlands National Institute for Public Health and the Environment (RIVM, Bilthoven). CCE was soon contributing to the work on critical loads and proposed a method to the Task Force on Mapping for modelling and mapping critical loads in each EMEP grid cell based on methods adopted in the Task Force's Mapping Manual. However, the first maps were produced using different grids (figure 5.3).

Towards the first effect-based protocol

In 1991 the Task Force on Mapping and the Working Group on Effects reported on progress in critical loads mapping at the 5th session of the Working Group on Abatement Strategies (EB.AIR/WG.5/10), which was already preparing for negotiations on a revised sulphur protocol. CCE gave a presentation on the feasibility of a European critical loads map. One of the maps presented at that session showed critical loads at which 99% of the forest soils would be protected (see figure 5.3).

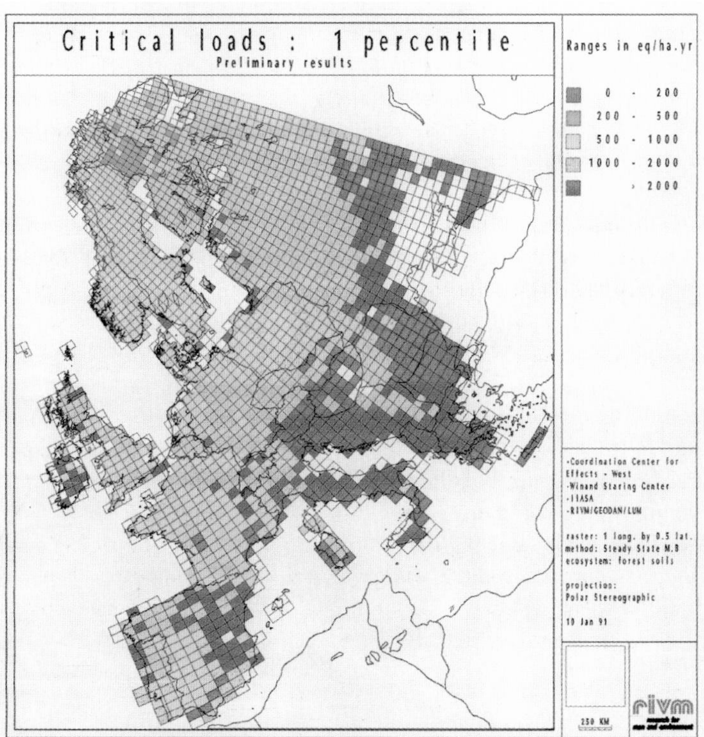

Figure 5.3. One of the first quantitative critical load maps for Europe, showing modelled deposition value ranges (in equivalents of acidity/hectare) that would protect 99% of forest soils. Areas most sensitive to acidification are shaded red

Already in 1990 European maps of simple critical loads, in effect qualitative sensitivity classes, developed by the Stockholm Environment Institute, were being tested in integrated assessment models. The Task Force on Integrated Assessment Modelling reported on preliminary results at the third session of the Working Group on Abatement Strategies in 1990. It was stated "...it must be stressed that the data set of critical loads as applied to derived sensitivity classes was taken as just one example to illustrate basic features of the critical loads approach. As soon as the current international mapping efforts provide complete data sets for critical loads, similar analyses will be undertaken using the officially supplied data" (EB.AIR/WG.5/R.7, para. 4). The mapping programme (the Task Force on Mapping supported by CCE) produced the first such map in 1991. CCE and SEI collaborated to compare the maps in the framework of integrated assessment (Hettelingh et al. (1991)).

Prior to submission of national data, the maps of critical loads produced by CCE were not based on the countries' own information but on a "background" database computed and mapped using information on European soils, forest coverage and meteorological characteristics. Even so, the approach used, which produced maps showing equal ecosystem protection percentages in each EMEP grid cell, strengthened the notion of cross-border "equity", important to achieve consensus agreement. The first European map of critical loads of sulphur-based acidity that also included national contributions was produced by the Mapping Programme[8,9] following a scheme illustrated in figure 5.4. By 1991, 14 Parties had nominated NFCs, which participated in the development of the first critical loads map[8]. For other countries the background database was still used for the map. Note figure 5.4 also shows how "exceedance maps" of critical loads can be computed, though for strategy development the integrated assessment modellers computed these.

According to Mr. Michael Quinion of World Wide Words, the word "exceedance", spelled with an "a", only seems to appear in the fourth edition of the American Heritage Dictionary and in the Oxford English Dictionary database of 1836. The term became widely accepted in the vocabulary of the Parties to the Convention to express the excess of deposition over critical loads.

Towards the multi-pollutant, multi-effect protocol

Since 1991 an increasing number of ICP Mapping NFCs have participated in the development of critical load maps. This active participation is of vital importance for agreement on the further development of modelling and mapping methodologies. Currently, ICP Modelling and Mapping benefits from the participation of 25 Parties to the Convention, and their NFCs have presented the results of their work in the seven CCE Status Reports (see www.rivm.nl/cce) published since 1990. The modelling and mapping work draws from a significant pool of knowledge, including that of other ICPs and scientific research in natural sciences.

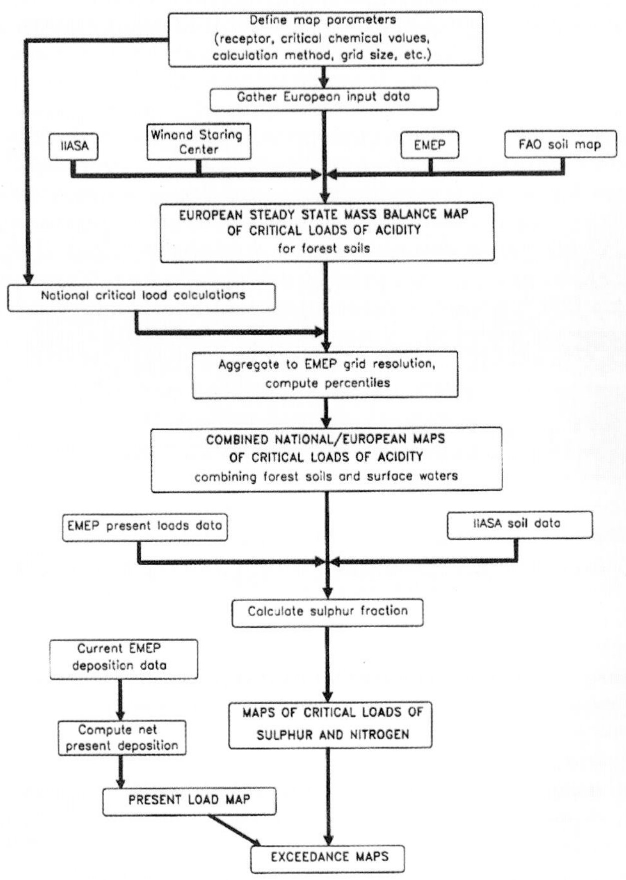

Figure 5.4. The procedure to produce the first European critical loads map of sulphur-based acidity in support of the revision of the first sulphur protocol[8]

When revising the 1988 Protocol on Nitrogen Oxides the Executive Body agreed to extend the critical load concept to include critical loads of nutrient nitrogen, critical loads of nitrogen-based acidity and critical levels of tropospheric ozone, since nitrogen oxides contribute to those three kinds of adverse effects. The inclusion of ozone required integrated assessment models to have quantified knowledge on critical levels of ozone. This was provided through collaborative efforts between the Mapping Programme and ICP Forest, ICP Vegetation and the Joint Task Force on the Health Aspects of Air Pollution.

Critical load maps combining acidification and eutrophication[10,11] were used to support the negotiations of the 1999 Gothenburg Protocol to Abate Acidification Eutrophication and Ground-Level Ozone[13]. The results were also used by the European Commission to support the European Union (EU) Directive on National Emission Ceilings for certain pollutants (2001/81/EC).

Recent European critical load maps now distinguish between ecosystems (see figure 5.5). This enables better understanding of the protection of, or potential damage to, ecosystems across Europe.

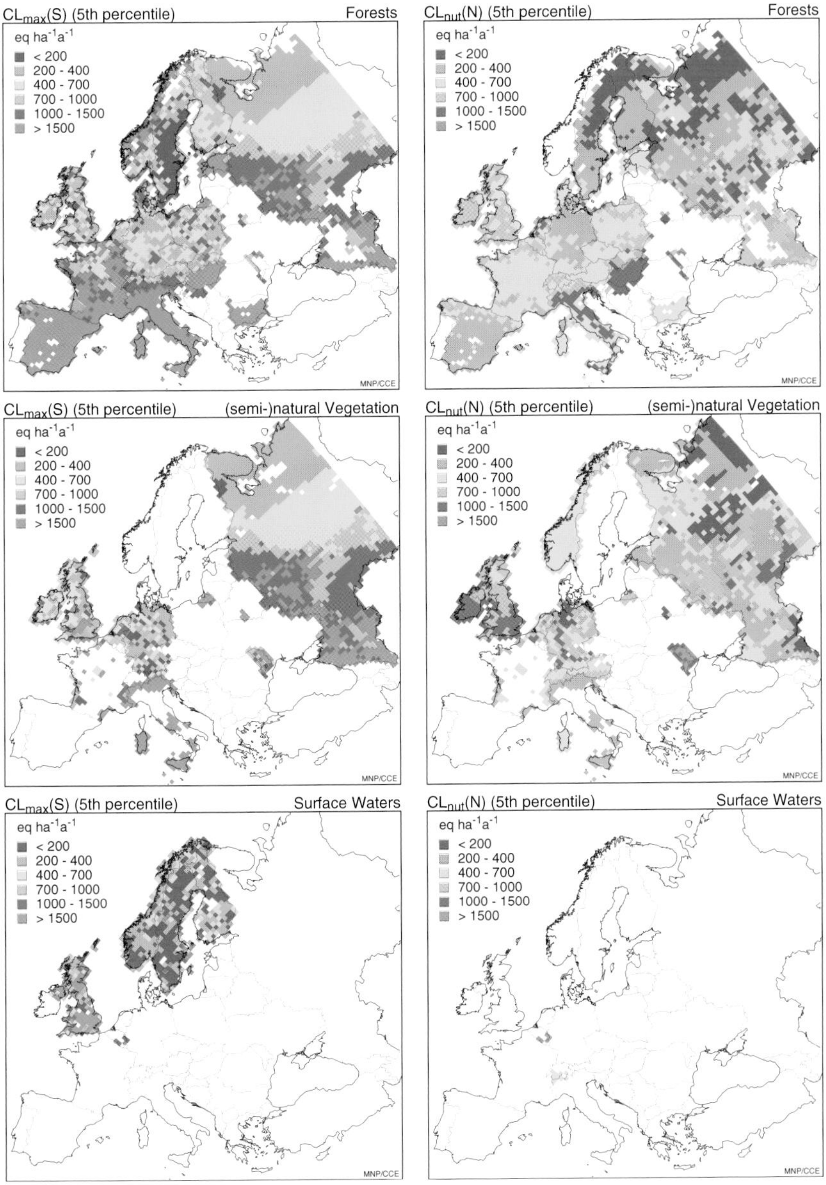

Figure 5.5. The 5th percentiles (protecting 95% of the indicated ecosystems) of the critical load of acidity (left) and the critical load of nutrient nitrogen (right) on the EMEP 50 km x 50 km grid for three different ecosystem classes (forests, semi-natural vegetation and surface waters)[12]

Has the risk diminished?

The area of ecosystems which are unprotected from acidification has diminished since 1980, clearly illustrating the accomplishment of European air pollution control policies (figure 5.6). The protection of ecosystems increases rapidly between 1980 and 2010. For eutrophication, the picture looks less optimistic (figure 5.7). While the red shaded (most unprotected) area is smaller in 2010 than in 1980, the decrease is far less than with acidification.

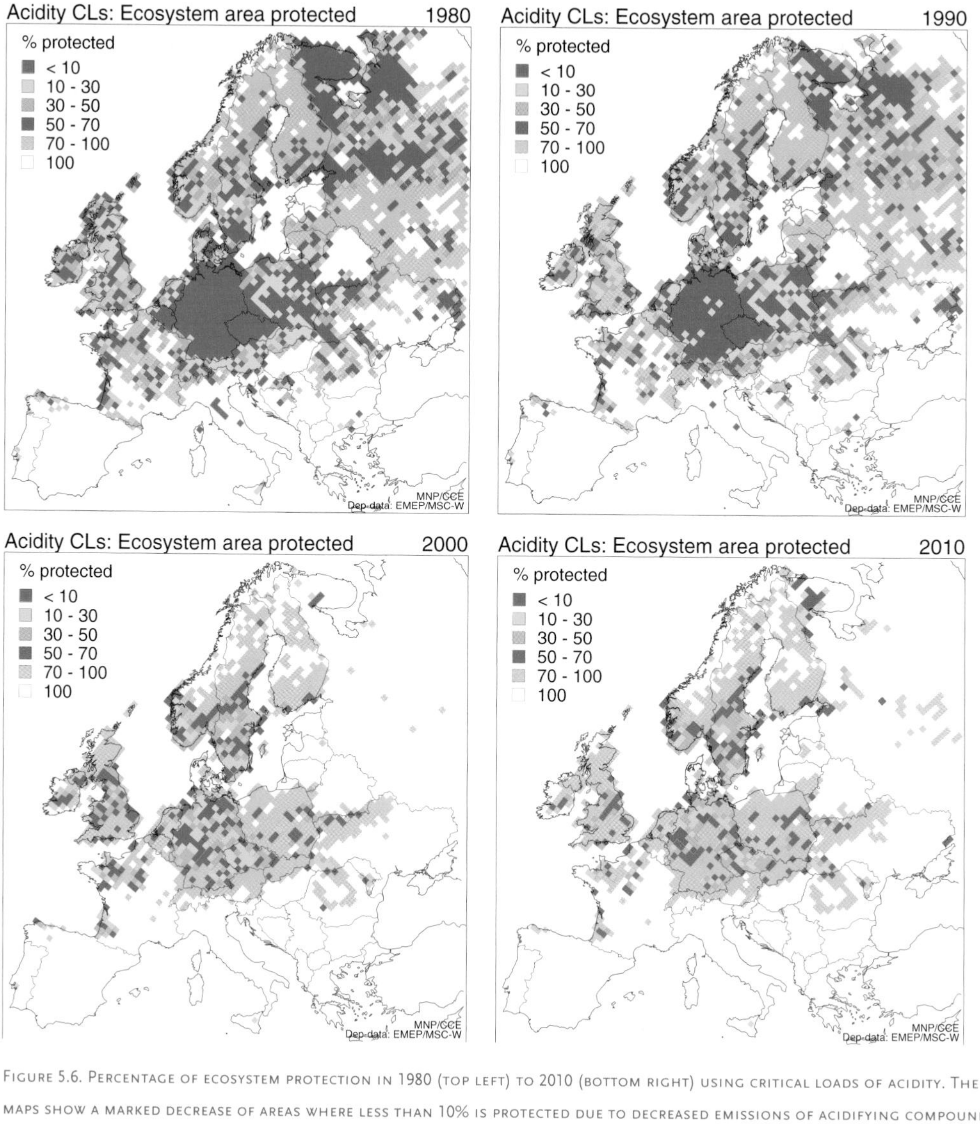

Figure 5.6. Percentage of ecosystem protection in 1980 (top left) to 2010 (bottom right) using critical loads of acidity. The maps show a marked decrease of areas where less than 10% is protected due to decreased emissions of acidifying compounds between 1980 and 2010. Acid deposition in 2010 is simulated using emissions agreed for the 1999 Gothenburg Protocol

Although the area of modelled protected ecosystems is increasing, the important question is "what is seen in the environment?" ICP Waters has already identified the start of chemical recovery in surface waters both in Europe and in North America[14] though biological systems seems to respond more slowly. With respect to the European forest condition, decreasing concentrations of sulphur in the needles of Norway spruce and Scots pine have been noted by ICP Forests[15], however, the forest soils will take considerably longer to recover[16]. So there is some evidence to reflect what is seen on the maps, but there are clearly some delays in the response.

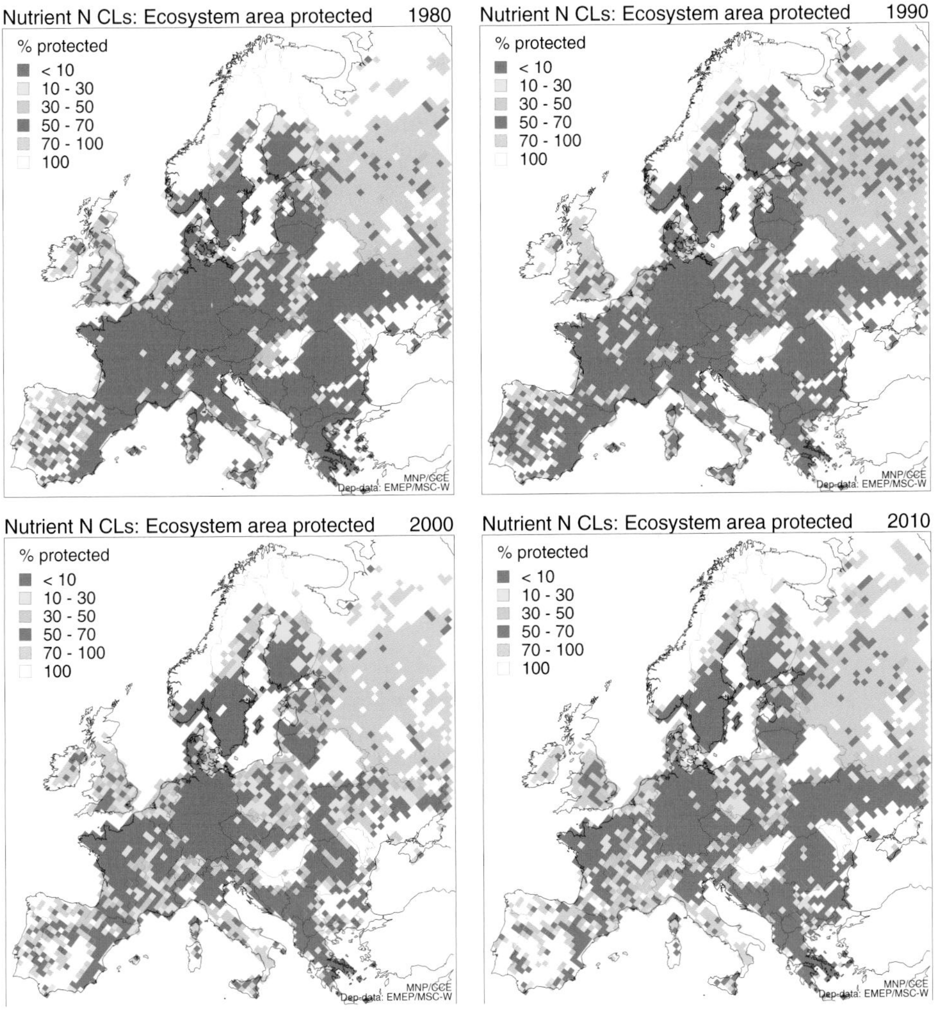

Nutrient N CLs: Ecosystem area protected 1980

% protected
< 10
10 - 30
30 - 50
50 - 70
70 - 100
100

MNP/CCE
Dep-data: EMEP/MSC-W

Nutrient N CLs: Ecosystem area protected 1990

% protected
< 10
10 - 30
30 - 50
50 - 70
70 - 100
100

MNP/CCE
Dep-data: EMEP/MSC-W

Nutrient N CLs: Ecosystem area protected 2000

% protected
< 10
10 - 30
30 - 50
50 - 70
70 - 100
100

MNP/CCE
Dep-data: EMEP/MSC-W

Nutrient N CLs: Ecosystem area protected 2010

% protected
< 10
10 - 30
30 - 50
50 - 70
70 - 100
100

MNP/CCE
Dep-data: EMEP/MSC-W

Figure 5.7. Percentage of ecosystem protection in 1980 (top left) to 2010 (bottom right) using critical loads of N (eutrophication). The maps show that areas where less than 10% is protected continue to occur across Europe due to nitrogen depositions in 2010. The deposition of eutrophying nitrogen compounds in 2010 are simulated using emissions listed in the 1999 Gothenburg Protocol

Further analysis of the time delays of recovery of or damage to surface waters and soils requires an extension of critical loads modelling work. At its 17th session, in December 1999, the Executive Body o the Convention underlined the importance of dynamic modelling of recovery (ECE/EB.AIR/68, para. 51(b)) to enable the assessment of time delays of recovery in regions where deposition falls below critical loads and of damage in regions where critical loads continue to be exceeded.

Conclusions and challenges

In the Convention's earlier years, the monitoring programmes established inter alia acidification effects in soils and surface waters, changes in nutrient nitrogen balances, damage to materials and reductions in crop yields. ICPs under the Working Group on Effects succeeded in providing an effect-related basis for the development of European air pollution control policies. This knowledge gradually developed to include specific dose-response relationships between loads and adverse effects. Most recently, the modelling and mapping of critical loads on a European scale have provided scientific and technical support of air pollution abatement policies that could now evolve from effect-related to effect-based assessments.

The use of critical loads to support European air pollution abatement policies has been successful. Critical loads supported the negotiations of the Protocol on the Further Reduction of Sulphur Emissions (Oslo, 1994), and the Protocol to Abate Acidification, Eutrophication and Ground-level Ozone (Gothenburg, 1999), and also supported the EU Directive on National Emission Ceilings (2001/81/EC). Over time, these agreements have become increasingly complex, extending from consideration of a single pollutant and a single effect to address multiple pollutants and multiple effects. The critical load concept has also contributed to the cost-effectiveness of European air pollution policies, since impacts (benefits) can be compared to the economic and technical consequences (costs) of policy alternatives.

In addition to improved information on environmental indicators such as critical loads, levels and recovery, the revision of the Gothenburg Protocol, whose preparations are already under way, is likely to focus on information regarding the impacts of ozone and particulate matter on human health. The Working Group on Effects collaborates closely with the World Health Organization through the Joint Task Force on Health, to develop information for inclusion in integrated assessment modelling.

Monitoring now reveals recovery of bio-geochemical balances, most notably in surface waters. Policies to reduce the deposition of sulphur compounds are being followed by improvements to water quality. However, soils are known to recover more slowly. Therefore, information on time delays of damage and recovery could become a relevant element in the assessment of European emission reduction targets.

In 2004 the Executive Body appreciated the progress achieved in the application of dynamic modelling and approved work-plan elements to continue to assess dynamic processes in soils and surface waters.

Thus, threats related to acidification, eutrophication, ozone, heavy metals and POPs are being gradually reduced. However, some issues still remain unsolved whilst developing knowledge leads to the identification of new problems[17]:

- Acidification: deposition on forests is higher than the average deposition across an EMEP grid cell. The result is that forest-specific exceedances of critical loads are likely to be higher than those computed with average deposition (as was done in the past). Therefore, integrated assessment of emission reduction alternatives might now point to a need for additional measures to protect forest ecosystems from acidification;
- Eutrophication: many ICP Forest plots show signs of nutrient imbalances and also elevated nitrate leaching. Similarly, half of the ICP Waters sites exhibit a high degree of nitrogen saturation. The measures in the 1999 Gothenburg Protocol will ease the problem. Nevertheless, the current commitments are known to be insufficient to prevent further accumulation of nitrogen in ecosystems in the long term;
- Ozone and particulate matter: current levels of ozone and levels of fine particles in many European and North American cities still lead to adverse health effects. Also, due to the multi-pollutant environment in urban centres, materials - whether used in constructions or in objects of cultural heritage – corrode faster and are soiled more rapidly than in the surrounding rural regions. Current levels of ozone also affect crops, forest trees and semi-natural vegetation over most of Europe and North America;
- Heavy metals: though emissions of lead, cadmium and mercury have decreased, these metals are expected to continue to accumulate in soils and reach concentrations sufficient to affect biota (aquatic biota in the case of mercury). The cadmium content of agricultural soils is also of concern because of its possible effects on human health.

The medium-term work programme of the Working Group on Effects foresees extending multiple effect assessments to address synergies with climate change and nitrogen processes including biodiversity effects. This could provide alternative effects-based end points for integrated assessment modelling with options to assess cost effectiveness of measures to reduce both “classical” as well as “climate change” air pollutants. This may provide opportunities for cost-efficient policies that take account of linkages between climate change and air pollution abatement policies.

Increasingly complex effects-based policies require robust scientific and technical knowledge. Close cooperation or even integration of activities of several ICPs to address difficult problems of modelling and measuring effects of multiple pollutants will continue to be an important challenge. The current voluntary funding mechanism of effect-based coordinating activities may not provide a sufficiently stable basis for maintaining the current level of coordination activities.

The interaction between science and policy under the Convention has become successfully linked with its consensus-based procedures. The Convention has established an organizational structure that is consistent with the underlying scientific network. This has created a stable framework to ensure the build-up of information, the development of research, and the application of the work to policy through inter alia dedicated workshops, official reporting mechanisms and scientific publications.

Collaboration with other relevant international activities is also recognized as important and the effects programmes are involved in joint research projects, monitoring activities, pooling of data and exchange of information. Within Europe, there is collaboration between the Convention and the European Commission's Clean Air For Europe Programme. At a more global scale there are links with Asia, e.g. the Acid Deposition Monitoring Network for East Asia, and links with Parties in North America continue to flourish. Environmental policies will continue to benefit from the success of the Convention especially for multi-pollutant, multi-effect approaches that include interactions between air pollution and other environmental issues.

Acknowledgements

We wish to thank: Ms.Berit Kvaeven, Ms. Merete Johannessen Ulstein, Ms. Brit Lisa Skjelkvåle, Mr. Thomas Haußmann, Mr Martin Lorenz, Mr. Harry Harmens, Ms. Gina Mills, Mr Till Spranger, Mr Vladimir Kucera, Mr Johan Tidblad, Mr Lars Lundin, Mr Martin Forsius, for their contributions on ICPs and Mr Michal Krzyzanowski for his contribution on the Task Force on Health, Ms..Willemijn Tuinstra for sharing historical material on the Convention, Mr. Max Posch and Mr. Jaap Slootweg for making computations to produce the European maps in this chapter.

References

1 Nilsson J (ed.), Andersen, B, Dickson, W, Eriksson, E, Henriksen, A, Kämäri, J, Nilsson, I (1986), Critical loads for nitrogen and sulphur, Report from a nordic working group, Nordic Council of Ministers, Miljø rapport 1986:11, Stockholm, 232 p.

2 Nilsson, J and Grennfelt, P (1988) Critical loads for sulphur and nitrogen, Report of a workshop held in Skokloster, Nordic Council of Ministers, Miljø rapport 1988:15, Stockholm, 418 p.

3 Malanchuk, John L., Nilsson, Jan (1998) The role of nitrogen in the acidification of soils and surface waters, Nordic Council of Ministers, Miljø rapport 1989:10, Stockholm.

4 Achermann, B, Bobbink, R (2002) Empirical critical loads for nitrogen, proceedings of an expert workshop, Berne, 11-13 November 2002 Swiss Agency for the Environment Forests and Landscape, Environmental Documentation No. 164.

5 Karlsson, PE, Selldén G, Pleijel, H (eds.) (2003) Establishing ozone critical levels II, UNECE Workshop Report, IVL report B1523, Göteborg, 379 pp.

6 UNECE-WHO (1997) Health effects of ozone and nitrogen oxides in an integrated assessment of air pollution, proceedings of an international UNECE-WHO workshop, Institute for Environment and Health, University of Leicester, Leicester.

7 WHO (2003), Health risks of persistent organic pollutants from long-range transboundary air pollution, Joint WHO/Convention Task Force on the Health Aspects of Air Pollution, WHO Regional Office for Europe, Copenhagen, 252 pp.

8 Hettelingh, J-P, Downing, RJ, De Smet, PAM (1991) Mapping Critical loads for Europe, CCE Status Report 1991, Coordination Center for Effects, National Institute of Public Health and the Environment (RIVM), Bilthoven, The Netherlands.

9 Hettelingh, J.-P., M. Posch, M., P.A.M. De Smet, R.J. Downing, 1995, The use of critical loads in emission reduction agreements in Europe, Water, Air an Soil Pollution 85:2381-2389.

10 Hettelingh J-P, Posch, M, De Smet, PAM (2001) Multi-effect critical loads used in multi-pollutant reduction agreements in Europe. Water, Air and Soil Pollution 130: 1133-1138.

11 Posch M, Hettelingh, J-P, De Smet, PAM (2001), Characterization of critical load exceedances in Europe. Water, Air and Soil Pollution 130: 1139-1144.

12 Posch M, J.-P. Hettelingh, J. Slootweg, R.J. Downing (eds), 2003, Modelling and Mapping of Critical Thresholds in Europe. Status Report1 2003, Coordination Center for Effects , National Institute for Public Health and the Environment (RIVM), Bilthoven, The Netherlands, 132 pp.

13 Bull KR, B. Achermann , V. Bashkin, R. Chrast, G. Fenech, M. Forsius, H-D. Gregor, R. Guardans , T. Haußmann, F. Hayes , J-P. Hettelingh, T. Johannessen, M. Krzyzanowski, V. Kucera, B. Kvaeven, M. Lorenz , L. Lundin, G. Mills, M. Posch, B-L. Skjelkvåle, M.J.Ulstein, 2001, Coordinated effects monitoring and modelling for developing and supporting international air pollution control agreements. Water, Air and Soil Pollution 130: 119-130.

14 Stoddard, JL, Jeffries, DS, Lükewille, A, Clair, TA, Dillon, OJ, Driscoll, CT, Forsius, M, Johannessen, M, Kahl, JS, Kellog, JH, Kemp, A, Mannio, J, Monteith, D, Murdoch, PS, Patrick, S, Rebsdorf, A, Skjelkvåle, BL, Stainton, MP, Traaen, TS, van Dam, H, Webster, KE, Wieting, J, and Wilander, A (1999) Regional trends in aquatic recovery from acidification in North America and Europe 1980-95. Nature 401:575-578.

15 Lorenz, M, Mues, V, Becher, G, Muller-Edzards, Luyssaert, Raitio, H, Fürst, A, Langouche, D (2003) Forest Condition in Europe, Federal Research Centre for Forestry and Forest Products, 2003 technical report, Hamburg, Germany.

16 De Vries, W, Reinds, GJ, Posch, M, Sanz, MJ, Krause, GHM, Calatayud, V, Renaud, JP, Dupouey, JL, Sterba, H, Gundersen, P, Voogd, JCH and Vel, EM (2003). Intensive Monitoring of Forest Ecosystems in Europe. Technical Report. EC, UN/ECE 2003, Brussels, Geneva, 161 pp.

17 Working Group on Effects (2004), Review and assessment of air pollution effects and their recorded trends, Technical Report prepared by the Bureau of the Working Group on Effects in collaboration with the International Cooperative programmes (ICPs) and the Task Force on the Health Aspects of Air Pollution (in prep.)

Integrated assessment modelling - the tool

Rob Maas, Markus Amann, Helen Apsimon, Leen Hordijk and Willemijn Tuinstra

Integrated assessment modelling has played a vital role in policy negotiations aimed at the abatement of transboundary air pollution in Europe. Its goal is to facilitate the design of an international cost-effective and effect-oriented policy, taking into account equity criteria as well as the relevant differences in environmental sensitivities in Europe. Over the past decade integrated assessment models of air pollution have become increasingly complex. Acidification has gradually been linked to eutrophication and to the local exposure of the population to ozone and fine particles. Currently also the links with the hemispheric transport of pollutants as well as the interactions with climate change are considered. In the past decades the Task Force on Integrated Assessment Modelling has played an important role as the interface between science and policy within the Convention.

Outline

This chapter describes the developments in modelling and in the design of the science-policy interaction over the past 25 years as well as the prospects for the near future. The first part focuses on the rise of integrated assessment models during the 1980s. The second part describes the further developments during the 1990s and the last part gives some future prospects.

The rise of integrated assessment modelling

In the early 1980s several institutes started to model acidification in Europe, based on the first source-receptor or "blame" matrices developed by EMEP. One of the projects was the Regional Acidification INformation and Simulation (RAINS) model, which started in 1983 at the International Institute for Applied System Analysis (IIASA) in Laxenburg, Austria. This project was an opportunity for collaboration between scientists of both Eastern Europe and Western countries long before the fall of the Berlin Wall.

Dealing with differences in Europe

In the 1980s a series of protocols to the Convention on Long-range Transboundary Air Pollution were adopted reduce pollutants like sulphur dioxide (SO_2), nitrogen oxides (NO_x) and volatile organic compounds (VOCs). These first-generation protocols contain, inter alia, quantitative goals for national emission reductions that impose equal percentage reductions on all countries in relation to their emissions in a selected base year (so-called flat-rate reductions). It was clear that these were not enough to prevent harmful effects to public health and nature. But it was also clear that, in a second round of commitments, a further tightening of uniform percentage reductions would lead to high costs, and these reductions would not be environmentally effective in all parts of Europe or North America. Why take additional measures in less populated areas with less sensitive ecosystems? To make the policy strategy more cost-effective, an effect-based approach, which minimizes the abatement costs for Europe as a whole taking into account the differences in Europe was adopted. For example, the London-Paris-Ruhr triangle has the highest concentration of industry, traffic and people; the north of Europe is more sensitive to acidification than the south; the potential for cheap abatement measures is larger in the South and the East; the prevailing wind is from the south-west.

From cost-benefit analysis to cost-effectiveness analysis
In 1986, at the fourth meeting of the Executive Body, the Task Force on Integrated Assessment Modelling was established "to explore the possibilities to develop an analytical framework for a regional cost-benefit and cost-effectiveness analysis of concerted policies to control air pollution." This was four years before the start of the negotiations in 1990, which led to the second Sulphur Protocol in 1994 (Oslo). Already in 1985 the Group of Experts on Cost and Benefit Analysis at its second session discussed national applications of integrated assessment models of costs and benefits of sulphur emissions control. This Group also recommended that further development of models should be coordinated by the UNECE secretariat, since this would be a suitable task for international cooperation "in order to economize on scarce intellectual resources." Furthermore, the Group of Experts considered that "...the IIASA model (i.e. RAINS) might constitute a valuable tool for European cost-effectiveness analysis..." In a report in 1986 to the Executive Body, the Group of Experts presented several national and international models. At that time the tasks attributed to integrated assessment models were quite ambitious. They should also be able "...to incorporate so-called intrinsic values of the environment..." and ".... special attention should be paid to the identification of resources at risk and the distribution of both costs and benefits over time and space...." Until the establishment of the Working Group on Abatement Strategies in 1988, which became, in 1992, the Working Group on Strategies, the Task Force on Integrated Assessment Modelling reported to the Group of Experts on Cost and Benefit Analysis. Within the Task Force however the attention shifted from cost-benefit analysis towards cost-effectiveness analysis. The Task Force became a multidisciplinary group that combined and interpreted knowledge from various scientific disciplines and stakeholders. It developed models that covered the whole cause-effect chain with the aim of providing useful information to decision makers.

Focus on sulphur

The second Sulphur Protocol, which was signed in 1994 in Oslo, was the first to derive its quantitative reduction obligations from the cost-effectiveness and effect-based principles. Its reduction obligations were based on the results of modelled linkages between the SO_2 emissions of each country and the exposure of different ecosystems, taking into account the sensitivity of such ecosystems to acidification. For this purpose, the EMEP Meteorological Synthesizing Centre-West in Oslo produced source-receptor matrices that describe the atmospheric dispersion of sulphur from each source across Europe. These "blame"-matrices were linked with a map of the critical loads of ecosystems (compiled by the Coordination Center for Effects (CCE) in Bilthoven, Netherlands, on the basis of nationally reported data and approved by the Task Force on Mapping). The critical load is defined as the highest annual deposition level at which adverse effects on natural ecosystems are unlikely to result in the long term. Critical loads vary greatly with soil type and other local characteristics.

Various models

The cost-effectiveness analysis was based on estimates of the potential and costs of further emission reductions in each country; compiling this information produces cost curves that indicate the abatement measures achieved for certain costs. The RAINS and the CASM models produced such cost curves, while the other models used the RAINS cost curves as input. By applying optimization

techniques, a minimum cost solution (aimed at an accepted Europe-wide ambition level of ecosystem improvement) served as the starting point for negotiations. Negotiators received the results of three different models: Abatement Strategies Assessment Model (ASAM) (Imperial College, London), CASM (Stockholm Environment Institute, York) and RAINS (IIASA, Laxenburg). Using three models was at that time an accepted way of dealing with the uncertainties in modelling. The Task Force developed harmonized scenario assumptions and explored the implications of methodological differences on the results.

Integrated assessment models

The Task Force on Integrated Assessment Modelling met for the first time in February 1987 in Geneva and was chaired by Mr. Adrian Sinfield of the United Kingdom. At this first meeting, experts from Finland, Germany, the Netherlands, Norway, Sweden, the United Kingdom and the European Commission as well as from IIASA took part. Modelling groups (RAINS (IIASA) and Acidrain (United Kingdom Department of the Environment)) gave presentations of the models and the Task Force formulated criteria for model evaluation.

At the second meeting in 1988 at IIASA in Austria, the Task Force, chaired by Mr. Leen Hordijk of the Netherlands, discussed the features of RAINS, Acidrain and BICRAM (the model of the Beijer Institute's Centre for Resource Assessment and Management) and received a review report by Mr. Davis Streets from Argonne National Laboratory, United States. About a year later the "Harwell" model, the predecessor of ASAM, was also presented to the Task Force, and BICRAM was transformed into CASM (Coordinated Abatement Strategy Model). Acidrain, ASAM, CASM and RAINS remained the most important models used by the Task Force and the Working Group on Strategies up to the second Sulphur Protocol in 1994.

After 1994 the Task Force, chaired by Mr. Rob Maas of the Netherlands, embarked on a multi-pollutant, multi-effect modelling approach and the RAINS model became the core model for policy negotiations.

In search of cost-effectiveness

Scenario development is an iterative process between the Task Force on Integrated Assessment Modelling and the Working Group on Strategies (now the Working Group on Strategies and Review). At the request of the Working Group, the Task Force produces a number of model calculations and presents the results at the next meeting of the Working Group. Policy discussions in this forum lead subsequently to refined requests to the Task Force. In this process of developing scenario calculations a pattern has emerged. The first requests of the Working Group on Strategies in 1989 concerned the costs and effects of current national emission reduction plans in comparison with flat-rate emission reduction strategies. In addition, scenarios were developed to calculate the hypothetical effect of so-called maximum technologically feasible reductions and of equipping all power plants with best available technology not entailing excessive costs. Early impact analyses were based on preliminary sensitivity maps from the Stockholm Environment Institute (SEI), which were used before the European critical load maps became available. Already then, it became clear that no feasible emission control strategy could bring acid deposition below the critical loads everywhere in Europe. It also illustrated the conflict between equity and efficiency. Flat- rate emission reductions as applied in the early protocols do not lead to cost-effectiveness; for the same amount of money an optimized allocation would lead to greater environmental improvement.

Target loads

After it became clear that the critical loads could not be met everywhere in Europe, the so-called target load concept was proposed. According to this, national governments should determine target loads for their territories taking into account, apart from the ecological impacts, also the technical, social, economic and policy considerations. The optimization models would then identify the cost-minimal international allocation of emission reductions. Applied in an iterative way, this process would eventually lead to full achievement of critical loads. However, this turned out to be problematic. In the absence of clear and generally accepted guidelines, the selection of national target loads was a rather arbitrary process, which could impose significant reduction burdens on other countries. While the Working Group on Strategies invited all Parties to submit their own target loads, not all Parties succeeded in doing so. At the seventh meeting of the Working Group, in 1992, several scenarios for achieving submitted target loads were proposed. At its eighth meeting, after having analysed the modelling results from the Task Force, the scenarios based on achieving target loads were abandoned and alternative methods for setting environmental targets were sought. Exploratory calculations evaluated target deposition levels set throughout Europe at 50 and 100% above the critical loads, respectively. Also scenarios aimed at protecting an equal share of ecosystems in all EMEP grid cells, o at reducing the difference between present deposition and critical loads everywhere by an equal percentage, were explored.

Gap closure

An acceptable solution was finally found using the so-called gap closure approach for target setting. This followed a suggestion from the Norwegian delegation at the seventh meeting of the Working Group to “reduce the present exceedance of critical loads by the same percentage everywhere”. The final negotiating scenario aimed to cut the then present excess deposition above the critical loads by 60% in each EMEP grid cell. In this way the strategy would “close the gap” between current deposition and the environmental long-term target of achieving all critical loads. The negotiators took one of the RAINS scenarios, based on the gap closure concept, and used it as a starting point for the final negotiations that led to the adoption of the Oslo Protocol in 1994. This was the first international air pollution agreement based on scientific model calculations aimed at cost-effectiveness and taking into account spatially differentiated environmental effects. The Protocol contributed to the sharp decrease in SO_2 emissions during the 1990s (see figure 6.1).

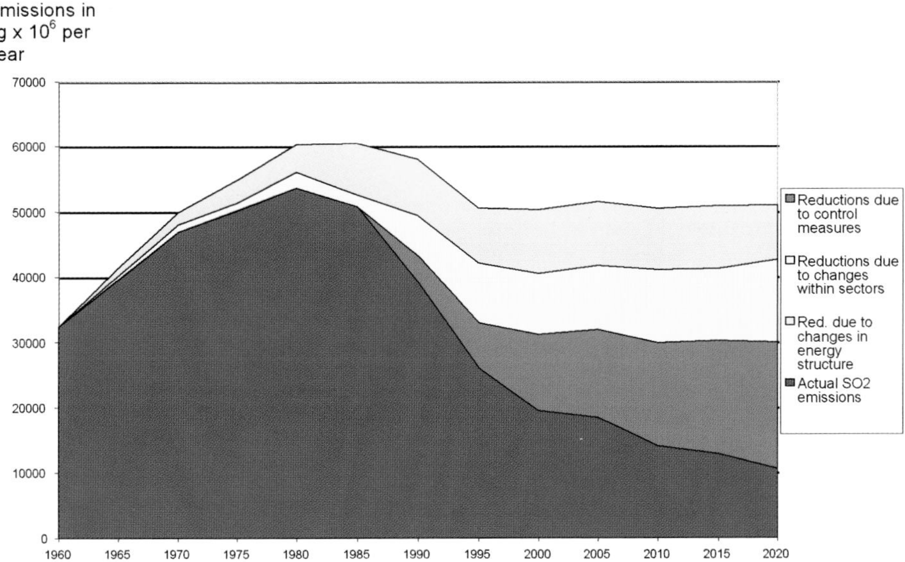

FIGURE 6.1. THE PREVENTION OF SO2 EMISSIONS IN EUROPE 1960-2020: ACTUAL LEVELS COMPARED TO HYPOTHETICAL LEVELS TAKING INTO ACCOUNT ENERGY CONSUMPTION GROWTH

SOURCE: IIASA

Further development of integrated assessment models

After the 1994 Oslo Protocol integrated assessment models became more complex in an attempt to explore more cost-effective solutions for a combination of pollutants and effects. Acidification was linked to eutrophication and to ozone exposure.

Towards a multi-pollutant multi-effect approach

It was estimated that the Oslo Protocol resulted in a cost saving of several billion euros per year due to the optimized distribution of abatement efforts compared to a flat-rate approach aimed at the same ecosystem protection level. Moreover, for those countries making large emission cuts to protect ecosystems elsewhere, substantial additional local benefits, such as reduced damage to buildings from decreased SO2 concentrations, provided extra justification. The success of the Oslo Protocol encouraged negotiators to embark on an effect-based multi-pollutant approach for the review of the 1988 Protocol on Nitrogen Oxides. As NOx contributes to the eutrophication of ecosystems (resulting in a decrease in biodiversity) as well as to acidification, it was expected that higher cost savings could be reached if ammonia (NH3) and sulphur were also incorporated in the optimization procedure. Because NOx and VOCs both contribute to ground-level ozone formation it was decided to integrate the review of the NOx Protocol with those of the 1994 Sulphur Protocol and the Protocol on VOCs

(once they entered into force) into one "multi-pollutant multi-effect" strategy. On 1 December 1999, Environment Ministers of the UNECE region signed, in Gothenburg (Sweden) the first multi-pollutant, multi-effect protocol; this included specific national emission ceilings, different for each country, for SO_2, NO_x, NH_3 and VOCs that were to be met by 2010. The Protocol is cost-effective (see figure 6.2) and will contribute to larger protection of ecosystems against acidification (see figure 5.6) and better protection of the population from ozone (figure 6.3).

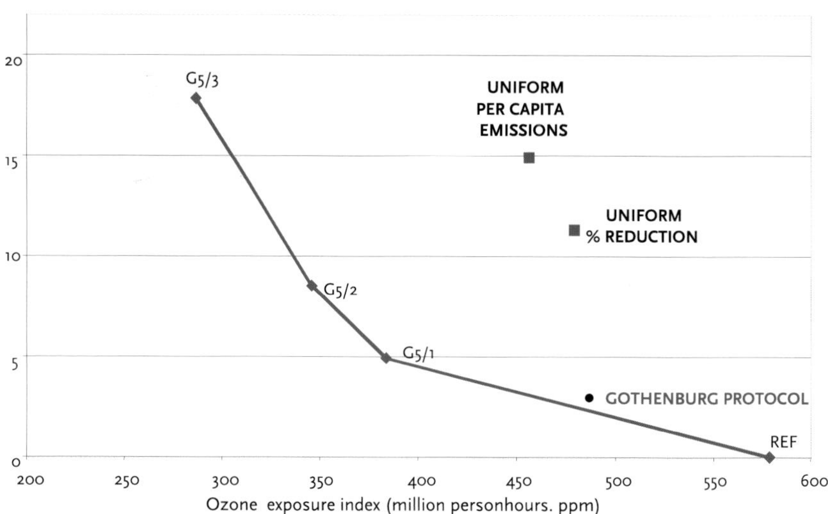

Figure 6.2. Cost-effectiveness of the Gothenburg Protocol. Costs and the level of ozone exposure compared with the cost curve of optimized solutions (the numbers G5/3 etc. refer to different scenarios produced by the RAINS model, scenario G5/2 was the "negotiating" scenario for the Gothenburg Protocol). Some non-optimized alternatives are shown. The ozone exposure index is the annual accumulated level of exceedance of an air concentration of 60 parts per billion (ppb) for the whole of the European population

Source: IIASA

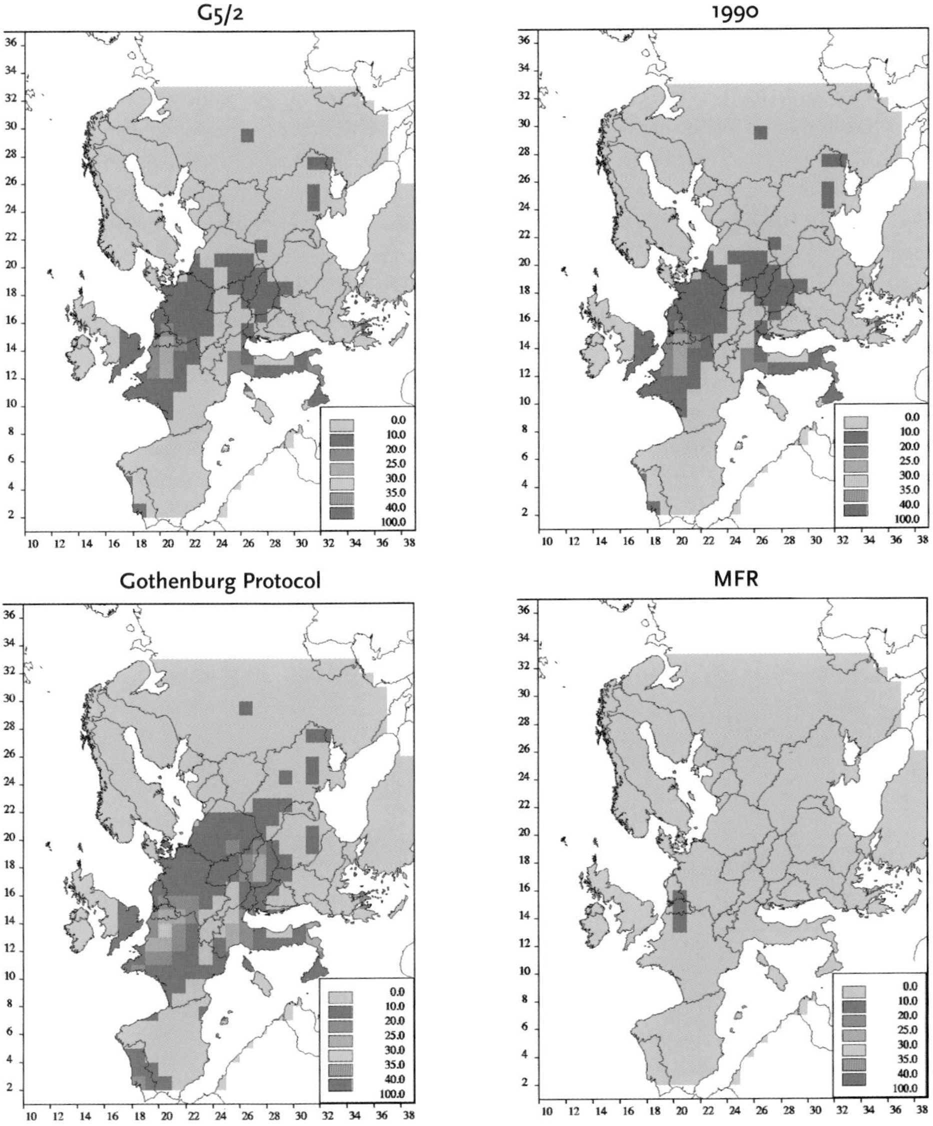

G5/2

1990

Gothenburg Protocol

MFR

Figure 6.3. The number of days with ozone above 60 ppb (a threshold set for human health effects) in 1990 (top left) and in 2010 for the G5/2 "negotiating" scenario (top right), for the emissions agreed in the Gothenburg Protocol (bottom left) and for the maximum feasible emission reduction scenario (bottom right)

Source: IIASA

Harmonization of models

The Gothenburg Protocol is based on scientific work over the period 1994-1999. Because of the increasing complexity of the approach, the modellers decided to join forces - more cooperation instead of competition. The first step was to harmonize the output of the models. It appeared that differences in results between RAINS, ASAM and CASM were mainly caused by the choice of input data and only partly by differences in cost-calculation and optimization methods. For all three models the modelling of air dispersion was based on the work of EMEP and critical loads data were provided by the Working Group on Effects from national inputs compiled by CCE. It was agreed that, where possible, all models would take the same officially submitted emission data (and projections) as the basis for calculations and that the same cost-calculation methodology would be applied (i.e. the socia costing method based on the technical lifetime of equipment and a real discount rate of 4%). In orde to avoid duplicating work, modelling groups decided on a division of labour: Imperial College specialized in agriculture-related emissions and in uncertainties, SEI in traffic and IIASA in energy anc the integration of the other findings in the RAINS model. As the RAINS modelling group was the first to incorporate ozone formation in the modelling framework, RAINS became the central model in support of the protocol negotiations (see figure 6.4). At the time of the adoption of the Gothenburg Protocol, the role of IIASA in the scientific work under the Convention was formalized by establishing the Convention's Centre for Integrated Assessment Modelling (CIAM) there. Imperial College explore new aspects not covered in the original range of effects such as the importance of particulates and implications for human health, adapting ASAM to show that strategies to reduce acidification would also be effective in reducing population exposure to secondary sulphate, nitrate and ammonium particulate matter.

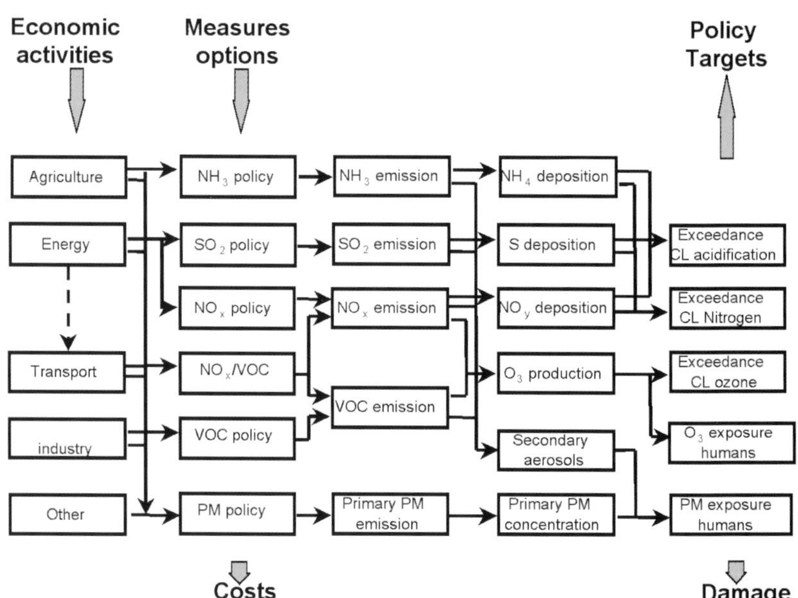

Figure 6.4. Structure of the RAINS model

Robustness

The Convention's Task Forces on Integrated Assessment Modelling and on Emission Inventories and Projections have both worked to increase the reliability of the officially submitted emission data and the consistency of emission projections (taking into account exogenous assumptions on economic growth and current environmental policies). This process of quality improvement still continues.

It is recognized that the credibility of model results among policy makers increases if input data reflect national statistics to the maximum extent possible without compromising international consistency and transparency. Also, the quality of the model results is directly dependent on the quality of national data submitted. In order to stimulate the learning process, all input data are made public via the Internet and extensive bilateral review sessions with each country are organized at CIAM. Moreover, uncertainty analyses became a crucial part of the work-plan; for the Gothenburg Protocol hundreds of sensitivity runs were made to assess the robustness of the optimization results. The design of the RAINS model was optimized to make the results more transparent and robust. In this way the revised model approach avoids small and uncertain exceedances of the low critical loads found in a few areas that can dominate the calculated emission reductions for the whole of Europe.

Success factors: consensus, people, transparency

The strong points of the integrated assessment modelling work under the Convention are its procedures to stimulate consensus on input data and methodology and its organizational position as an interface between science and policy. The Task Force on Integrated Assessment Modelling has formed an interface between the scientific groups under the Convention (EMEP and the Working Group on Effects) and decision makers that negotiate protocol obligations in the Working Group on Strategies (and Review). New scientific findings on emissions, dispersion and effects were incorporated in the RAINS model and model results were presented to the Working Group on Strategies, which in the iterative process described above defined ambition levels and the new scenarios required.

The UNECE secretariat of the Convention in Geneva played an important role in taking care of the relevant reporting mechanisms under the Convention. It also helped establish informal reporting mechanisms that were essential for timely model development, e.g. provisional critical loads and EMEP data were made available to modellers prior to their formal approval by the Working Group on Effects and the EMEP Steering Body.

The senior key scientists and the negotiators involved in all this work created a collective memory, which avoided the problem of "old" discussions being repeated over and over again. This also contributed to the effectiveness of the Task Force. Furthermore, integrated assessment modellers have made effective use of the Internet to increase the transparency of their work. Data, reports and models are all available on the CIAM, EMEP, CCE or Convention web sites. The availability of the model has stimulated the use of RAINS by experts for national purposes and this has enhanced the quality of the model's review. In several countries national versions of the RAINS model have been built, and national experts have improved the credibility of the model results to policy makers. Negotiators in the Working Group on Strategies need to be briefed by people they trust and who understand the model and its complexity.

Building trust in model results

To encourage the trust in science, participation in the Task Force has been open not only to national experts, but also to policy makers and representatives of non-governmental organizations. Environmental groups and industry have made use of these possibilities to scrutinize the models (as well as the underlying work of EMEP and the Working Group on Effects), identify weaknesses and prepare their own model runs. In an atmosphere where there is a willingness to understand the view of the other and where there are procedures to manage conflicts, assessments and decision-taking are effectively linked. Policy preferences are constructed during this process. Important also are the occasional training workshops for policy makers to brief them on the state of the art and the continued reports on the cost and effectiveness of possible policy strategies. For the Gothenburg Protocol it took more than 30 modelling runs before policy makers had an appreciation of the relationship between costs and environmental improvements so that they could define a generally acceptable ambition level.

Pitfalls

As well as strengths the integrated assessment work under the Convention also has weaknesses. Despite the openness, transparency and extensive external reviews, the increased complexity of the model leads to a situation where only a limited number of experts, those intensively involved in the process, understand the RAINS model in detail. Lack of trust in the model is a serious risk, therefore, even more attention is being paid to scientific peer review procedures and the intercomparison of results with national integrated assessment models. To some extent RAINS results can also be compared with ASAM results. CASM is no longer used, but a new integrated assessment model - Merlin - is currently being developed at the University of Stuttgart (Germany).

Another risk is, paradoxically, the Convention's focus on consensus, which may lead to a "closed shop," where dissident views are seldom heard. A challenge for the future will be to remain open to different views to retain a certain amount of healthy scepticism. While models now include advanced statistical methods for quantifying some types of uncertainties, other, and perhaps more fundamental, types of uncertainties, e.g. in the model structure, could receive less attention because they are not easily quantified, though they might be equally important for policy analysis.

Future prospects

There is a growing demand for more complex models for finding a more cost-effective balance between local efforts and those at the regional and the global scales. In order to maintain a credible scientific basis for effect-based international agreements a large number of research questions have to be tackled, while taking care of the pitfalls mentioned above.

Linking to the urban and the global scales

After the Gothenburg Protocol it was decided to extend the multi-pollutant, multi-effect approach further and try to link the transboundary air pollution problem with the health risks of air pollution at the local level, especially those from fine particulate matter (PM). While very small particles are subject to long-range transport in the same way as sulphur and nitrogen oxides, the overall human exposure to particles is dominated by the high population densities in European cities, where local sources make substantial

contributions. Thus, the balance between local and generic measures will be crucial for the cost-effectiveness of an abatement strategy. A number of research projects have been started to address the interplay between local and transboundary air pollution.

It has also become increasingly clear that hemispheric background concentrations of ozone and PM have a critical influence on the achievability and costs of air quality targets in Europe. Thus, the European scale is too limited for comprehensive assessment of cost-effective effect-based strategies. Because the Convention currently covers a large part of the Northern hemisphere, an extension of the modelling domain would be possible. This could then provide a more meaningful framework for addressing emissions outside the current EMEP modelled area. In addition, the contributions from sources outside Europe and the UNECE region could be included in the analyses, providing the opportunity for targeting some longer-lived precursor emissions (e.g. methane, which contributes to ground-level ozone) that have been ignored in the past (see figure 6.5). The resulting extension of the multi-pollutant approach to include these pollutants could be accompanied by extending the scope of the effects to include those resulting from greenhouse gases. This could lead to increased cost-effectiveness through increased integration.

	PM	SO_2	NO_x	VOC	NH_3	CO_2	CH_4	N_2O	CFCs HFCs SF_6
Health impacts: PM	√	√	√	√	√				
O_3			√	√					
Vegetation damage: O3			√	√			√		
Acidification		√	√		√				
Eutrophication			√		√				
Radiative forcing: - direct						√	√	√	√
- via aerosols	√	√	√	√	√				
- via OH			√	√			√		

Figure 6.5. The multi-pollutant multi-effect framework extended to greenhouse gases

Uncertainties will remain

Uncertainty treatment will remain a crucial part of integrated assessment in the coming years. Therefore, investigation into the robustness of emission reduction strategies in relation to key assumptions will continue to be of great importance. The text box below gives an overview of elements that still need improvement. Over the past decade policy makers have shown an increasing interest in scientific uncertainties. On the other hand, scientists have also pointed to the fact that there is uncertainty about the actual implementation of the emission reductions that were agreed, for example, in the Gothenburg

Protocol. Will all countries ratify? Will all countries fully meet their obligations? Or will there be technological breakthroughs that could easily lead to cheaper solutions and greater emission reductions than foreseen in the models? Integrated assessment models cannot cover all aspects of society and can only give a conditional view of future developments. Even with the scientific progress already made, the future itself remains our biggest uncertainty.

Unfinished business

Over the past 25 years many new scientific questions were raised and many new findings followed. This improved the state of the art in integrated assessment modelling, but it also led to new questions and elements of uncertainty:

1. Information on the contributions of shipping and aviation to air pollution has improved, but the willingness to take action within the framework of the International Maritime Organization and the International Civil Aviation Organization is still uncertain, while the relative share of shipping and aviation emissions is increasing;
2. Estimates of the effectiveness and costs of ammonia abatement measures have improved, but an assessment of the environmental effectiveness of changes in the EU Common Agricultural Policy is still needed;
3. Estimates of the formation of secondary inorganic particles have improved, but the lack of knowledge about primary particle emissions and about the natural sources of particle exposure requires improvements in emission estimates;
4. It is clear that the costs of additional abatement measures for SO_2, VOCs and NOx emissions will increase, but further analysis is needed of the possibilities for technological breakthroughs or behavioural changes that may be expected in the foreseeable future;
5. Knowledge about the linkages between climate change abatement measures and those for air pollution has increased, but further efforts are needed to bridge the communication gap between climate change and air pollution experts in both the science community and the policy arena;
6. Methods to assess ozone formation have improved (including a new Eulerian model developed by EMEP), but more analysis is needed to assess the future trends in global background ozone;
7. Knowledge about the linkages between regional pollution concentrations and urban background levels has increased, but more research is needed to assess the cost-effectiveness of local measures to reduce the exposure of the population;
8. Methods to model ecosystem-specific deposition and to map sensitive ecosystems have improved. These take into account base cation depositions and dynamic processes in the soil and freshwater systems, but more data are needed to harmonize the spatial scale of the data reported by the various countries and to make sure that all sensitive ecosystems are taken into account;
9. Methods to model the pathways of particulate matter exposure have improved, but it is still unclear which species of particulate matter are really causing health problems. Integrated assessment models will have to analyse the effects of strategies for several plausible dose-response relationships;
10. Methods to assess scientific uncertainties were improved following an increasing interest in uncertainties from the side of the policy makers, but more attention could still be paid to the uncertainties regarding the actual implementation and enforcement of protocol obligations.

The role of the secretariat: building the protocol tree

Lars Nordberg, Keith Bull, Radovan Chrast, Oddmund Graham, Andrzej Jagusiewicz, Peter H. Sand, Arne Tollan and Henning Wuester

This chapter, written by some of those who served in the secretariat over the past 25 years, provides observations from the perspective and perception of the Convention secretariat in Geneva. It shows that the services provided by this forum grew over time and became an integrated part of the Convention's machinery. It also shows that the secretariat works, not only upon requests by the Executive Body and its subsidiary bodies, but also by taking its own initiatives in support of the Convention. The chapter addresses issues relevant to the United Nations Economic Commission for Europe (UNECE) secretariat but not the role of the United Nations Conference Services which provides meeting facilities, documentation, translation and interpretation. UNECE is one of the five regional commissions of the United Nations. Established in 1947, it is a subsidiary body of the Economic and Social Council (ECOSOC), which operates under the General Assembly. It should be noted that the Convention never became an element of the regular UNECE work-plan, since the Executive Body is an independent treaty body.

Outline

The first section addresses the choice of UNECE as the forum for negotiations and as secretariat for the Convention. It explains the political environment, how the rules of the game were developed and the first success after the adoption of the Convention, the EMEP Protocol dealing with the structural financing of the EMEP activities. The second section addresses the setting-up of cooperative schemes for monitoring, science and policy development. The next section deals with how the secretariat handles reporting and publications and the promotion of international transparency and exchange of information. The section 'Prominent methods of work' handles the secretariat's methods of work including inter-secretariat cooperation and the advantages of an non-political secretariat. In the section 'Innovative approaches' the role of the secretariat is described as supportive, and sometimes even more than supportive, in various innovations within the Convention such as integrating science into negotiations, as well as facilitating innovative developments regarding, for instance, critical loads, integrated assessment modelling and compliance monitoring. The last section deals with considerations for the future.

Choice of forum for negotiations: UNECE

It was a long and politically sensitive process in the 1970s, which led to constructive cooperation on air pollution in Europe and North America. The United Nations 1972 Stockholm Conference on the Human Environment noted transboundary air pollution as an issue of major international concern and the Conference on Security and Co-operation in Europe (CSCE) Final Act of Helsinki in 1975 further highlighted that issue. A high-level meeting in Geneva in 1979 led to the adoption of the Convention and the choice of UNECE as its secretariat. Nordic countries contributed resources for a United Nations trust fund for the purpose of the Convention in a time of political division and lack of willingness to cooperate closely in the region. The secretariat was intentionally very small in the beginning, benefiting from external non-politicized and expert consultancy services. The Executive Secretary of the UNECE was identified by the Parties as the secretariat for the Convention, since this function offered a neutral and recognized high-level United Nations mechanism for intergovernmenta cooperation which provided all necessary conference facilities and had a tradition of working with complicated East-West issues. In line with the UNECE terms of reference, the working languages are English, French and Russian, and the Convention and its associated protocols appear in equally authentic English, French and Russian versions and are deposited with the Secretary-General of the United Nations.

Handling East-West issues

The ECE of the 1980s was one of very few international bodies where East and West participated on ar equal footing and with equal interest in the outcome. Thus ECE meetings, as recorded in the reports drafted by the secretariat, became a thermometer for measuring the temperature in East-West relations. The choice of wording in meeting reports spoke volumes. The balancing act in choosing alternating chairpersons and vice-chairpersons from different sides of the Iron Curtain was another battleground, as was staff recruitment, requiring, under a gentlemen's agreement, that a leaving staff member from one side of the Curtain should be replaced by another from the same side. Such nicetie could lead to suboptimal choices; however, they were honoured by everybody and provided stability.

> It was not even considered remarkable when it was alleged that the Director of Personnel at the United Nations in Geneva was a KGB Colonel. Offices in Palais des Nations were thought to be wired by the Secret Services of one or both of the two sides. The mutual suspicion caused many staff members to conduct sensitive discussions, not in their offices, but rather in corridors and stairways. (See John Barron, 'KGB Today: The Hidden Hand', London, 1984, pp. 240-241.)

At that time, the unique role of UNECE as a well-functioning meeting ground for East-West contacts had its curious sides. As a consequence of the division of Germany after the Second World War, and the four-power agreement on Berlin, the location in Berlin of the Environmental Agency or "Umweltbundesamt" of the Federal Republic of Germany became a regular test of East-West relations. When the Federal Republic of Germany was represented at UNECE meetings by experts from the Agency, this regularly set off a chain of official protest notes, responses and responses to the response, involving the delegations of the German Democratic Republic, the Federal Republic of Germany, the Union of Soviet Socialist Republic (USSR) and the Western power, which was handling common matters at that particular time. The secretariat gradually and discreetly "ritualized" the controversy by always circulating an advance provisional participation list, when necessary omitting institutions and cities, followed by standardized opening statements from both sides, subsequently appended to the meeting report, thereby preserving the formal legal position of each side.

Establishing the rules of the game

The positive outcome of meetings depends of course on many factors. Well-prepared background papers drafted by the secretariat, often based on external input, are needed, and draft recommendations and resolutions should be balanced between the maximum desirable and the politically possible. UNECE in the 1980s was almost unique in the sense that it was a common talking ground between East and West, and all Parties wanted it to stay that way. Diplomacy was often required, also on the part of the secretariat. The popular belief that diplomatic life is a merry-go-round

of lunches and cocktail parties ignores the fact that social events are breeding-places for mutual understanding and compromises.

Reaching agreement on international cost-sharing for EMEP

One particular test of secretariat prowess took place when the national contributions to the Protocol on Long-term Financing for the Cooperative Programme for Monitoring and Evaluation of the Long-range Transmission of Air Pollutants in Europe (EMEP) had to be calculated and agreed upon. The basis for the calculations was the United Nations assessment rates, and these rates themselves are based on a mix of population numbers and gross national products. Other variables in this particular case were the role of individual countries in emitting and receiving air pollutants, those receiving more than their own emissions feeling that this ought to be reflected. Some countries had a special role as hosts of the technical coordinating centres of EMEP, and some countries demanded special treatment because of small size or peripheral location. And what ought to be the minimum charge that every party to the Protocol should be expected to pay? (This share was eventually set at 0.02 %.)

With some 30 countries and such a set of variables, one can imagine the complexity of the situation and the time pressures to produce alternatives for negotiation. Delegations viewed every new scheme with scepticism: "What is in it for me?" After some 30 attempts to accommodate everybody the Protocol was agreed. Eastern countries could accept the agreement since a mechanism for mandatory contributions in kind was introduced for them. Signing took place at the second session of the Executive Body, September 1984.

> ECE had not entered the era of information technology in 1984. Personal computers hardly existed and the small table calculators of the Air Pollution Unit could not do the calculations needed for the negotiation of the EMEP Protocol. The saving solution was the ECE Forestry Division where Christopher Prins had access to a computer, and took on the job. He quickly made a spreadsheet programme, and a flow of tailor-made calculations and new demands were brought back and forth between the meeting room and Prins´computer by secretariat staff.

Setting up cooperative schemes for monitoring, science and policy development

An efficient follow-up of the Convention required a structure of bodies for environmental monitoring, scientific assessments and policy development. The first years saw a proliferation of such bodies, first and foremost of course the Executive Body for the Convention itself, which has been meeting annually since 1983 (between 1980 and 1983 work was carried out by the Interim Executive Body).

The Executive Body quickly established subordinate working groups:

- **Working Group on Effects** with subordinate working parties and international cooperative programmes for rivers and lakes, materials, and forests;
- **Steering Body for EMEP** with three coordinating centres (one chemical, two meteorological synthesizing centres);
- **Working Group on Specific Agreement on Emission Reduction** negotiating the 1985 Helsinki Protocol on Reduction of Sulphur Emissions or their Transboundary Fluxes by at least 30 per cent;

- **Working Group on Nitrogen Oxides**; and
- **Group of Experts on Cost and Benefit Analysis**.

The **Working Party on Air Pollution Problems** already existed under the Senior Advisers to UNECE Governments on Environmental Problems, and took responsibility for emission-reducing technologies under the Interim Executive Body.

The role of chairmen can be crucial for success. It goes without saying that a close and confident relationship between the chairmen and the secretariat is a must (in the UNECE of the 1980s there were only chair**men**). Many of the people serving the Convention in this capacity deserve honourable mention: Mr. V.G. Sokolovsky (USSR) was for many years Chairman of the Executive Body itself. He was always correct, carrying out the chairman's duties with much authority. Mr. Toni Schneider (Netherlands) served as Chairman of the Steering Body of EMEP. His style was strong, dynamic and efficient. His meetings always concluded on time. Mr. Jim Bruce (Canada), was Chairman of the Special Group which negotiated the Helsinki Protocol. Chairing a negotiation of conflicting views presents particular challenges, and Mr. Bruce combined a very pleasant and sociable style with a strong mind, never losing sight of the target of the negotiations. These key personalities were subsequently followed by other remarkable people, notably Mr. Jan Thompson (Norway) as Chairman of the Executive Body and Mr. Lars Bjorkbom (Sweden) as Chairman of the negotiating body, the Working Group on (Abatement) Strategies. The national experts taking part in the meetings of "bodies", "groups", "centres" and "Parties" made invaluable contributions, many as authors of technical reports and studies. However, the meeting costs and time required soon became a bottleneck for many Parties wanting to take an active part. Reorganization was needed.

Organization of the work on effects

The Interim Executive Body for the Convention at its first session in 1980 established the Working Group on Effects of Sulphur Compounds on the Environment. The Working Group was requested to collect and assess available information on dose-effect relationships, and the extent of estimated damage caused by sulphur compounds and the estimated benefits, including economic benefits, deriving from possible emission reductions for materials, including historic and cultural monuments, aquatic ecosystems and soil, groundwater and vegetation (ECE/ENV/IEB/2). The name of the group was later changed to the Working Group on Effects to reflect its modified mandate.

Following this decision and based on a series of consultations held from 1981 to 1983 by three groups of experts designated by interested Governments, the Working Group submitted to the Executive Body for consideration background technical papers reviewing the current knowledge on the effects of sulphur compounds on materials, including historic and cultural monuments, aquatic ecosystems, soil, groundwater and vegetation. These identified major gaps in current knowledge, proposed further in-depth studies and suggested establishing international cooperative programmes to deal with the problems.

While the Executive Body established just three international cooperative programmes (ICPs) in 1985, concerns about other effects have resulted in the present seven international cooperative effect-

oriented activities under the Convention. Each of these has a Task Force, mostly operating under the guidance of a lead country, which considers all related technical problems and approves documents for submission to the Working Group on Effects, while international coordination is provided by specific institutes/institutions, approved by the Parties and the Executive Body (see chapter 5).

Introducing health consideration into the work

In its article 7 the Convention invited the Contracting Parties inter alia: "... to initiate and cooperate in the conduct of research into and/or development of the effects of sulphur compounds and other major air pollutants on human health and the environment, ... with a view to establishing a scientific basis for dose/effect relationships designed to protect the environment."

In implementing the Convention and pursuant to its article 10, paragraph 4, the Executive Body established close cooperation with the World Health Organization (WHO) and invited it to provide summarized and assessed information on the health effects of major air pollutants (see report of the first session of the Interim Executive Body, 1980, ECE/ENV/IEB/2, annex I). The same invitation was directed to the interested Governments. Consequently, between 1980 and 1997 the WHO Regional Office for Europe presented the Executive Body with several technical reports on the health effects of air pollutants, namely sulphur oxides, nitrogen oxides, persistent organic pollutants (POPs) and heavy metals.

With further development of the effect-based approach and, in particular, during preparation of the 1999 Gothenburg Protocol to Abate Acidification, Eutrophication and Ground-level Ozone it was felt that successful implementation of the Convention would require a more systematic and better targeted assessment of the possible health effects of major pollutants from long-range transboundary transport. Hence, in 1997 the Executive Body and the WHO European Centre for Environment and Health established the Joint Task Force on the Health Aspects of Long-range Transboundary Air Pollution. Its aim is to quantify the contribution of transboundary air pollution to human health risks and to help define priorities for future monitoring and abatement strategies. The work of the Task Force is based on estimates of air pollution concentrations, in particular those derived by EMEP, and on the results of hazard assessment performed by WHO.

The Task Force has already prepared assessments of the health impacts of particulate matter, heavy metals and POPs from long-range transboundary air pollution and is continuing its activities to address the needs of the Executive Body.

Protecting the intergovernmental status of operations

The development of science-based approaches to negotiating protocols transformed the process. The original diplomatic and foreign-policy-dominated forum became the core of a number of scientific and expert networks. While this added significant value to the operations under the Convention, the secretariat, supported or driven by Parties and influential individuals, had to counterbalance this to make sure that the intergovernmental status of the framework remained at the centre of attention. It required a continuous effort to keep the focus of all activities on the intergovernmental process, either on the negotiation of new protocols or the review of existing protocols and their implementation. This sometimes implied that even useful scientific networks that had developed under the Convention had

to be redirected or terminated once they were no longer linked to the intergovernmental process. The appearance of the Implementation Committee in 1997 certainly helped re-establish some of the balance and further emphasis on its work is crucial to the survival of the Convention as an intergovernmental instrument.

THE LATE MINISTER ANNA LINDH SIGNING THE 1998 PROTOCOL ON POPs ON BEHALF OF SWEDEN

Ensuring formal consistency in the development of protocols

As the protocol tree developed, the demands on the formal process expanded. The Convention's bodies, including the Executive Body, always favoured simple non-formal approaches. Against that background, the secretariat often had to strike a difficult balance between covering all the necessary formalities to ensure due process and keeping that process lean and smooth. For a long time the Executive Body had not distinguished between conclusions of discussions and formal decisions. As the process became more complex in the second half of the 1990s, numbered decisions were introduced to highlight the formal nature of some of the Executive Body decisions. These often stemmed from a delegated authority in a protocol that the Executive Body exercised.

In ensuring formal consistency, the role of the Executive Body as the meeting of the Parties to the Convention and all of its protocols was key. Not overloading the protocols with details, but leaving it up to the Executive Body to determine the level of detail, also helped. It gave the necessary flexibility to form a web of formal and informal agreements, written decisions and established practices that provided the basis for operating the complex structure of a convention and eight protocols. In serving this structure, the secretariat had to demonstrate an awareness of the links, and this started in the drafting of meeting reports.

In connection with the final preparation of protocols and their subsequent adoption and signature, the secretariat worked closely with the legal adviser in Geneva and, in particular, with the United Nations Treaty Section in New York. Although this procedure is highly formal and follows very strict rules, the chief of the secretariat in the protocol-prolific 1990s many times had to find unconventional methods to secure a seemingly smooth process. High-level delegations coming to Geneva, Oslo, Aarhus or Gothenburg to sign protocols got what they wanted and never suspected that sometimes only a miracle or the intervention of a "Friend of the Convention" had made it possible.

Reports, information exchange and transparency

Reports and publications

In order to give the flow of technical-scientific reports a proper outlet and wider circulation, the secretariat started publishing the UN series 'Air Pollution Studies' in 1984. It contained only technical reports prepared for the UNECE Air Pollution Unit. Even so, drafting and editorial standards were high and there were problems in obtaining reliable data, not least from what were then Eastern bloc countries.

A 1985 report on forest damage in Europe is an illustration of using reliable data. The author of the report had compiled whatever was available from official sources, as well as from books, journals and expert opinions, some of which deviated dramatically from governmental sources. When the report – showing rather shocking figures of forest damage both for Western and Eastern Europe – became available in draft form at the United Nations press centre in the Palais des Nations, a journalist from the 'Süddeutsche Zeitung' picked it up and published an alarming article in his newspaper. Only hours later, UNECE Executive Secretary, Mr. Klaus Sahlgren, received a call from the Ambassador of the German Democratic Republic in Geneva, complaining that unofficial figures of forest damage had been used for his country, and requesting changes to the final version. Consequently, the final published report contained no reference at all to the German Democratic Republic[1].

In 1985, the Executive Body initiated a series of major reviews of national strategies and policies for combating air pollution that were to be undertaken every four years using national submissions and other official sources. The stated aim of the reviews was "to ascertain the extent to which the objectives and fundamental principles as laid down in articles 2, 3, 4 and 5 of the Convention have been met"[2].

Today, in the light of the 1998 Aarhus Convention[3], which guarantees access to environmental information as a fundamental civil right, it is hard to recall the significance of that decision. For throughout the Cold War period, government-held data – including air pollution data – were still treated as State secrets; and efforts to collect foreign data were part of the intelligence-gathering activities of secret services on both sides of the Iron Curtain[4].

The centre of information exchange under the Convention's article 8 was EMEP, which had already developed a transnational information flow "without equal in the environmental field"[5]. Yet even national emission inventories – on which EMEP depends for modelling – proved tough to obtain from some countries where they were considered politically sensitive and hence either withheld or censored

In the 1986 major review Romania reported that its SO_2 emissions in 1980 were 200,000 tons[6]. Everybody knew that this figure was totally fictitious; but since it had been personally approved by Mrs. Elena Ceausescu (wife of the country's dictator, self-proclaimed chemical expert, and since 1979 head of the National Council for Science and Technology), the official emissions could not be corrected until after her execution in 1989. The 1990 major review subsequently estimated Romanian SO_2 emissions for 1980 at 900,000 tons[7], and the 1998 major review finally put them at 1,055,000 tons[8].

Similarly, the annual surveys of forest damage and air pollution, initiated in 1986 under the International Cooperative Programme (ICP) on Forests, faced resistance from government agencies reluctant to publicize unwelcome news.

In the United Kingdom, Greenpeace bluntly accused Her Majesty's Forestry Commission of manipulating its national forest health data in Convention reports and of misinforming the public about the severity of air pollution damage[9]. As a result, the release of the 1989 Annual Forest Survey turned into a diplomatic issue. The Executive Body, upon the insistence of the United Kingdom's delegation, decided that not only all forest damage reports but also any UNECE press releases accompanying them would henceforth require advance approval by the Working Group on Effects, to give each government an opportunity to "sanitize" the text[10].

Promotion of transparency and exchange of information

Growing public attention, however, and the gradual rise of non-governmental organizations (NGOs) to observer status inevitably forced more transparency and new approaches to information disclosure. NGOs had already successfully turned some routine Convention meetings into lively media events. At a meeting of the Working Group on Specific Agreement on Emission Reductions, in 1984, demonstrators blocked the entrance to the Palais des Nations with a huge tree reportedly suffering from air pollution damage and others climbed a crane above the United Nations 'Bocage' building

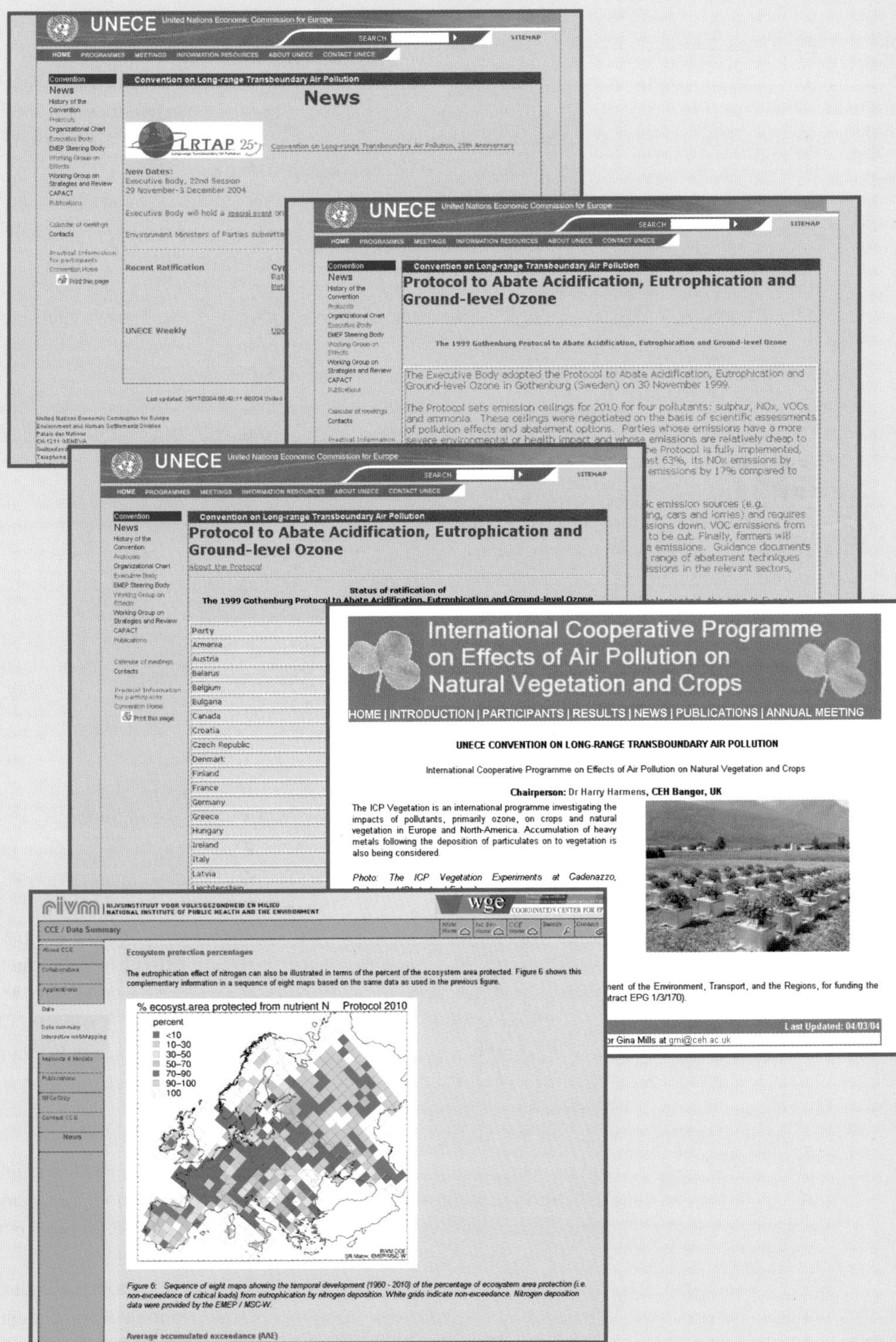

The Convention's web pages are maintained by the secretariat and provide a range of information on the Convention and its work. The pages also provide links to the web sites of the Convention's programme centres

displaying provocative banners. Since 1985, environmental NGOs have regularly attended Executive Body meetings, disseminating their alternative press material (such as ECO Bulletins and 'Acid News') in the process. The Convention's secretariat, for its part, began to take initiatives for public information. During the 1990s, stakeholder-friendly brochures and leaflets were produced by the secretariat, voluntarily co-funded by Parties; and in conjunction with the adoption of the 1999 Gothenburg Protocol, a United Nations film on acid rain was produced and shown on several international news channels, including CNN World Report.

Internet

With the increasing importance of the Internet, the secretariat developed a web site in the 1990s (www.unece.org/env/lrtap). It continues to provide information on the Convention and its subsidiary bodies. It includes links to web sites of the Convention's programme centres and provides access to meeting documents. The importance of the Convention is reflected by the site being one of the most popular of the UNECE web pages, the high number of "hits" prompting UNECE to provide a quick link from its own home page. Currently, information exchange under the Convention operates at multiple levels: EMEP, major reviews, reports of ICPs[11], data on recovery, and a wide range of expert networks and workshops. The Implementation Committee, established in 1997, periodically reviews compliance with the reporting requirements of the Convention and its protocols. According to the Committee's 2002 review, the quality and completeness of national reporting – including emission data – have notably improved, not least due to the naming (and shaming) of countries in non-compliance[12].

Establishing reporting procedures as a basis for future compliance monitoring

Reporting is one of the pillars of the Convention itself. The legal obligations to report on strategies and policies for air pollution abatement were developed as a key element of what constitutes a common framework for all Parties to the Convention. At the same time it had to serve the specific needs of the protocols, which only some Parties had ratified. While the original purpose of reporting was an exchange of information to provide the basis for policy negotiations, with the development of the compliance regime, precise information on the performance of Parties to the protocols was required.

In the early 1990s with only the first Sulphur and Nitrogen Oxides Protocols in force, it was possible to use an integrated structure for reporting by all Parties to the Convention. The main compliance-related information for these two protocols was provided through emission inventories. In the early days, there was general interest in a broad reporting scheme, given that little information on environmental policies was available internationally. This culminated in the publication of the 1994 and 1998 Major Reviews on Strategies and Policies, which provided an extensive compilation of information submitted by Parties and an analysis of that information by the secretariat.

With the second generation of protocols going beyond simple emission reduction requirements to include more specific obligations on the application of abatement technologies for certain emission sources, more specific reporting became necessary. Such information was needed for the Implementation Committee to review compliance. At the end of the 1990s, Parties faced many parallel and often overlapping international reporting schemes and rejected expanding any general reporting. The result was a major streamlining of the reporting requirements under the Convention

using a questionnaire, prepared by the secretariat, with specific questions for each relevant obligation of the, by then, seven substantive protocols. One of the first tasks that the Implementation Committee undertook was to review compliance with Parties' reporting obligations. This resulted in a significant improvement of the response rate and put in place a solid information database to review compliance by Parties with their substantive obligations. Since 2002 further streamlining and effective implementation have been achieved through the use of an Internet-based questionnaire linked to a secretariat database.

Prominent methods of work

The "lead country" approach

One gratifying aspect of secretariat work in the early 1980s was the easy access to expert assistance from Parties, whether on forest damage, corrosion of building materials, or the effects of air pollution on historical monuments. Several countries volunteered to host important meetings or serve as lead countries for various programme activities. With limited United Nations budget resources, such contributions in kind became vital for maintaining the scientific basis. Willing Parties also seconded key staff members to the secretariat for periods of up to one year. These contributions were crucial to the effective performance of the secretariat.

Inter-secretariat cooperation and external contacts

Regular contacts with the permanent diplomatic missions to the United Nations in Geneva were very important in the daily work of the secretariat. There were particularly frequent contacts with Switzerland, Austria, the Federal Republic of Germany, the United States and the Nordic countries. The, mostly young, Geneva diplomats responsible for environmental matters became very good two-way channels to governments. The special circumstances during the early years of the Convention have been described by Mr. Chossudovsky[13].

Collaboration by the Convention with the secretariats of other international institutions dates back to the forerunner of EMEP – the programme on long-range transport of air pollutants initiated in 1972 by the Organisation for Economic Co-operation and Development (OECD). The programme was transformed in 1978 into a cooperative programme by UNECE, the World Meteorological Organization (WMO) and the United Nations Environment Programme (UNEP). The Geneva-based European office of UNEP had a strong interest in learning from the UNECE Convention's work when it started on the road to the Vienna Convention (and its Montreal Protocol) for the Protection of the Ozone Layer[14]. Cooperation with such organizations has continued and has been further extended to include: WHO (WHO/EURO) with regard to the health effects of air pollution; water acidification studies carried out under the auspices of the WHO/UNEP Global Environment Monitoring System (GEMS); the European Forestry Commission of the Food and Agriculture Organization of the United Nations (FAO/EFC) with regard to pollution effects on forests; the International Institute for Applied Systems Analysis (IIASA) in Laxenburg (Austria)– for modelling of air pollution and the cost-effectiveness of emission reductions; and the World Commission on Environment and Development ("Brundtland Commission"), which established its secretariat in Geneva in 1984.

For purposes of monitoring air pollution in marine areas, memoranda of understanding were concluded with the Baltic Sea Commission (HELCOM) and the North-East Atlantic Commission (OSPARCOM). After the European Community became a party to EMEP in 1986, emission inventorie were coordinated with the CORINAIR programme now operated by the European Environment Agen (EEA), and large-scale surveys of the "forest condition in Europe" were organized jointly with the EC Directorate-General for Agriculture.

The Convention on Long-range Transboundary Air Pollution inevitably interacts with a number of oth environmental regimes, including some informal organizational linkages and institutional developments. Given that the same national delegates and experts often participate in decision-making for the Convention and for other multilateral environmental agreements, there has been a certain amount of mutual "institutional learning"[15], for example with regard to innovative mechanisms and procedures for compliance control[16], and regarding priority listing of pollutant[17].

Development of innovative schemes: the role of a non-political secretariat

Even though the Convention was negotiated and signed in the "post-Helsinki" atmosphere of détent with the 1975 Final Act of Helsinki calling for cooperation to control air pollution and its effects, a number of European countries still had serious problems with its implementation in the 1980s. The problems ranged from economic to geopolitical considerations and, in some countries, even include national security (data on air pollution, in particular when related to the location of specific sources, were considered as strategically important, requiring special protection). It was the non-political role of the secretariat and its ability to bridge the gaps using technical and scientific arguments that helpe with negotiations and facilitated reaching workable solutions.

In the early years of the Convention, Signatories and/or Parties to the Convention were principally divided into three main groups:

- A group of countries strongly supporting efficient internationally harmonized air pollution contro measures (mainly countries receiving the major part of their pollution from abroad and experiencing severe environmental damage);
- Countries opposing establishing internationally binding control measures arguing that any recommendation for remedial action had to be based on more complete knowledge of damage and the entire link between source of pollution and its effects (mainly countries producing most the air pollution and exporting it); and
- Countries sitting on the fence, not expressing any strong preference (mainly East European countries, basically not too happy with adopting any international legally binding control measures, and hence quietly supporting the second group).

Under these circumstances the apolitical secretariat played a crucial role by:

- Actively initiating comprehensive reviews of available scientific knowledge (e.g. preparation of background documents for the first meetings of groups of designated experts);
- Drafting reports on the results of the expert groups in such a way that (i) well-known facts were clearly presented; (ii) ongoing scientific progress was shown; (iii) the dangers of continuing uncontrolled air pollution were explained; and (iv) long-term advantages of adopting effective remedial measures were duly described;

- Assisting in organizing international scientific collaboration in addressing the most acute problems related to air pollution; and
- Providing updated knowledge and information not only to decision makers and to professional communities, but also to the general public in the UNECE region.

Innovative approaches

Integration science into negotiations but keeping it separate from policy

A key factor in the success of the Convention and its protocols has been the way that science has contributed to political decision-making. This has been made easier by the new political environment though the secretariat has been a major factor in ensuring the effective communications between scientific experts and decision makers of all Parties. The formal structure of the Convention largely separates scientific activities from negotiations and, while this has provided a level of protection for the scientific work, the effects-based approaches developed since about 1990 have demanded scientific input. However, through the use of reports and through presentations from individual scientists and the Convention's scientific programme centres, the secretariat has ensured that scientific messages have been clear and well understood by all Parties throughout the region. Furthermore, it has been crucial that the communications be two-way, building mutual confidence and maintaining a dialogue between scientist and policy-maker whilst optimum solutions for pollution control were discussed and agreed.

Moving from the first-generation flat-rate protocols to the second-generation effects-based protocols changed the role of the science. It required much more targeted input from expert bodies set up under the Convention into formal negotiations. The secretariat had an important role to link the different bodies. It met with some reluctance by the scientists who feared that their contribution would be misused in the political process and that they would be held responsible.

The work on integrated assessment modelling that evolved throughout the 1990s was essential to the application of science as it provided the link for other scientific areas such as critical loads and atmospheric modelling and thus created an effective science-policy base for discussions. A key to making this work was a clear separation of scientific and technical work on the one hand, and policy discussions on the other. It was crucial to emphasize the expert nature of bodies like the Task Force on Integrated Assessment Modelling, which were close to the negotiations. While experts in such bodies were nominated by governments (and by accredited NGOs), they were there to contribute their expert knowledge and not to represent the political position of their countries. This also meant stopping the work of expert bodies before it entered into policy choices. The secretariat ensured both the formal lines of communications as well the informal ones were established between all relevant bodies of the Convention and that these links functioned in an acceptable and effective way. This was the basis for the confidence building that was so important in the negotiation of the 1994 Oslo and 1999 Gothenburg Protocols, and at the ministerial adoption session for the Gothenburg Protocol scientists were invited to make presentations highlighting the scientific basis of the Protocol.

Over the years there have been many brochures and booklets describing the work of the Convention. Some were prepared and published by the secretariat, others were developed in cooperation with one or more Parties

Integrated assessment modelling and cost considerations

While critical loads were identified in the 1988 Sofia Protocol as the means for developing future emission control strategies, it was the development of integrated assessment modelling that provided the real basis for negotiations in the 1990s. Bringing together the atmospheric models, the maps of critical loads and the costs of abatement technologies, the integrated assessment models provided a way of developing optimized scenarios showing environmental benefits and their associated costs. Part of the secretariat's role was to make sure that the official channels of communication ensured that data and models met with the necessary approval from the relevant scientific and technical bodies and that results were available when required. In addition, special informal channels of communications were agreed between the secretariat and the scientific and technical groups to enable data to be exchanged quickly and the modelling to meet the tight time schedule set for the negotiations. The secretariat also had the task of ensuring that the informal exchanges met subsequent approval by the Convention's appropriate bodies. Many trivial matters also had to be solved by the secretariat.

Early when the scientific community was dealing with critical loads it introduced the term "exceedance" for loads above the critical one. That word, being scientific jargon, was initially not accepted by the United Nations linguists and editors. They requested that another term be used. The Chief of the Convention secretariat had to wear down the formal in-house resistance until the term was ultimately accepted.

In recent years, as the Convention has moved to consider the review of its Gothenburg Protocol, the secretariat has provided guidance for the development of the Expert Group on Techno-economic Issues, led by France, which has brought national experts together to provide technical input on the costs and effectiveness of control technologies to integrated assessment modelling.

Monetary benefits

While integrated assessment models have provided information on the costs of control technologies, the value of benefits from the models was often seen simply in terms of meeting critical loads, the thresholds at which harmful effects take place. There has long been interest from Parties in estimating the economic benefits of emission controls and to this end the Task Force on Economic Aspects of Abatement Strategies was established in 1991. It identified that the major benefits were associated with the protection of human health and building materials, and in the preparations for the Gothenburg Protocol benefits were calculated for the most prominent abatement scenarios. For practically all countries the benefits were two to five times the calculated costs. The Task Force also drafted a guidance document on economic instruments for the Gothenburg Protocol, which was based on a review of experience compiled in the secretariat. The Network of Experts on Benefits and Economic Instruments has continued the work of the Task Force in recent years, but despite support from the secretariat, there is still no satisfactory assessment of the monetary benefits from reduced air pollution damage to ecosystems.

The new sophisticated Protocol was presented to the media by Mr. Lars Björkbom (Chair, Working Group on Strategies), Mr. Jan Thomson (Chair, Executive Body), Mr. Kjell Larsson (Swedish Environment Minister), Mr. Lars Nordberg (secretariat) and Mr. John Beale (United States) (from left to right) at a press conference on 30 November following the adoption of the 1999 Gothenburg Protocol

Integration of technical annexes into protocols

The secretariat has always been aware that technical control options could make or break a compliance regime of any of the protocols. However, during the Cold War it was hardly envisaged that technology cooperation would materialize. That is why the first Sulphur Protocol , based on simple flat-rate reduction obligations, was not backed by any technological guidance on how to meet its objectives.

With the political climate getting warmer, the secretariat could increasingly contribute to the further development and integration of technical annexes into protocols. Subsidiary groups dealing with this task were the Working Party on Air Pollution Problems, the Working Group on Technology and, finally, the Working Group on Abatement Techniques.

Progress has been quite impressive when moving from the simple flat-rate regime to the multi-pollutant and multi-effect strategies, based not only on recommendatory best available technology (BAT) and mandatory limits on emissions, but also on structural change in the most polluting sectors, i.e. energy, transport and agriculture, and relying inter alia on cleaner technology and less polluting fuels and agricultural practices. This flexibility in choosing control options together with product control and management measures (as in the Protocol on Heavy Metals and the Protocol on POPs) attracted less developed countries in the UNECE region to joining the Convention and its protocols.

Guidance on BAT has been extended over a wide range of mobile sources, starting with road vehicles, and then covering off-road vehicles and machines, ships and aircraft. However, new emission sources were targeted rather than existing ones. The same rule has been applied to stationary sources, which soon overtook the mobile ones in the total volume of technical annexes. However, a horizontally-

integrated multi-media approach has prevailed, thereby avoiding transferring pollution between environmental media (e.g. the work of the Task Force on By-products).

Workshops on technology and capacity-building

Care has also been taken to include in the protocols' technical annexes state-of-the-art techniques based on operating experiences identified by task forces and expert groups serviced by the secretariat. Another recurrent forum in which the secretariat deployed resources were seminars and target-oriented workshops on exchange of information on technical control measures held since the early 1980s and open to all Parties to the Convention. These were often particularly targeted towards countries in transition, almost half of the UNECE member States at one time, in order to provide for a region-wide exchange of information in the three working languages of UNECE. They also greatly contributed to the development of guidance under the technical annexes, helped to explain different control measures and time scales including emission standards of the European Union (EU) and demonstrated the technical and economic feasibility of "best available control technologies".

The secretariat had no significant sources for financing capacity-building for emission control techniques in countries in transition. After the fall of the Berlin Wall however, it could devote increased attention to exchange of information on technology and related operational experience and costs. Many ways and means were successfully explored, including guidance on standard-setting and enforcement.

Protecting experts and the process from becoming irrelevant in a competitive world

Having established approaches for incorporating science into policy-making, the Convention has a need to maintain its scientific and technical groups to ensure that the process itself can be maintained. It is too easy to believe that the steps already taken to cut emissions are sufficient to address the problems of air pollution. There is also increasing competition from other environmental and political issues as well as from newly developing political situations such as the expansion of the EU.

The secretariat has been aware of the importance of such issues for many years and has sought to promote the Convention and its work through enhancing its visibility and ensuring the transparency of methods and results. It has also aimed to develop cooperation rather than competition in particular with programmes and organizations with related interests. Effective cooperation with WMO, EEA and WHO has been achieved through sharing the lead roles in some of the Convention's bodies.
Some Parties have expressed concern that the UNECE Convention in Europe might be overshadowed by EU interests, in particular the European Commission's Clean Air for Europe (CAFE) programme. However, the secretariat, the Bureau of the Executive Body, scientific experts and programme centres, and many Parties to the Convention have tried to develop a parallel-track approach to ensure that the Convention and CAFE both support and use the same science and results to enable the development of legal instruments under the umbrella of each. In this way there are mutual benefits and competition is avoided. But such efforts have not always been easy, for example, to get the EU to accept the critical loads approach for its own policy development was a major step; this also was facilitated by numerous secretariat contacts, both formal and informal.

Development of implementation and compliance monitoring

In the 1990s the Executive Body recognized that some of its earlier protocols had arrived at their target dates – the time at which Parties should have met emission targets. To look into Parties' compliance with their obligations the Executive Body, at its session in 1997, established the Implementation Committee to provide reports on how individual Parties were meeting their reporting and emission reduction obligations.

This was a new area of work for the secretariat and, while the first cases considered by the Committee were submissions from countries that knew they were failing to meet their obligations, the secretariat soon found itself in the position of referring Parties that had failed either to report or to cut their emissions as required. The secretariat was also responsible for the Committee's communications, inviting Parties to explain to the Committee why they were failing and informing Parties of the decisions of the Executive Body related to their non-compliance. Such a role has been vital for the successful functioning of the Committee, and in a large majority of cases Parties have been ready to respond to all requests from the secretariat.

The compliance regime is intended to be non-confrontational and non-judicial, bringing pressure through thorough review and presentation of facts linked to legal obligations. The secretariat's role has ensured due process and consistency in the approach, giving overall credibility to the work of the Committee. However, in referring cases to the Committee, the secretariat plays an active role in initiating reviews where Parties might prefer to keep quiet. This is a substantial shift in the role of the secretariat as it becomes a guardian of the protocols.

In its contacts with Parties to the Convention and the protocols, the secretariat provides information to support and assist the speedy ratification of agreements, their timely implementation and transparent compliance monitoring.

Further considerations for the future

The institutional framework set up by the Executive Body will continue to develop for the purpose of intergovernmental cooperation on science, monitoring, policy and implementation. The secretariat will play a major role in this process, as already reflected in this chapter. While the primary aim of the Convention is to foster agreements on emission reductions in the UNECE region, it also provides incentives for worldwide action involving other regions. The secretariat is increasingly participating in interregional and inter-agency cooperation and promotion of the Convention, e.g. in East Asia with the Acid Deposition Monitoring Network for East Asia (EANET). It also supports introducing hemispheric approaches to the assessment and abatement of air pollution.

The Convention sets an example for action in developing countries. The Swedish International Development Cooperation Agency (Sida) now designs subregional programmes on air pollution with reference to elements of the Convention. This process will certainly continue and the secretariat remains alert to new initiatives and directions.

UNITED NATIONS ECONOMIC COMMISSION FOR EUROPE
UNECE PRESS RELEASE COMMUNIQUÉ DE PRESSE CEE-ONU
COMMISSION ÉCONOMIQUE DES NATIONS UNIES POUR L'EUROPE

Press Release ECE/ENV/03/P02
Geneva, 31 January 2003

Air pollution and climate change – tackling both problems in tandem

Scientists and policy makers should no longer treat air pollution and climate change as distinct problems, because the two are very closely related. The recent Workshop on Linkages and Synergies of Regional and Global Emission Control, organized under the UNECE Convention on Long-range Transboundary Air Pollution by the International Institute for Applied Systems Analysis (IIASA), looked at the numerous links between these two policy areas. It concluded that these links are so important that they merit close cooperation.

Air pollution affects the regional and global climate both directly and indirectly. Ozone in the lower layers of the atmosphere contributes to global warming even more than some greenhouse gases included in the Kyoto Protocol, and particulate matter in the atmosphere also has important climate impacts. However, although black carbon, or soot particles, has a warming effect, other particles, for instance sulphates and nitrates, may cool the climate. The current high levels of sulphates and nitrates mask the effects of climate change to some degree. Through cuts in sulphur and nitrogen emissions necessary to protect human health and the environment the climate impacts of the greenhouse gases may actually show more quickly. On the other hand, measures to cut black carbon emissions, for instance from diesel combustion, will have double benefits, protecting both human health locally and also the climate regionally and worldwide.

Methane has a direct negative impact on climate (it is one of the Kyoto Protocol greenhouse gases) and it contributes to ground-level ozone levels. Methane emissions (mainly from agriculture, energy and waste management) have grown very rapidly since pre-industrial times. Cutting these emissions will reduce health- and ecosystem-damaging ozone levels and reduce the extent of climate change.

While indications of the climate impacts of increasing greenhouse gas concentrations can already be seen in the rise of mean temperatures and the increase in the numbers of extreme climate events (floods and droughts), most impacts are likely to happen over the next 50-100 years. Some gases, like carbon dioxide, stay in the atmosphere for a very long time, so measures to reduce emissions only start to show an effect after a few decades. In contrast, ozone, black carbon and methane can be controlled to show effects much sooner (10-20 years). Cutting these pollutants could help reduce some climate impacts while waiting for longer-term measures to pay off.

.../

UNITED NATIONS ECONOMIC COMMISSION FOR EUROPE
UN/ECE PRESS RELEASE COMMUNIQUÉ DE PRESSE CEE-ONU
COMMISSION ÉCONOMIQUE DES NATIONS UNIES POUR L'EUROPE

Press Release ECE/ENV/01/07
Geneva, 31 August 2001

Nitrogen pollution threatens Europe's forests

Extreme weather conditions, parasites and air pollution wreak havoc on the crowns of a quarter of all trees. In particular, nitrogen pollution is a major threat to Europe's forests, which are struggling to absorb annual depositions of 14 kg or more per hectare. And despite steep cuts in sulphur pollution (current depositions of 9 kg per hectare), past emissions continue to take their toll on forest soils. Both nitrogen and sulphur – emitted from intensive livestock farming, vehicle exhaust, fossil fuel burning and other sources – cause acidification when soils become saturated. The problem is particularly acute in central and western Europe, but less so in Scandinavia and south-western Europe.

These are the main findings of the 2001 report on 'Forest Condition in Europe'[1] published jointly by the United Nations Economic Commission for Europe (UNECE) and the European Commission. The annual report of the UNECE International Cooperative Programme on Assessment and Monitoring of Air Pollution Effects on Forests includes data from 38 countries. The Programme has been monitoring forest condition in Europe for 15 years. Its 6000 forest plots constitute one of the world's largest bio-monitoring networks. The Programme provides important information on the effect of clean air policies implemented under the UNECE Convention on Long-range Transboundary Air Pollution. Its findings are also relevant to international processes on biodiversity, climate change and sustainable forest management.

Crown condition varies from region to region and from one species to another. In Scandinavia and the Baltic region, there are fewer damaged trees. In some central European forests, which were particularly badly hit in the past, crown condition is recovering. Moreover, this year's focus on Aleppo pine (*Pinus halepensis*) gives this Mediterranean tree species a relatively clean bill of health.

In south-eastern Europe, however, long periods of drought, high temperatures [...] have led to a sharp increase in the proportion of damaged and dead [...]ion also deteriorated in central European plots with high atmospheric [...]

[...]le on http://www.icp-forests.org/RepEx.htm

UNITED NATIONS ECONOMIC COMMISSION FOR EUROPE
UN/ECE PRESS RELEASE COMMUNIQUÉ DE PRESSE CEE-ONU
COMMISSION ÉCONOMIQUE DES NATIONS UNIES POUR L'EUROPE

Press Release ECE/ENV/01/03
Geneva, 26 June 2001

AIR POLLUTANTS MAKE TRANSCONTINENTAL JOURNEY

"Contrary to received opinion, peaks of summertime smog are not caused by local polluters alone," says Kaj Bärlund, Environment Director at the United Nations Economic Commission for Europe (UNECE). "Whether air pollution levels in your area comply with air-quality standards or breach them may actually depend on how much pollution it receives from across the ocean."

Leading European and North American scientists have agreed that there is strong evidence for intercontinental movements of fine particles and ozone across the northern hemisphere between North America, Europe and Asia. They presented their findings at a recent conference on air pollution across the Atlantic and the Arctic, hosted by the United States Environmental Protection Agency (EPA) and Environment Canada within the framework of the UNECE Convention on Long-range Transboundary Air Pollution.

The new findings show that fine particles and ozone travel not only across borders but also across oceans. This implies that it may not be enough to take local measures such as clamping down on car use during pollution peaks to meet air-quality standards, since some of the pollution is emitted overseas.

Fine particles are emitted by many sources, including motor vehicles, particularly those that run on diesel, industry and other combustion sources. Some particles are small enough to penetrate the lungs. They are blamed for several health problems, such as increased risk of heart and lung disease. They can also carry carcinogenic substances and have been associated with premature deaths. Ground-level ozone, also known as summer smog and not to be confused with stratospheric ozone that forms the ozone layer, is a secondary pollutant caused by industrial and motor vehicle emissions and the use of certain products such as solvents and paints. It irritates the eyes and is known to damage lung function, particularly in children and asthmatics. It also causes leaf injury in plants, including crops and trees, and causes mainly organic materials like paint or rubber to disintegrate.

.../

For the use of information media, not an official record. Issued by the United Nations Information Service.
UN/ECE Information Office, CH-1211 Geneva 10
Phone: (+41 22) 917 44 44
Fax: (+41 22) 917 05 05
E-mail: info.ece@unece.org
Internet home page: http://www.unece.org

Destiné à l'information; ne constitue pas un document officiel. Publié par le Service de l'information des Nations Unies.
Bureau d'information CEE-ONU, CH-1211 Genève 10
Téléphone: (+41 22) 917 44 44
Télécopie: (+41 22) 917 05 05
Courrier électronique: info.ece@unece.org
Site Internet: http://www.unece.org

UNITED NATIONS ECONOMIC COMMISSION FOR EUROPE
UNECE PRESS RELEASE COMMUNIQUÉ DE PRESSE CEE-ONU
COMMISSION ÉCONOMIQUE DES NATIONS UNIES POUR L'EUROPE

Press Release ECE/ENV/03/P27
Geneva, 23 December 2003

Protocol on Heavy Metals enters into force and new work on persistent organic pollutants agreed

The 19 new Parties to the Protocol on Heavy Metals are to celebrate its entry into force next Monday, 29 December.

The Protocol, signed by 35 countries and the European Union at its adoption in Aarhus, Denmark, in 1998, is the seventh to take effect under the Convention on Long-range Transboundary Air Pollution of the United Nations Economic Commission for Europe (UNECE).

Since the announcement earlier in the year that the Protocol would enter into force, three more countries – Austria, Bulgaria and Monaco – have ratified it. All 19 Parties, i.e. Austria, Bulgaria, Canada, the Czech Republic, Denmark, Finland, France, Germany, Luxembourg, Monaco, the Netherlands, Norway, the Republic of Moldova, Romania, Slovakia, Sweden, Switzerland, the United States and the European Community, are expected to attend the first meeting of the Parties to the Protocol, which will take place at the time of the next session of the Convention's Executive Body scheduled for December 2004. Their discussions are likely to focus on the three priority metals covered by the Protocol – lead, cadmium and mercury.

Meanwhile new work on persistent organic pollutants (POPs) has already been agreed at the first meeting of the Parties to the 1998 Protocol on Persistent Organic Pollutants, which took place in Geneva in conjunction with the Convention's most recent session of its Executive Body.

This Protocol became effective in October and this was the first chance for countries to consider future work on these toxic substances. They agreed a work-plan for 2004, targeted at reviewing the provisions of the Protocol to see if they are effective, and to establish a new Task Force on POPs, which will also address longer-term work. The Task Force will meet in March.

.../

For the use of information media, not an official record
UNECE Information Service, CH-1211 Geneva 10
Phone: +41(0)22 917 44 44
Fax: +41(0)22 917 05 05
E-mail: info.ece@unece.org
Internet home page: http://www.unece.org

Destiné à l'information; ne constitue pas un document officiel
Service de l'information de la CEE-ONU, CH-1211 Genève 10
Téléphone: +41(0)22 917 44 44
Télécopie: +41(0)22 917 05 05
Courrier électronique: info.ece@unece.org
Site Internet: http://www.unece.org

THE UNECE SECRETARIAT REGULARLY ISSUES PRESS RELEASES TO INFORM THE PRESS AND THE PUBLIC ON MAJOR EVENTS

Promoting political and geographical expansion

Looking back now over the lifetime of the Convention, political changes both large and small have taken place throughout the UNECE region. The secretariat, being non-political, has been able to adopt a UNECE-wide perspective throughout, acknowledging changes and problems within the region whilst considering them in the broader context of the global environment. It has sought to bring together countries and their experts from the region to ensure the best possible participation in the Convention's work.

Being part of the United Nations system, the secretariat continues to provide a secure and practical mechanism for promoting communications between Parties and experts. Promoting the ratification of the Convention and its protocols, though sometimes slow and not always easy in times of political change, has been key to ensuring participation by UNECE States. At present the Convention has 49 Parties (including the European Community as a Party in its own right) and two Signatories (the Holy See and San Marino), which have signed the Convention but not ratified it. This leaves just five UNECE member States that are not Parties to the Convention: Albania, which has indicated a willingness to become a Party on several occasions, but which has encountered problems because of political change; Andorra; and three Central Asian States, Tajikistan, Turkmenistan and Uzbekistan. These Central Asian States have recently been involved in regional workshops and have indicated their intention to move towards accession in the near future.

A recently approved UNECE project proposed by the secretariat and funded by the United Nations Development Account will provide guidance to politicians and experts in Central Asia, particularly in Kazakhstan which is already a Party to the Convention, to assist the five Central Asian countries to accede to and implement the Convention and its protocols.

From regional to global

The regional approach of the Convention has already been used as a steppingstone for global action, namely the preparation of the 2001 Stockholm Convention on POPs, negotiated under UNEP, which takes the 1998 Protocol on POPs as a point of departure. Likewise the UNEP initiative on mercury has been taken with the 1998 Protocol on Heavy Metals in mind.

The Gothenburg Protocol demonstrated how several air pollutants could be addressed at the same time and the co-benefits from doing this. Now it is important to consider links to sectoral policies and to other related issues such as climate change. When these are considered the geographic and political scale of the problem changes; air pollution needs to be related to the global scale and consideration given to changes taking place outside the UNECE region. Such an outreach implies that air pollution should also be seen in the context of economic development and poverty in the world and as a possible element in national development plans. The Convention and its secretariat will no doubt address these challenges in the coming years.

References

1 Economic Commission for Europe, "Effects of Acidifying Depositions and Related Pollutants on Forest Ecosystems", Air Pollution Across Boundaries: Air Pollution Studies No. 2, ECE/EB.AIR/5, UN 1985, pp. 7-30.

2 Work-plan for the implementation of the Convention, ECE/EB.AIR/7, UN 1986, annex IV, section 1.1.2.

3 Convention on Access to Information, Public Participation in Decision-making and Access to Justice in Environmental Matters, and its 2003 Kiev Protocol on Pollutant Release and Transfer Registers.

4 After the fall of the Berlin Wall, when the archives of the former German Democratic Republic's secret service (infamous Stasi) became publicly accessible, the UNECE secretariat discovered that one of its own staff members – under the code name 'Newton' – had regularly reported all EMEP data to the country's Ministry of State Security, along with detailed reports on his colleagues and superiors and on prominent government delegates at Convention meetings.

5 J.C. di Primio, "Data Quality and Compliance Control in the European Air Pollution Regime", in: D.G. Victor, K. Raustiala & E.B. Skolnikoff (eds.), The Implementation and Effectiveness of International Environmental Commitments: Theory and Practice, MIT Press: Cambridge/MA 1998, pp. 283-303, at 297.

6 Strategies and Policies for Air Pollution Abatement, ECE/EB.AIR/14, UN 1987, p. 42 (table 1).

7 ECE/EB.AIR/27, UN 1991, p. 39 (table 5).

8 ECE/EB.AIR/65, UN 1999, p. 85 (table 2). Romania's annual SO2 emissions further increased to 1,517,000 tons by 1989, but have since reverted to 912,000 tons reported as of 1994; see V. Vestreng, Review and Revision of Emission Data Reported to CLRTAP, EMEP/MSC-W Note 1/2003, p. 74 (table 1).

9 When the Bough Breaks, Greenpeace UK: London 1988; "Britain's woodlands in a worse state than they cared to admit", Acid News No. 2/May 1988, pp. 8-9.

10 Report of the 8th session of the Executive Body, ECE/EB.AIR/24, UN 1990, para. 31.

11 For example, see the consolidated technical report submitted to the 18th session of the Working Group on Effects: K. Bull (ed.), Trends in Impacts of Long-range Transboundary Air Pollution, WGE/CEH 1999.

12 Summary report in: Yearbook of International Co-operation on Environment and Development (2003/2004), pp. 92-94.

13 See Evgeny M. Chossudovsky, "East-West" Diplomacy for Environment in the United Nations, Geneva: UNITAR 1988, UN publication E.88.XV.ST26.

14 Many key delegates represented their governments both at UNEP and Convention meetings – notably Mr. Richard Benedick (United States), Mr. Martin Holdgate (United Kingdom), and Mr. Willem Kakebeeke (Netherlands).

15 See the Convention experience cited by P.M. Haas & D. McCabe, "Amplifiers or Dampeners: International Institutions and Social Learning in the Management of Global Environmental Risks", in: Learning to Manage Global Environmental Risks, vol. 1 (The Social Learning Group, MIT Press: Cambridge/MA 2001), pp. 323-348

16 For example, the same legal expert drafted the rules of 'Implementation Committees' under the UNEP Montreal Protocol on Substances that Deplete the Ozone Layer, and under the Convention Protocols on VOCs and SO2; P. Széll, "The Development of Multilateral Mechanisms for Monitoring Compliance", in: Sustainable Development and International Law (W. Lang ed., Graham & Trotman/Nijhoff: London/Dordrecht 1995), pp. 97-109.

17 Compare the 1998 Convention on Long-range Transboundary Air Pollution's Protocol on Persistent Organic Pollutants and the 2001 UNEP Convention on Persistent Organic Pollutants.

Compliance and consensus

Chapter 8

Patrick Széll, Volkert Keizer and Tuomas Kuokkanen

Review of compliance by the Parties with their obligations under the protocols to the Convention on Long-range Transboundary Air Pollution is a comparatively recent activity. Only in the past six years has there been a standing body, the Implementation Committee, to review compliance. The Committee considers cases of non-compliance drawn to its attention by submissions from Parties or referrals by the secretariat. It also systematically evaluates information reported by Parties and assesses Parties' progress in fulfilling their protocol obligations. The Committee was created at a time when many multilateral environmental agreements recognized that, without regular and efficient scrutiny of Parties' compliance, a treaty had little real value. But, as other agreements which operate a compliance scrutiny system (e.g. the Montreal Protocol and Espoo Convention) have found, the activity is politically sensitive and so the Committee and Executive Body must act with a cautious blend of determination and sensitivity to ensure that their supervision is effective without being alienating.

Outline

The following chapter considers first the structure, functions and workings of the Implementation Committee during its early, formative years. There is then a review of the technical aspects of its work. The Convention and its protocols are technical in nature and the Committee's analyses and recommendations are founded on a clear understanding of how the various protocol obligations, and the flexibilities built into them, are meant to function in practice. The chapter concludes with a short section on how the Convention's decision-making rules operate. From the outset in 1979, for every Convention body - be it the Executive Body, the Working Group on Strategies and Review or the Implementation Committee - the key word has been consensus.

Throughout the text decisions of the Convention's Executive Body and documents submitted to it are cited; these documents and decisions can be found on the Convention's web site: www.unece.org/env/lrtap.

Operation of compliance review under the Convention

Establishment of the Implementation Committee

In 1997, the Executive Body established the Implementation Committee to review compliance with all the protocols to the Convention (Executive Body decision 1997/2). It developed the Committee's structure and functions in the light of experience already gained in operating such a committee under the Montreal Protocol and in furtherance of its own decision on compliance taken three years earlier when adopting the 1994 Sulphur Protocol.

The Committee consists of nine Parties to the Convention. Each member of the Committee must, according to the mandate, be party to at least one protocol. The independent quality, personal expertise and continuity of participation of the individual members of the Committee are all important for the success of its work though, formally speaking, the members represent the Parties from which they come.

The Implementation Committee has three main functions: to review compliance with reporting obligations, to consider any submission or referral and to prepare in-depth reviews of compliance wit specified obligations in individual protocols. The non-compliance procedure can be triggered by means of submissions by Parties or referrals by the secretariat. A submission may be brought either by one or more Parties against another Party or by a Party with respect to itself. If the secretariat becomes aware of a case of possible non-compliance, it may bring the matter to the attention of the Committee by means of a referral.

The Implementation Committee makes recommendations to the Executive Body – the entity to which it is answerable. In accordance with paragraph 9 of its mandate, the Committee is required to report on its activities at least once a year to the Executive Body and make such recommendations as it considers appropriate. Upon consideration of a report and any recommendations from the Committee, the Executive Body may decide upon measures of a non-discriminatory nature to bring about full compliance with the protocol in question.

Review of compliance by Parties with their reporting obligations

Under its mandate, the Implementation Committee reviews periodically compliance by the Parties wi the reporting requirements of the protocols. Parties are required to report both information on strategies and policies that serve as a means of reducing emissions and information on their emissions.

With regard to information on strategies and policies, the Committee reviews both the timeliness anc completeness of reporting. While most Parties eventually submit complete reports, a number have failed to respect the deadlines. The quality of national reporting has improved markedly over the year though the reports have been, and continue to be, uneven in length, depth and content.

To achieve its goal, the Committee has used various innovative means to put gradual pressure on Parties to comply with their reporting obligations. These range from merely noting the non-compliance of a Party in its report, to advising the Executive Body to urge the head of delegation of th Party, together with an expert familiar with the data that should be reported, to visit the secretariat to discuss how and when the material can be presented.

The completeness of emission data reporting has improved significantly since the Implementation Committee began to review it as a matter of course each year. For example, the level of emission data reported for the 1985 Sulphur Protocol was 99% in 2003 while it had been 86% in 1998. Similarly, the level reported for the 1988 Protocol on Nitrogen Oxides was 99% in 2003 while in 1998 it had been only 82%. Parties have clearly made a great effort to fulfil their reporting obligations because of the scrutiny carried out by the Committee and the related decisions of the Executive Body (e.g. Executive Body decisions 2001/4, 2002/9 and 2003/9).

Despite such improvements, the situation is not yet satisfactory and the Committee has constantly found it necessary to remind Parties of the importance of complying fully with their reporting obligations, in particular with their obligations to report on strategies and policies.

Parties are obliged to report to the Executive Body on their strategies and policies developed in accordance with the protocols. To help the process the secretariat circulates a questionnaire every two years and publishes the responses received.

Consideration of submissions by Parties and referrals by the secretariat
By the end of 2003, the Implementation Committee had considered a total of ten individual submissions and referrals relating to the compliance by individual Parties with substantive obligations. Five were self-submissions and five were referrals by the secretariat (see table 8.1).

In seven of the ten cases, the Committee, and subsequently the Executive Body, concluded that there had been non-compliance: namely the cases of Norway, Finland, Italy, Greece, Ireland and Spain. The three exceptions were Slovenia, Sweden and Luxembourg. As Slovenia's submission concerned its potential non-compliance between 2005 and 2007, there could be no non-compliance till 2005 at the earliest and so the decision of the Executive Body, based on the recommendation of the Committee, was merely advisory in nature. With regard to Sweden's submission, it became apparent in 2003 - as a result of a reappraisal of its volatile organic carbon (VOC) emission data and method of calculation - that Sweden had in fact been in compliance with the 1991 Protocol on VOCs from the outset. A similar outcome seems likely in the case of Luxembourg but the Committee recently postponed finalization of its recommendation to the Executive Body until it had received clarification on one point regarding that country's calculations. All the submissions and referrals handled by the Committee so far have been non-contentious in nature. The Parties involved have not questioned the finding of non-compliance but rather have sought to explain the background and the factors that led to the breach.

In most of the ten cases, the Parties have identified one or more sectors that have been proved particularly problematic for them. For instance, the main reason for the failure by Norway to reduce its VOC emissions in accordance with the 1991 VOC Protocol was the delay in developing the necessary technologies to control emissions in the offshore oil sector, which was responsible for a large share of Norway's emissions. In Ireland, the extraordinary economic growth in the 1990s caused an unexpectedly large increase in its VOC emissions. In addition, so-called fuel tourism between Northern Ireland and the Republic increased Ireland's emissions. In Finland, emission reductions in the road transport sector - its largest source of VOC emissions - had fallen below expectations due to the economic recession in the beginning of the 1990s. As a consequence, the renewal of its vehicle fleet was slower than anticipated. The mobile source sector was one of the principal causes of Italy's, Greece's and Spain's difficulties as well. One problem that has been common to many of the referrals and submissions has been the uncertainty and/or inaccuracy of the national data.

The Implementation Committee has first considered the background to the submissions and referrals and then the pertinent provisions of the protocol in question. It has then determined whether the concerned Party has failed to comply with its obligations. Finally, it has produced a recommendation to the Executive Body. To date, the Executive Body has adopted all the recommendations presented to it by the Committee.

TABLE 8.1. SUBMISSIONS AND REFERRALS BROUGHT BEFORE THE IMPLEMENTATION COMMITTEE.

Party	Protocol	Obligation	Submission/ referral	Action
Slovenia	1994 Sulphur	Article 2, paragraph 5 (b), limit value	Self-submission	- Executive Body decision 2000/1 - Further decision pending
Norway	1991 VOC	Article 2, paragraph 2, emission reduction	Self-submission	- Executive Body decision 2001/1 - Follow-up decisions 2002/2 and 2003/1 - Further decision pending
Finland	1991 VOC	Article 2, paragraph 2, emission reduction	Self-submission	- Executive Body decision 2001/2 - Follow-up decision 2002/3 - Closed pursuant to decision 2003/2 (Finland achieved compliance)
Italy	1991 VOC	Article 2, paragraph 2, emission reduction	Self-submission	- Executive Body decision 2001/3 - Follow-up decisions 2002/4 and 2003/3 - Further decision pending
Sweden	1991 VOC	Article 2, paragraph 2, emission reduction	Self-submission	- Executive Body decision 2002/5 - Closed pursuant to decision 2003/4 (Sweden in compliance all along)
Greece	1988 NOx	Article 2, paragraph 1, emission reduction	Secretariat referral	- Executive Body decision 2002/6 - Follow-up decision 2003/5 - Further decision pending
Ireland	1988 NOx	Article 2, paragraph 1, emission reduction	Secretariat referral	- Executive Body decision 2002/7 - Follow-up decision 2003/6 - Further decision pending
Spain	1988 NOx	Article 2, paragraph 1, emission reduction	Secretariat referral	- Executive Body decision 2002/8 - Follow-up decision 2003/7 - Further decision pending
Luxemb.	1991 VOC	Article 2, paragraph 2, emission reduction	Secretariat referral	- Pending
Spain	1991 VOC	Article 2, paragraph 2, emission reduction	Secretariat referral	- Executive Body decision 2003/8 - Further decision pending

One can identify three main elements in the recommendations of the Committee and the related decisions of the Executive Body. First, there has been a conclusion of non-compliance. Second, the Party concerned has been urged to fulfil its obligations as soon as possible. Third, the Party has been requested to provide periodic progress reports to the Committee. Depending on the circumstances of the matter, the Committee and Executive Body have used different nuances of language in their reports. For instance, their recommendations "express disappointment", "note with concern", "remain concerned", "urge" or "strongly urge" in order to increase gradually the pressure on Parties in breach.

Regarding the third of these elements, each Party found in breach is called on to report by a specified date on the steps that it has taken to achieve compliance, in particular to set out a timetable that specifies the year by which it expects to be in compliance, to list the specific measures taken, or scheduled to be taken, for fulfilling its emission-reduction obligations under the protocol and to set out the projected effects of each of these measures up to and including the year of compliance. The purpose of such requirements is to put pressure on the Parties in question to bring about full compliance as quickly as possible. The Committee has placed a heavy emphasis on the preparing of timetables and on offering practical suggestions to accelerate emission reductions. Each year it has reviewed the steps taken by those Parties to which Executive Body decisions have been addressed and as necessary, made recommendations for follow-up decisions by the Executive Body until the Parties concerned have achieved compliance. Thereafter, the Executive Body decides that there is no reason for the Implementation Committee to continue to review a particular submission or referral.

To date, of the ten countries for which individual proceedings have commenced, the Executive Body has decided in two instances to close the proceedings. While Finland achieved compliance (Executive Body decision 2003/2), in the case of Sweden, as noted above, it was eventually established that it had been in compliance all along (Executive Body decision 2003/4). In the case of Luxembourg, a similar outcome to that of Sweden seems likely.

In-depth reviews

In accordance with its mandate and at the request of the Executive Body, the Implementation Committee regularly prepares reports on Parties' compliance with the principal obligations in a given protocol. The aim has been to review a different protocol every year. So far, the Committee has conducted four in-depth reviews on: the 1985 Sulphur Protocol; the 1988 Nitrogen Oxides Protocol; the 1991 VOC Protocol; and the 1994 Protocol on the Further Reduction of Sulphur Emissions. In 2001, it noted with regret that as many as a third of the Parties to the 1991 VOC Protocol were not in compliance, and that this was in stark contrast to the 1985 Sulphur Protocol and 1988 Nitrogen Oxides Protocol where compliance was achieved by almost all Parties.

The difference between such in-depth reviews and the Committee's consideration of submissions and referrals is that in-depth reviews are collective in nature and are principally concerned with the overall effectiveness of the protocol under scrutiny, while referrals and submissions are concerned with the performance of individual Parties in respect of a particular protocol obligation. This said, in-depth reviews have provided raw material for triggering referrals by the secretariat. The Committee has stated that, even though it may become aware of an instance of non-compliance while carrying out in-depth reviews, due process dictates that the Executive Body should not take any measures unless and

until the Committee has properly and individually reviewed the matter, including listening to any arguments that the Party concerned might wish to make. The Executive Body may, however, take general measures as a consequence of the findings of an in-depth review to promote and improve implementation by the Parties to a particular protocol.

Key points

In the light of the above, one may conclude that the operation of the Implementation Committee has added value to the management of the Convention. Even though the Committee and Executive Body have only limited powers, they have succeeded, through the application of innovative means, to put gentle pressure on Parties that are in breach. Thereby, it has also sent a clear message to all Parties about the need to take their obligations seriously.

The completeness and timeliness of emission data reporting has undoubtedly improved since the Committee started regularly examining Parties' compliance with their reporting obligations. The Committee's workload in reviewing individual submissions and referrals has steadily increased and, although it has been difficult at times to get Parties in breach to accelerate their schedules for achieving compliance as much as the Committee and the Executive Body would wish, the pressure applied has achieved positive results.

So far, no Party has challenged the proceedings or the findings of the Committee. On the contrary, they have been very supportive of the activities of the Committee and, for the most part, have cooperated fully and constructively with its requests, even when they have been criticized in its recommendations. Most have been ready – indeed keen – to explain the difficulties they have experienced in trying to fulfil their obligations and, in its turn, the Committee has always sought to offer practical suggestions that Parties might follow in order to facilitate and accelerate full compliance. True to the spirit and intention of the Parties to the Convention when establishing the implementation process in 1997, the Committee has at all times operated on the principle that a cooperative and facilitative approach to those in breach of their protocol commitments is more likely to produce positive results for the Convention and for the environment than a confrontational approach.

Some technical aspects of compliance review

The protocols to the Convention deal with complex technical issues. As a result, the assessment of compliance with the obligations that they contain is heavily dependent on making technical judgements. The first substantive protocol - the 1985 Sulphur Protocol - placed a flat-rate requirement on all Parties to reduce their national emissions by 30%. Subsequently, the negotiating States adopted a less confrontational style and developed protocols containing more flexible obligations. Whilst flexible provisions can be very helpful in getting politically sensitive obligations agreed, they could make the assessment of compliance more difficult.

Flexibility - two autonomous tracks

The 1988 Nitrogen Oxides Protocol and subsequent instruments provided Parties with flexibility by creating basic obligations that simultaneously followed two autonomous tracks reflecting the two main types of existing national strategy:

1. **Control of total emissions** through imposing flat-rate reductions, or a standstill, in most of the protocols and by establishing effect-based targets, country emission ceilings, in the 1994 Sulphur Protocol and the 1999 Gothenburg Protocol to Abate Acidification, Eutrophication and Ground-level Ozone. This approach has the advantage of allowing the Parties a wide range of implementation possibilities, but has a downside that compliance assessment is completely dependent on the quality of the emission data reported; and
2. **Use of state-of-the-art** abatement technology, at first only through non-binding guidance set out in technical annexes which give examples of best available technology (BAT), and later through mandatory emission limit values (ELVs) and standards, which are the backbone of the national strategy in many countries (e.g. in Germany since 1974). An advantage of this approach is that compliance with ELVs and standards can be easily verified. The downside is that the only possibility for implementation is to apply those ELVs or standards.

In this respect the term 'autonomous' does not deny the interrelation between the two tracks, but stresses that in general a Party has to comply fully with the obligations under each of them. Occasionally however, for a specific pollutant and by way of exemption or to allow for an alternative approach, one of the tracks is abandoned and the other made to prevail. Thus, a Party will be exempted from meeting its overall reduction obligation so long as it complies with all its BAT obligations, or it will be exempted from application of certain BAT obligations provided that its overall reduction targets are still met.

Such a double approach, both technology-oriented and using (effect-oriented) overall emission targets, has been used in the Netherlands since 1984. Because progress on one track will influence a country's position on the other, reliance on the two-track approach helps it to meet its obligations no matter what its national strategy. This, in turn, has allowed the Implementation Committee to focus it in-depth reviews of the 1998 Nitrogen Oxides Protocol and the 1991 VOC Protocol simply on national emission obligations (see EB.AIR/2000/2, para. 26 and EB.AIR/2001/3, para. 46). For practical reasons, the in-depth review of the 1994 Sulphur Protocol dealt with other obligations only when they permitted clean-cut conclusions to be drawn about compliance (see EB.AIR/2002/2/Add.1, para. 32). With one exception (i.e. the Slovenian case which concerns article 2, para. 5(b), of the 1994 Sulphur Protocol), all the referrals and submissions made to date to the Committee have related simply to national emission obligations.

The total emissions track

Over the years, various concepts for improving implementation have been developed by the negotiating States with a view to further stimulating ratification and implementation of the protocols to the Convention. Thus:

- **Alternative base years** are permitted under the 1998 Nitrogen Oxides Protocol, the 1991 VOC Protocol, the 1998 POPs Protocol and the 1998 Protocol on Heavy Metals while the emission reduction obligations of countries with a large territory and/or relatively low emissions have been modified. This latter modification has resulted in a management area approach, which has made the concept of transboundary fluxes operational (see the 1991 VOC, 1994 Sulphur and 1999 Gothenburg Protocols) and for a standstill instead of a reduction (see the 1991 VOC Protocol). Denmark was able to become a Party to the 1994 Sulphur Protocol by reason of a temporary exemption that enabled it to discount unforeseen short-term problems in its power supply;

- **Individual national emission ceilings** have been included in the 1994 Sulphur and 1999 Gothenburg Protocols. They are based on scientifically and technologically sound cost-effect optimization, which takes costs of abatement as well as deposition patterns, human health and sensitivity of ecosystems into account. The optimization is directed towards reaching environmental quality and human health targets in Europe at the lowest overall cost. To make this approach work, implementation by as many countries as possible is of great importance. The national ceilings in the protocol annexes were established on the basis of national bids made in accordance with an agreed modelled scenario. The procedure further enhanced the prospects of increasing levels of ratification and compliance; and
- **Special regimes for North America** have been developed under the 1994 Sulphur and 1999 Gothenburg Protocols because the exchange of acidifying substances between Europe and North America is limited and EMEP covers only Europe. Notwithstanding this, the United States did not sign the 1994 Sulphur Protocol.

As an exemption a Party may under the 1998 Protocols on POPs and Heavy Metals abandon the total emission track for a specific pollutant, if it cannot achieve the requirements, after complying with all its BAT obligations for that pollutant.

The abatement technology track

All protocols after the 1985 Sulphur Protocol contain BAT obligations, but consensus about the meaning and scope of BAT is not easy to achieve. To facilitate ratification and to improve the prospects of implementation, protocols have either modified the obligation or replaced BAT by less absolute concepts like "BAT which is economically feasible" or "BAT not entailing excessive cost". The approach of individual protocols varies, which has consequences for the assessment of compliance. For instance:

- **Mandatory or recommendatory technical annexes** may be used. The 1988 Nitrogen Oxides and 1991 VOC Protocols require the application of national emission standards, taking into consideration the technical annexes. In the subsequent protocols, ELVs for stationary and new mobile sources, as well as product standards, are obligatory. However, for stationary sources (other than new large combustion sources under the 1994 Sulphur Protocol) equivalent strategies may - subject to various conditions - be used instead of ELVs;
- **The state of the art on control technology** is not necessarily reflected in obligatory ELVs; for instance, ELVs for large combustion sources in the 1994 Sulphur Protocol, derived - via the European Union's Large Combustion Plant Directive - from 1983 German legislation, reflect the technology of the early 1980s. All annexes that describe BAT refer to the need to update the descriptions regularly, but only the 1988 Nitrogen Oxides Protocol definition has been revised - in 1991, 1994 and 1996; and
- **Different timescales, areas, sources and standards.** Different timescales have been specified for countries with economies in transition (see the 1998 POPs and the 1999 Gothenburg Protocols) and for existing sources. In the 1991 VOC Protocol, BAT for existing sources has been restricted to specific areas, while ELVs for those sources in the 1994 Sulphur and 1999 Gothenburg Protocols are restricted to specific categories. Canada and the United States have been exempted from the BAT track under the 1994 Sulphur Protocol and they apply only national legislation under the 1999 Gothenburg Protocol. For members of the European Union and the European Economic Area,

compliance has been assisted through increased reliance by the protocols on the European Union's description of BAT as well as its product standards and ELVs.

After 1991, protocols have allowed for alternative strategies in certain cases by partly abandoning the technology track for particular obligations, provided that equivalent reductions are reached or overall reduction targets are still met. To accommodate Canada, the 1998 Protocol onHeavy Metals expressly allowed a Party with a very large land area to exchange BAT for a 50% overall reduction in its emissions.

Effects on compliance assessment

The wide variety of obligations on both the total emission and the technology track has consequences for compliance assessment. Accurate emissions data are essential for assessing compliance under the total emission track. This goes for all the alternatives developed in the various protocols. Further improvement in the reliability of Parties' emissions data reporting is essential not least to avoid "creative calculation" by Parties that find themselves in difficulty with compliance. The data need to be reliable not just in a relative sense for enabling flat-rate reductions to be compared to a base year's figures, but also in an absolute sense for making assessments vis-à-vis an emission ceiling. Using and assessing these data can be difficult for the Implementation Committee. For instance:

- The Committee relies on data as reported by the Parties. In the case of referrals or submissions, evaluation of data by outside technical experts is possible. To date, however, there have been no instances of such experts evaluating data for the Committee;
- The protocols provide no clear definition of which emissions make up a Party's annual emissions, though definitions in the Convention and the 1991 VOC, 1994 Sulphur and 1999 Gothenburg Protocols may be read as indicating that, for those Protocols, they are emissions of an anthropogenic nature (see EB.AIR/2001/3, para. 40) originating from areas under the jurisdiction of a Party. In the referral concerning Luxembourg, the Committee accepted that VOC emissions from managed forests were non-anthropogenic (see EB.AIR/2003/1, para. 53). The definition of "sulphur emissions" in the 1994 Sulphur Protocol implicitly includes emissions from ships in territorial waters; and
- Although uniform emission reporting guidelines in practice harmonize national calculations satisfactorily, there are some snags. The application of guidelines is not mandatory for the 1985 Sulphur and 1988 Nitrogen Oxides Protocols and is only partly mandatory for the other protocols. Provided they can show justification, Parties may recalculate their emissions. Such recalculations have been successfully presented to the Committee by, amongst others, Sweden and Luxembourg (see EB.AIR/2003/1, paras. 23 and 48). Methods for estimating road transport emissions are not fully harmonized and how to deal with emissions from ships and air traffic is still under discussion. Irrespective of these guidelines, the accuracy of VOC emission estimates is relatively poor.

Different timescales for applying BAT and straightforward exemptions do not complicate the assessment of compliance, though increased flexibility in the definition of BAT can make such assessment more difficult. Thus:

- It is not easy to judge whether national emission standards follow the guidance set out in a technical annex and it can be even more difficult to assess whether an alternative strategy has the

equivalent effect it claims. Only in the 1999 Gothenburg Protocol does the onus of proving such equivalence lie with the Party that uses the exemption; and

- The updating of BAT definitions may have an impact on the assessment of compliance, though in practice this is not very likely. When the 1999 Gothenburg Protocol comes into force for sulphur, nitrogen oxides and VOC, two BAT descriptions will exist under two protocols for the same source and the same pollutant (e.g. for VOCs the 1991 VOC and 1999 Gothenburg Protocols). If a country is a Party to both treaties, the more stringent BAT requirement of the latter Protocol will prevail. But when a country is Party only to the Protocol on VOCs, its compliance with BAT will be tested only against what is an evidently obsolete version.

External factors may further complicate compliance assessment. For instance, a Party may decide prematurely (before it has made adequate progress with preparing the necessary national legislation) to ratify a protocol hoping thereby to advance the national introduction of BAT; and some European Union countries have sought to demonstrate their compliance with particular protocol requirements merely by citing the title of the related European Union rules by which they are bound, instead of a clear indication of their transposition into national legislation (see EB.AIR/2003/1/Add.1, paras. 37 and 43).

Decision-making under the Convention

Rules of procedure and the tradition of consensus

From the outset, the Executive Body and its various subsidiaries, including the Implementation Committee, have made their decisions on the basis of consensus. The practice has been so consistent that delegates and commentators have tended to assume that consensus is expressly required by the rules. But this is not the case. It is true that the Convention and its protocols do specify consensus within the Executive Body for the adoption of amendments to treaty articles and annexes and for the amendment of certain decisions that have been incorporated into protocols by reference. But for the large majority of Executive Body and subsidiary body decisions, the Convention and its protocols are silent on the decision-making rules to be applied and as a result, in such cases, the actions of those bodies will be governed by whatever has been laid down in the applicable rules of procedure.

The Executive Body decided at its first session in 1983 to apply the rules of procedure of UNECE but that certain amendments might have to be made in order to suit its own purposes (see ECE/EB.AIR/1, para. 14). Rule 35 of those rules states that: "Decisions of the Commission shall be made by a majority of the members present and voting." Applied mutatis mutandis to the Convention, this means that all decisions of the Executive Body and its subsidiaries, save those expressly requiring consensus under the terms of the Convention or its protocols, shall be taken by simple majority vote.

Despite the unambiguous nature of this rule, the Executive Body has never deviated from its determination to establish consensus before acting. There were two main reasons for this. First, most multilateral environmental agreements have traditionally sought to work through consensus believing this to be, at least in the longer term, in the best interests of the environment; and second, at the time of the Cold War, the UNECE member States understandably felt a need to work, as far as possible, cooperatively in sectors such as the environment. But whatever the motivations, the practice of consensus is now so deeply rooted in the Convention system that it would be a great surprise if it were to be questioned. Where the rules of procedure are concerned, it might even be argued that the Executive Body has, through long and consistent practice, modified its 1983 decision by implication.

Consensus – advantages and disadvantages

The tradition of consensus within the Executive Body has ensured that all Parties remain in step and that, when necessary, strenuous efforts are made to accommodate the wishes, concerns and needs of all who are bound by the treaty in question. Consensus has fostered cohesion within the Executive Body and, since there are no dissenters, added strength and authority to its decisions. But inevitably these have come at a price; the pace of advance under the Convention and its protocols has been slower and more tentative than it would have been under majority voting.

Unlike a requirement for unanimity (which historically is the basic rule of international law on decision-making), consensus has allowed those Parties not present when an Executive Body decision is taken to be discounted and has also enabled them to acquiesce in the outcome of decisions without having to express openly their agreement or disagreement to them. Similarly, in contrast to a majority voting system, consensus has avoided the alienating effects of Executive Body decisions that do not sufficiently take into account the legitimate interests of the outvoted minority and the damaging consequences that such divisive action can have for the Convention system.

Non-Party participation in decisions under individual protocols

The Convention is rare among multilateral environmental agreements in the number of protocols that it has spawned. Even more unusual is the extent to which the Executive Body and its subsidiaries have, at their meetings, made no distinction between Parties and non-Parties. For practical purposes, non-Parties to a particular protocol are treated as if they were already Parties to it. They fill bureau seats and chair committees even though various matters that they thereby have to deal with inevitably relate to protocols by which they are not bound. They are called on to speak in debates on protocols that do not bind them according to when they seek the floor, not – as is normally the case for observers – after the Parties have spoken. They even participate in the adoption of Executive Body decisions pertaining to those protocols since consensus does not require them to be named or their vote counted. The position would, of course, be different if a vote were ever taken since the Convention and its protocols as well as the UNECE rules of procedure (as applied mutatis mutandis) make it clear that only the Parties to the instrument in question may vote.

The Convention's Implementation Committee considered this issue at its seventh meeting (May 2001) in relation to its own mode of operation. With a Committee composed of only nine members, each representing a Party rather than appointed in his or her personal capacity, it was seen that if members were excluded from all aspects of the Committee's work that related to protocols to which their countries were not Party, there could at times be few members involved in discussion and even no quorum. The Committee adopted a pragmatic approach and, in particular, concluded that if a country was a member of the Committee but not a Party to the protocol that was the subject of a submission or referral, it should be able to contribute fully to the process at stage (a) discussion of the factual background to the case, and stage (b) identification and analysis of the legal and other considerations

involved. It should, however, withdraw from the proceedings for stage (c) the Committee's preparation of its conclusions and recommendations on the case.

A similar situation could, of course, arise where a member of the Committee comes from a Party that is the subject of a submission or a referral. Indeed, it has already occurred in a number of the self-submissions made to the Committee (e.g. by Norway and Italy). In those cases, the Committee has adopted the approach described above for cases relating to protocols to which a Committee member's country is not a Party. The approach has worked well in practice, which is perhaps not surprising given that self-submissions are consensual in nature. The Committee may, however, need to review its practice in the event of one or more of its members belonging to a Party that is involved in the more confrontational atmosphere of proceedings launched by the secretariat in respect of a Party or by one Party in respect of another Party.

Scope for majority voting

As indicated above, to date no vote has ever been called within the Executive Body. Consensus has been, is now and for the foreseeable future is likely to remain, the most effective and the most acceptable basis for decision-making under the Convention and its protocols, despite its inevitable tendency to dilute and slow down action in tackling the major environmental problems with which the Convention is concerned. It is "efficient" because Parties are more likely to respect an Executive Body decision if they subscribe to its terms than if they are driven reluctantly into observance by means of a majority vote; and it is "acceptable" because within UNECE, and indeed at the international level in general, Parties to treaties continue to see consensus-based decision-making as an important symbol of the sovereign equality of States.

Public participation and the role of NGOs

Chapter 9

Christer Ågren and Les White

To a certain extent the public and industry have participated, either directly or indirectly, from the early days of the Convention on Long-range Transboundary Air Pollution. Public pressure, for example that generated by deep concern over forest dieback (Waldsterben) in the early 1980s, helped bring the Convention to adopt its first Protocol on Sulphur in 1985.

Public and industrial participation is usually organized through the involvement of non-governmental organizations (NGOs): environmental NGOs and industrial NGOs. Both participate in meetings under the Convention.

A fairly new tool that has helped develop public participation, and stakeholder involvement, is the Internet, which has both improved accessibility to information (transparency) and enhanced opportunities for wider consultations. Information about the Convention (including meeting documents) and data from Convention activities are available on the Convention's web site (www.unece.org/env/lrtap/) or through its links to the sites of the various programme centres.

Outline

While environmental NGOs were very actively engaged in the Convention's developments during the 1980s, such a high level of activity and involvement could not be sustained over time. This gradual fading of interest does not, however, apply to Christer Ågren, who is still engaged in monitoring and reporting the work of the Convention and who is the author of the first section of this chapter.

The interest and involvement of industry in the work of the Convention has grown over time. In the second part of the chapter Les White provides "An industry view" on developments such as integrated modelling and cost-effectiveness. This view is focused on Europe and the "traditional air pollutants", i.e. sulphur dioxide (SO_2), nitrogen oxides (NO_x) and volatile organic compounds (VOCs). However, a wide range of industrial NGOs have participated in the work under the Convention and there are no doubt other perspectives from other industries' NGOs, e.g. the chemical industry in relation to the Protocol on POPs and the Protocol on Heavy Metals and agriculture in relation to ammonia in the 1999 Gothenburg Protocol.

The role and views of environmental organizations

By Christer Ågren

Environmental demands are ever more frequently met with the excuses such as "we as a country cannot proceed alone", "it would impair our international competitiveness" or "it would be pointless, since anything we could do would have little effect on the general situation". The final escape is usually "the problem can only be solved by international agreement". The Convention on Long-range Transboundary Air Pollution came about precisely to overcome this reluctance. Under it, too, many countries have made great efforts to reach concrete proposals for internationally agreed measures. Although they fail to have global application, these measures nevertheless affect the greater part of the "international competition", since the Convention is supported by a total of 48 countries in Europe and North America, as well as by the European Community.

Today it goes without saying that countries have to cooperate in order to resolve transboundary environmental problems, but this was far from obvious for many countries only 30 years ago, when talks about an international treaty to control air pollution started. Some environmental groups became aware of the transboundary dimensions of the acid rain problem relatively early, and carried out international activities – e.g. postcard actions and demonstrations - already in the 1970s (see figure 9.1). In general, however, the international process of negotiation that took place during the second half of the 1970s, leading up to the signing of the Convention in 1979, attracted very little attention from environmental groups. The event that really opened the eyes of a wide range of environmental non-governmental organizations (ENGOs) to the Convention, was the 1982 Stockholm Conference on the Acidification of the Environment. This was organized by the Swedish Government in the hope that it would encourage enough ratifications to bring the Convention into force, and would stimulate national and international acid rain abatement action.

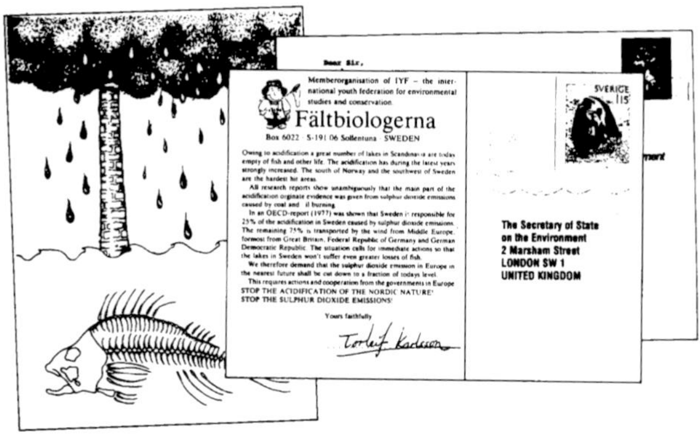
Dear Sir,

Memberorganisation of IYF – the international youth federation for environmental studies and conservation.

Fältbiologerna

Box 6022 · S-191 06 Sollentuna · SWEDEN

Owing to acidification a great number of lakes in Scandinavia are today empty of fish and other life. The acidification has during the latest years strongly increased. The south of Norway and the southwest of Sweden are the hardest hit areas.

All research reports show unambiguously that the main part of the acidification originate evidence was given from sulphur dioxide emissions caused by coal and oil burning.

In an OECD-report (1977) was shown that Sweden is responsible for 25% of the acidification in Sweden caused by sulphur dioxide emissions. The remaining 75% is transported by the wind from Middle Europe, formost from Great Britain, Federal Republic of Germany and German Democratic Republic. The situation calls for immediate actions so that the lakes in Sweden won't suffer even greater losses of fish.

We therefore demand that the sulphur dioxide emission in Europe in the nearest future shall be cut down to a fraction of todays level.

This requires actions and cooperation from the governments in Europe.

STOP THE ACIDIFICATION OF THE NORDIC NATURE!

STOP THE SULPHUR DIOXIDE EMISSIONS!

Yours faithfully

Torleif Karlsson

SVERIGE 115

The Secretary of State
on the Environment
2 Marsham Street
LONDON SW 1
UNITED KINGDOM

Figure 9.1. In 1979 thousands of postcards with demands to cut emissions of acidifying sulphur emissions were sent to the Governments of the United Kingdom, the Federal Republic of Germany, and the German Democratic Republic. The postcard action was carried out by youth environmental organizations in Sweden and the United Kingdom.

Watchdogs and lobbyists

Internationally coordinated air pollution activities by ENGOs started in summer 1981, and one of the first targets was to prepare inputs to the Stockholm Conference. As from that date, environmental organizations have kept a close eye on developments under the Convention, as well as on the various countries' national activities on matters concerning transboundary air pollution. From the Convention's entry into force in March 1983, ENGOs have been acting as observers at selected meetings under the Convention, especially those involving preparations for, or negotiations of, new protocols. They have also continuously monitored developments under the Convention, as well as connected side events, such as the ministerial meetings held in Ottawa in March 1984, where the so-called 30-per-cent club was formed, and in Munich (Germany) in June 1984, where that club grew from 10 to 16 countries.

In the 1980s, the period when transboundary air pollution and acid rain were at the top of the political agenda, the ENGO delegation attending the Convention's meetings usually consisted of some three to

six persons, representing international (e.g. World Wide Fund for Nature, Friends of the Earth and Greenpeace) as well as various national environmental groups. At negotiating meetings, the NGOs produced and distributed a daily newsletter (ECO Magazine), commenting on the negotiations, as well as providing facts and analyses (see box). The role of the ENGOs was, and still is, to simultaneously act as watchdog, lobbyist, media contact, information resource and link between the previously fairly closed negotiation process and the outside world.

The watchdog function includes keeping a close watch on each country's position and ensuring that national delegates provide a fair and correct representation of the country's official policy. By presenting facts and arguments, environmental groups try to influence national positions, and thus the outcome of negotiation – an activity known as lobbying. The progress, or lack of progress, in negotiation is of high general interest and public concern, and is therefore usually reported by the media. Since the media are not allowed into the meeting rooms, press briefings and personal contacts are used as the means for communicating developments via the media to the public.

Drastic emission cuts necessary

Excerpts from a joint press release by Friends of the Earth International and Greenpeace, published during a meeting of the Convention's Executive Body in Geneva, 11-14 November 1986: "Addressing the conference seven years to the day after the Convention was signed, [the environmental organizations] expressed disappointment at the lack of real progress achieved in the intervening years. Criticizing the poor level of ratification of the 30% Sulphur Protocol signed in Helsinki last year, [they] pointed out that the environmental movement was seeking more drastic reductions of 90% in sulphur emissions in Europe, with 80% reductions to be achieved by 1993. [The environmental organizations] are also seeking 75% reductions in nitrogen oxides emissions by 1995 from 1980 levels, and 75% reductions in the formation of ozone. These demands are based upon actual scientific knowledge of the ecological tolerances of the most sensitive habitats..."

Competing concerns and new arenas

In the early 1980s, transboundary air pollution in general, and its impact on forests and freshwaters in particular, became one of the top environmental priorities in large parts of Europe, as well as in North America. By the end of that decade, however, other pollution problems - primarily the depletion of the ozone layer and climate change - gained increasing attention. Faced with the reality of limited resources, many ENGOs increasingly chose to give less priority to regional air pollution, and thus also to the Convention, in order to be able to tackle these new environmental concerns. These moves were made in full awareness of the fact that the problems caused by regional air pollution were far from being solved.

There were of course other reasons contributing to the Convention being moved down the agenda, including the fact that it is always difficult to maintain media attention, and consequently also public interest and concern, on one topic for a long period of time. In the late 1980s, the European Community gradually became more active on air quality and on directives to reduce emissions, e.g. the Large Combustion Plant Directive. By the mid-1990s, several new initiatives had been brought up on the European Union (EU) agenda, including the Auto-oil Programme, a new air quality framework directive, the Integrated Pollution Prevention and Control (IPPC) Directive, and an acidification strategy, to mention only a few. As a result of the Maastricht and Amsterdam treaties, the European Parliament was given a stronger position in the EU decision-making process, often resulting in more progressive environmental legislation than previously. Consequently, since the early to mid-1990s, both national and international ENGOs in Europe have devoted increasing efforts and resources trying to influence and improve EU environmental legislation, including air quality legislation.

The fact that many international and national ENGOs which were heavily involved in the Convention's activities in the 1980s to a large extent moved their attention to other issues and other arenas during the 1990s, does not at all imply that they have lost interest in the Convention. The work under the Convention has continued to be closely monitored, primarily by the Swedish NGO Secretariat on Acid Rain, and developments have been, and still are, continuously reported to an informal network of national and international European ENGOs. Environmental groups, as well as others, are also being informed through articles in the Swedish NGO Secretariat's magazine "Acid News". Moreover, at events of higher political interest, such as the final stages of negotiation leading up to new protocols to the Convention, ENGOs usually mobilize themselves to put pressure on national decision makers.

Changing driving forces

As time has passed, the dominating motives behind air pollution abatement, the so-called driving forces, have changed. At the time of establishing the Convention, the main driving force was the problem of acidified freshwaters in Scandinavia and Canada, and the initial aim was to reduce the emissions and transboundary flows of sulphur pollution. Within a few years of adoption of the Convention, and even before it had entered into force, the problem had widened to include also the widespread and increasing damage to forest ecosystems. At about the same time, it also became clear that sulphur was not the only transboundary air pollutant causing acidification and forest damage; the Convention would also need to deal with nitrogen oxides, ammonia, volatile organic compounds and ground-level ozone.

While damage to ecosystems continued to be the main concern throughout the 1980s, the damaging impact of air pollutants on human health became an issue of growing concern in the 1990s. Only slowly was it realized that health damage due to air pollution was not restricted to local pollution in traffic-dense cities or heavily industrialized areas, but that much of the damage was caused also by transboundary pollution, and this was especially the case with ozone and fine particles. This fact was picked up by the Convention in the second half of the 1990s, and introduced into the negotiations leading up to the 1999 Gothenburg Protocol. Damage to human health is now the main political driving force for air pollution control in Europe and North America, as well as in other parts of the world where air pollution is on the political agenda.

Role of the Convention

In the 1980s the Convention was the leading international forum for developing and agreeing strategies and policies for air pollution abatement in Europe. It was also a main source of information on, for example, emissions, transboundary fluxes, depositions and air pollution effects, although, at that time, most of this information was not easily accessible to the public.

Over the past five to ten years, however, the EU has gradually grown in importance as the main forum for air pollution abatement policy in Europe, especially for the current 25 member States. It should, however, be remembered that the EU does not cover as many countries as the Convention, and that many EU activities (such as the acidification and ozone strategies, and the National Emissions Ceilings Directive) build to a large extent on work done under the Convention. The same is true for the ongoing EU Clean Air for Europe (CAFE) programme, which is being developed in close cooperation between the EU and the Convention.

As regards information on air pollution, the European Environment Agency (EEA) has become a source of increasing value. But the Convention still has a strong, and in some cases unique, position regarding some types of information, such as the EMEP atmospheric modelling and emission inventories and the Working Group on Effects mapping of critical loads and monitoring of environmental effects.

So even if the Convention is no longer the only European forum for international policy development, it still plays an important role as such, and it still provides a wide variety of useful products and services, which are frequently used outside the Convention, inter alia by the EU CAFE programme and nationally by most European countries. It also provides inspiration and input to activities outside of Europe, such as the global UNEP Convention on Persistent Organic Pollutants and regional cooperation in, for example, Asia.

The Convention's various activities gather a wide range of expertise for exchanging views and ideas and for developing new methods and concepts to be used in air pollution policy. Moreover, the fact that air pollution is increasingly recognized as a Northern hemispheric rather than a regional problem, also underlines the role of the Convention both as a link between the whole of Europe and North America and as forum for communication and cooperation with Asia.

Improve communications

With the exception of air pollution specialists, it is probably fair to conclude that today the Convention is not well known by national or local environmental NGOs, although it is probably safe to assume that most international ENGOs have a somewhat greater knowledge (see figure 9.2). It is also worth noting that even for those Convention-specific products that are used nationally, such as EMEP data or critical loads maps, there appears to be very limited knowledge as to their origins. The level of awareness about the Convention is generally much lower now than in the 1980s, and this is not confined to ENGOs, but applies equally to other groups, such as politicians, civil servants, industry groups, the media and the general public.

FIGURE 9.2. THE HIGH-PROFILE DAYS OF THE MID-1980S WHEN GREENPEACE MEMBERS IN AUSTRIA, BELGIUM, CZECHOSLOVAKIA, DENMARK, FRANCE, GERMANY, NETHERLANDS AND THE UNITED KINGDOM CLIMBED, DURING THE INTERNATIONAL ACID RAIN WEEK (APRIL 1984), POWER STATION AND OIL REFINERY CHIMNEY STACKS TO BRING PUBLIC AND GOVERNMENTAL ATTENTION TO THE PROBLEM OF ACID RAIN CAUSED BY SULPHUR DIOXIDE EMISSIONS

SOURCE: GREENPEACE

Air pollution, and especially its impact on human health, is still high on the agenda in Europe and North America, and of increasing concern in parts of Asia. Clearly much effort is still needed to bring emissions down to "acceptable" levels. As described above, the Convention has some unique features that put it in a position to play a significant role in the further development of international air pollution policies. But in order to do so effectively, the Convention must gain, or recapture, a higher, more visible profile in the eyes of national decision makers and other stakeholders (e.g. environmentalists and industry).

During the past few years, the Convention has discussed various ways of improving its information and communication systems, and some improvements have been made. But an effective communications strategy is needed, and it should not only focus on the Convention but must also aim at increasing the awareness and knowledge about air pollution problems and their solutions in general. Over the years environmental groups have contributed to these aims, and, provided that the level of involvement increases, they could certainly contribute even more in the future. Obviously, effective communication is costly, and since the Convention's secretariat does not have funds for such activities, the resources will have to be provided by the Convention's Parties.

Maintain core activities

Research and monitoring of the environment are of fundamental importance, not only for increasing our understanding of the world we live in but also for keeping a watch on known problems and revealing new ones. Research and monitoring of the environmental problems associated with air pollution have long been coordinated under the Convention. Through its subsidiary bodies the Convention has helped generate a lot of valuable data. It has also promoted the exchange of knowledge and experience, thus in turn influencing the decisions of various countries with regard to their measures for curbing emissions. So far, a few countries have voluntarily undertaken to fund the coordination of these activities. There seems to be general agreement on the injustice of letting a handful of countries bear the whole cost of an activity that is so fundamental to the effectiveness of the Convention, especially as it is to the advantage of all Parties. Consequently, it is becoming increasingly urgent to establish a stable financing mechanism, not only for the Convention's effects work, but also for its integrated assessment modelling. It is these activities that have enabled cost-effective international agreements for lowering emissions to be reached. The modern strategies employed by the Convention have brought forth smart solutions that have saved billions of dollars, on account both of their cost-effectiveness and the prevention of damage that air pollution would otherwise have caused. It is therefore deplorable that some countries are still blocking agreements that are vital for the progress of the Convention.

Speed up ratification

Quick ratification of protocols by countries is vital for several reasons. It is only after entry into force that their obligations become legally binding. Moreover, the methodology adopted for the Gothenburg Protocol of a stepwise approach to long-term environmental objectives implies reviewing the agreements, and revision cannot take place before the protocol has come into effect. Then there is the question of credibility. In recent years the ratification of agreements concerning the environment has tended to be increasingly drawn out. This has been the case not only with the Convention but also with the Kyoto Protocol and annex VI to the International Maritime Organization's International Convention for the Prevention of Pollution from Ships (MARPOL). It is a great paradox that nations should, after using great resources and much effort to reach compromise solutions, and agree and sign international agreements, either delay ratification or even ignore it. Should this trend continue, it would undoubtedly undermine public confidence in international agreements to save the environment. Indeed it has already started to do so because some agreements have become indefensibly diluted and several countries have neglected to fulfil their commitments. It is therefore imperative that those countries that have not already done so should ratify without further procrastination.

Ensure compliance

The Implementation Committee of the Convention plays an increasingly important role for scrutinizing the way various protocols are complied with. It has revealed that several countries have failed to fulfil their legally binding commitments, either to bring down emissions or to report on their national situation in this respect. Despite the sharp reprimands issued by the Executive Body of the Convention (on which all Parties to the Convention are represented) several countries have still not reduced their emissions as required by the protocols. And despite repeated reminders from the Convention's secretariat, some countries have not even taken the trouble to assemble and report the basic information needed by the Committee for carrying out its compliance work. Inadequate reporting is especially serious, because the information that is being asked for is essential not only for tracking compliance with agreed commitments, but also for providing material for the coming reviews and revisions of the protocols.

The usual way of "reminding" negligent countries is to send a polite letter. But since that evidently is insufficient, rather more drastic methods, such as "naming and shaming" the offenders, is an obviou next step. The failure of countries to comply is in any case a clear indication of the inadequacy of present ways of dealing with the problem. Consequently, the Convention has every reason to revise its methods. Both the carrot and the stick are needed – measures to encourage countries to participate actively in the procedures, as well as to get them to act more quickly, and possibly to punish offender

Revise the Gothenburg Protocol

The use of the critical loads approach, developed under the Convention in the late 1980s, has enhanced the cost-effectiveness of emission abatement. Combined with the new multi-effects and multi-pollutant concept, it has resulted in more countries being actively involved in the elaboration of emission abatement strategies. The 1999 Gothenburg Protocol certainly marked a step forward, in th it made clear that international agreements could be made to rest on scientific grounds and in accordance with the critical loads approach. Its environmental aims are clearly expressed, and all the Parties have had a hand in setting the targets. It has, moreover, been based on a thorough analysis of cost-effectiveness, spreading commitments to attain its aims at the lowest possible cost. On top of a this, an analysis of the economic benefits from implementing the Protocol was made, which showed that the overall gain would exceed the outlay many times over.

But the emission reductions that the Signatories undertook to achieve by 2010 are totally inadequate. In the case of some countries and some pollutants the national emission ceilings were so liberal as t allow even higher emissions than would result from existing legislation. The reason for these anomalies is that the ceilings of the Gothenburg Protocol were in effect set by the Signatories themselves, there having been no proper negotiation. In a great majority of cases the figures are an expression of what the countries believed their emissions would be in 2010 as a result of existing legislation. In other words, they did not propose any further cuts.

There will nevertheless be possibilities for improvement when the Protocol comes up for review and revision in 2005. This will provide an opportunity for establishing new and stricter emission ceilings. must be obvious that the sooner we can bring about a reduction in these emissions to levels that nature and people can tolerate without being harmed, the less will be the damage and the quicker the recovery.

The process itself is important

In the public debate, much focus is on the specific commitments laid down in the various protocols, and rightly so. But one significant aspect of the process of negotiation that is often overlooked is that it hastens the production of new data, both because the negotiations require it and because there is often a deadline for concluding the agreement. The fact that negotiations are taking place is also important for the formation of opinion, since it usually attracts the attention of the media. Consequently, the mere existence of the Convention and all the activities and data that it is generating

is of great value for promoting the environmental cause. No matter whether the protocols are "good enough" from an environmental point of view, the process is still going on and there is always pressure from public opinion both to get the existing protocols ratified and respected and to continue the work to better protect public health and the environment.

Future stakeholder involvement

There are many ways by which the Convention could be made more attractive for stakeholder involvement, for example by setting up a fund for reimbursing travel costs of environmental organizations and by announcing upcoming meetings more effectively. While these types of practical arrangement, as well as the status given to stakeholders, are of some importance, in the end it is the profile of the Convention in general, as well as the perceived usefulness of each meeting, that decides the level of stakeholder involvement. Environmental organizations are rational and will target their efforts and resources towards activities where they think their input will bring the best results. Provided that the necessary resources are available, stakeholders are generally keen to get involved even at the early stages of policy development. Since the Convention's activities can be expected to provide inputs to policy development, not only for the Convention itself but also for the EU and individual countries, there ought to be a natural interest among both national and international NGOs to become more involved in the Convention.

The resulting level of stakeholder involvement in the Convention is dependent primarily on the profile of the Convention, i.e. the perceived political influence at international and national levels, the priorities and resources of the organizations and the meeting procedures and arrangements that keep stakeholders involved and part of the process. Seen from the perspectives of national and international ENGOs in Europe, the Convention and its activities are, as noted above, generally not well known today. Partly as a result of this lack of awareness, the Convention is not regarded as being decisive - or even a major player - in the development of policies and legislation for air pollution abatement. Consequently, most environmental groups currently focus their efforts on influencing national or EU policy development.

Authorities and decision makers have slowly but surely come to realize that public acceptance is key to progress in adopting and implementing policy, including measures to cut air pollution. Public acceptance is highly dependent on awareness and understanding, which can be improved through information, transparency and involvement. Therefore, continued progress in the Convention's work regarding communication, research and monitoring, and stakeholder involvement is crucial. Public acceptance is also dependent on the credibility of the process itself and this is why the Convention must also make progress on ratification, compliance and revision. These tasks may be challenging, but they must be dealt with. While the Convention undoubtedly has contributed to reducing air pollutants emissions in Europe over the past 25 years, there is still much to be done in order to effectively protect human health and the environment. It is to be hoped that the Convention will take on this challenge, and continue to be a major player in the struggle for clean air.

Chapter 9

An industry view

By Les White

In making the "industry contribution" to this celebratory book, it is perhaps only natural to dwell on what has taken place in Europe over the 25 years of the Convention to combat the concerns about long-range transport of air pollutants. It is quite an impressive picture as one traces the journey from those simple first protocols to the complex multi-pollutant, multi-effects basis of the Gothenburg Protocol. It is also clear that the establishment of the Convention, and the many and varied programmes under it, have served to catalyse and drive the development of a number of important related EU directives such as the Large Combustion Plant Directive and, more recently, the National Emission Ceilings (NEC) Directive. In this brief "industry view" this journey is traced from its relatively simple beginnings to the present world of multi-effects integrated assessment modelling. In concluding, time is taken to think about where things might go from here.

From simple beginnings to effects-driven approaches

The first decade following the signing of the Convention saw the development of three important "beginning" protocols aimed at taking the first steps to control the emissions of sulphur dioxide (SO_2), nitrogen oxides (NO_x) and volatile organic compounds (VOCs). Unlike their later revisions, these early protocols were not based on a detailed assessment of the relationship between emissions from individual countries and their environmental impacts but simply required fixed cuts in emission for each Party. A 30% reduction for SO_2 and VOCs and a cap on NO_x emissions were all referenced t 1980 emission levels.

The establishment of EMEP in 1977, creating a Europe-wide air monitoring programme and later the development of a robust transboundary dispersion model, were key steps in paving the way for the development of a "polluter pays" approach to the allocation of burden sharing for the development o revised protocols during the 1990s.

The creation of the Coordination Center for Effects in 1991 to bring together, on a common basis, the extensive effects-related work of the Convention, was a further important step to provide a consistent effects database through the mapping of critical loads/levels for Europe.

Finally, the availability of robust integrated assessment models designed to examine control scenarios with a view to determining the relationship between the cost of emission controls and their environmental impact, opened the door to true polluter pays burden sharing, based on cost-effectiveness. In this regard, 1994 Protocol on Further Reduction of Sulphur Emissions, based on this approach, was a milestone in Europe. From an industry point of view this represented an important move towards ensuring environmental expenditure was targeted to deliver cost-effective responses to the problem of acidification. It also marked a significant shift away from early technology-driven approaches in Europe. This shift was to influence not just the future Convention process but also the design of legislation in the EU.

Technology versus environmental quality-driven legislation

Historically, two fundamental approaches have been used to underpin environmental legislation, the "technology-driven" approach and the "environmental quality-driven" approach.

Technology-driven: This approach is based on the notion of progressively reducing emissions of the pollutants of concern based on the application of available technology. The process involves an assessment of the capability of available technologies to derive an emission limit. Since here the only definition of "clean" is zero emissions, progressive updates of the legislation, with tougher emission limits, are made at regular intervals to reflect the developments in available technology. Concepts like the application of best available techniques (BAT), sometimes embracing the notion of "not entailing excessive costs" (BATNEEC), are derived from this approach.

Environmental quality-driven: In this alternative approach, the starting point is the establishment of environmental targets. For air-related legislation this could be air quality standards, based on human health concerns, or critical load/levels, based on ecological concerns. In the latter case, the vulnerability of ecosystems varies significantly, so the targets vary geographically.

The appropriate use of dispersion modelling allows the relationship between emission sources and their contribution to the environmental concern to be established. Using these relationships within an "integrated assessment modelling" framework then enables determination of the least-cost mix of measures required to deliver the target(s). Here, "clean" is the point at which the environmental targets are achieved. This approach accounts for the variation in the sensitivities of environmental receptors to air pollutants across a geographical area and indeed, in the case of ecological concerns, the variations in environmental targets themselves.

The quality-driven approach also allows for the appropriate accounting of Europe-wide standards when they are justified on the basis of preserving the internal market. For example, the setting of common vehicle emission standards throughout Europe, when considered with all other sources, may result in lower emission cuts from the other sources in countries where the internal market rather than environmental needs justified the vehicle standards.

Catalysed by the work under the 1994 Oslo Protocol, the environmental quality-driven approach has dominated the development of both the Convention and the EU air-related legislation over the past decade. Examples of this are the European Auto-oil programme, the 1999 Gothenburg Protocol and the parallel EU NEC Directive. It is what industry often refers to as "the rational approach" since it seeks to solve environmental problems in the most cost-effective way.

What has been achieved?

A focus on acidification: In this short "Industry view" it is not possible to cover all the elements targeted by the various protocols, so here the focus on acidification illustrates the important contribution that the Convention has made towards solving this problem. In addition, it gives an opportunity to show alternative ways of tracking progress in policy-relevant terms. The two familiar maps of figure 9.3 compare exceedances (expressed as an accumulation of exceedances over critical loads for all ecosystems within a grid square) as modelled for 1990 with that modelled for 2010 assuming the emission ceilings of the Gothenburg Protocol are achieved. Such maps are typical outputs from the integrated assessment modelling process used to develop that Protocol.

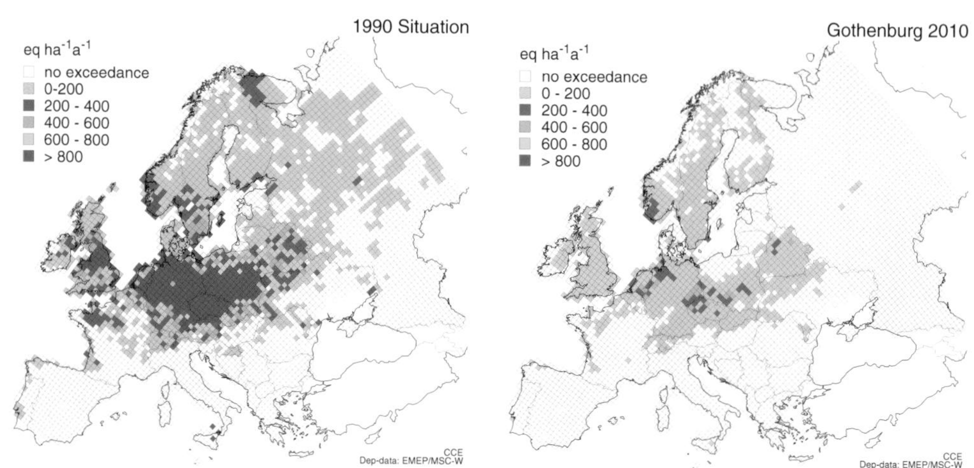

Figure 9.3. Average accumulated exceedance on 50x50 km2 grid cells of critical loads for acidification, for the emissions of 1990 (left) and for the emissions agreed in the Gothenburg Protocol (right). The figure is compiled using the CCE critical loads database of 2004 and depositions computed with the EMEP Lagrangian model

Source: RIVM-CCE

While the maps of figure 9.3 provide a helpful perspective on the extent of change of the exceedances of critical loads, unfortunately they do not provide information on the relationship between actual deposition and emissions required for protection, i.e. how far are we from achieving critical loads?

Alternative policy-relevant presentation of data: Figures 9.4 are derived from the same data used in the maps of figure 9.3 but "zoom in" on two EMEP grids: one grid is on the Nethrerlands/German border (EMEP grid 20-16) which was a "binding grid" in the integrated assessment modelling analysis of the RAINS model used to underpin the Gothenburg Protocol; the other grid is in the United Kingdom on the Wales/England border (EMEP grid 16-14). These figures show modelled sulphur and nitrogen deposition with time (from 1980) in relation to the critical loads target of achieving ninety-five per cent area protection from acidification.

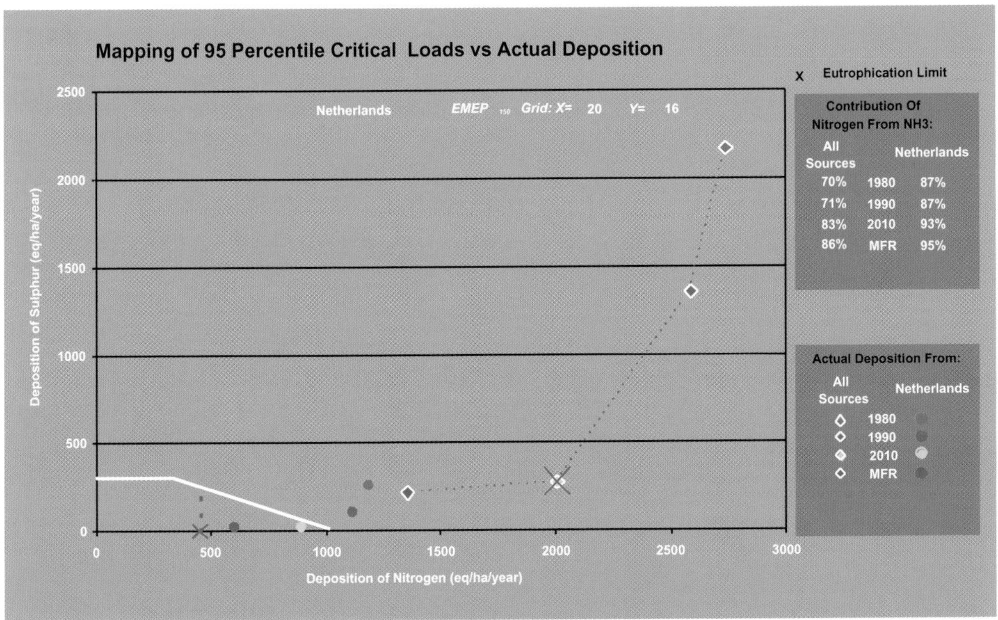

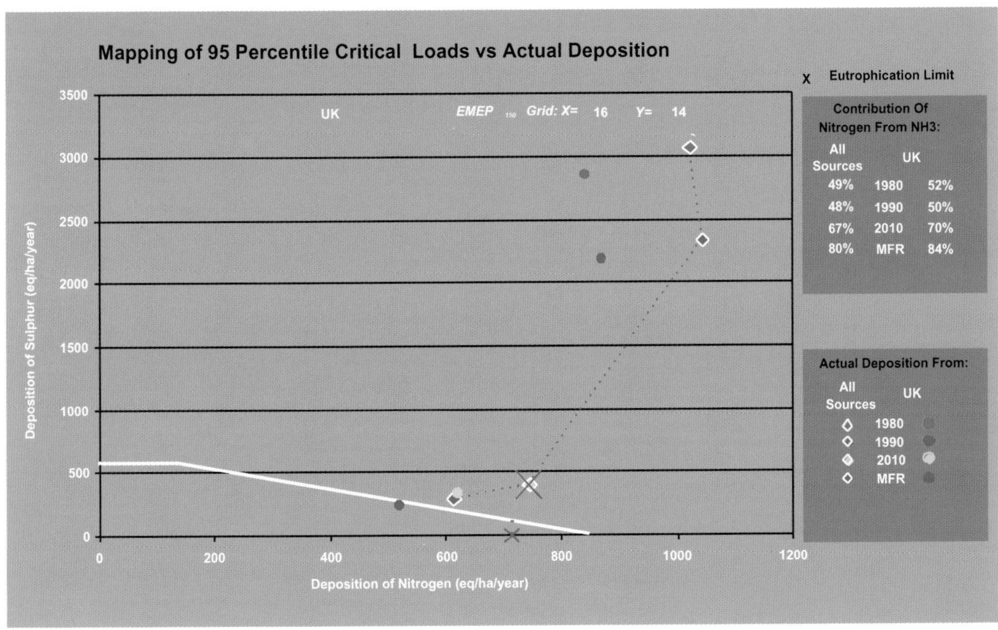

Figure 9.4. The relation between sulphur and nitrogen deposition and the target of 95% critical loads for two grid cells, one at the Netherlands/German border, the other at the Wales/England border in the United Kingdom. When the deposition is within the trapezoid (bold white outline) 95% the ecosystems (in terms of area) are protected against acid deposition

Source: CONCAWE based on RAINS modelling

The circular symbols in figure 9.4 indicate the acid (i.e. sulphur and nitrogen) deposition that the receiving country makes to itself. The acid deposition derived from the emissions from all countries is shown as diamonds and dotted lines. Comparing the plots of "all contributors" to "country to itself" for the Netherlands/German grid highlights the importance of the cooperative nature of the Convention for solving long-range air-pollution-related problems. According to the EMEP modelling results that underpin these plots, if the Netherlands was affected only by its own emissions, ecosystems in this area would be protected (at least to the 95 percentile level) by 2010. However, this is far from the case due to contributions from other countries. In contrast to this, the United Kingdom is by far the most significant contributor to its own problems and therefore benefits significantly from reductions in its own emissions. Such contrasting realities have surely featured in the negotiation phase of successive protocols.

These simple plots also demonstrate the enormous reductions in acid deposition that have been or will be achieved from already agreed European policies since 1980. They also show clearly the effect of the early policy emphasis on sulphur reductions. Significant nitrogen reductions are visible but only post-1990 (since it was only in 1993 that catalysts on all new cars in the EU became mandatory).

Figures 9.4 also serve to highlight the likely future need to focus on nitrogen rather than sulphur for policies to bring deposition levels below critical loads, e.g. in a revision to the Gothenburg Protocol. This is perhaps most acute in the Netherlands/German grid where a substantial reduction in nitrogen deposition is required to arrive at no-effect levels. Finally, again for this grid, the need for substantial reductions in agricultural sources is seen from the contribution of ammonia emissions to the overall nitrogen deposition, i.e. more than 80% in 2010. This alone will be a major policy challenge for the future.

Uncertainties in policy-relevant terms: As the approach to developing protocols has become more complex (e.g. multi-pollutant, multi-effect) there is increasing reliance on integrated assessment models to enable the interactions to be examined and expressed in policy-relevant terms. As such, the models provide an important bridge between "complex science" and "practical policy". This places a significant social responsibility on the scientific community to ensure that the effects of uncertainties are not invisible to the policy process but rather expressed in policy-relevant terms.

As policy measures move industry to the steeper part of the curve of "environmental improvement" versus cost, uncertainties become more important in avoiding "regret policy". One such uncertainty is the structural changes that have a potentially significant influence on national or sectoral burden sharing. This problem is minimized through the use of multiple time horizons in the development of policy.

Where from here?

One of the great future challenges for the Convention will be to find an appropriate role in the light of an expanding EU. The significant overlap between the European Commission's work on the NEC Directive and the Gothenburg Protocol serves as a forerunner of this challenge. The early work on the Commission's CAFE programme already signals the potential for a similar overlap in the planned revision to the Gothenburg Protocol. Having said this, the CAFE programme has, to date, relied

almost entirely on the databases and tools created through the various programmes and initiatives under the Convention. Solid scientific underpinning is the key to the development of sound policy. In this regard, in the ever-growing complexity of addressing concerns over long-range transboundary air pollution (fine particulates being the latest addition), the Convention has led the way in the past 25 years. Its mature scientific infrastructure places it in a strong position to do so in the future.

Johan Sliggers

To conclude this book this chapter focuses on the future. What lies ahead of the Convention on Long-range Transboundary Air Pollution and its protocols in a changing UNECE region? Can the Convention deliver what is needed in the coming decades? These are key questions for a convention that has proved successful and productive over the past 25 years.

The success and productivity of the Convention may be found in the way that it works:

- Science and technology: there are networks for monitoring, for gathering emissions data, for modelling and for compiling information on abatement technology;
- Science-policy interaction: scientists and policy makers work together effectively towards the goal of reducing air pollution, gathering the information required and developing the tools needed for policy-making;
- Innovation: the interaction of scientists and policy makers leads to innovative solutions for environmental problems. In addition, the Convention finds answers that recognize differences in national policies; and
- Of the countries and for the countries: countries develop the Convention and are responsible for it. There is little bureaucracy. The bulk of the work is either undertaken by lead countries or by programme centres, whose work-plans are approved by the countries, assisted by a small UNECE secretariat.

These characteristics and the flexibility of the people who do the Convention's work will continue to be needed to face the challenges ahead. In this way the Convention will still be an effective mechanism to combat international air pollution in the future.

Outline

This chapter will first look back to the 1999 Gothenburg Protocol because it marks a turning point in the work under the Convention. The chapter then will deal with the interrelation of the Convention with the work within the European Union (EU) and especially pay attention to the recently enlarged EU. In addition, the chapter will deal with:
Developments: topics that are being addressed at the moment;
Further needs: subjects that need to be addressed; and
Challenges: issues that need to be resolved.
Finally, the chapter concludes on the future of the Convention: a bright sky.

Gothenburg a turning point

In many ways the Gothenburg Protocol can be regarded as a turning point in the history of the Convention. The first protocols to the Convention (1985 Sulphur Protocol, 1988 Protocol on Nitrogen Oxides and the 1991 Protocol on Volatile Organic Compounds (VOCs)) addressed one substance at a time, are technically oriented (best available technology (BAT), emission limit values) and prescribed the same flat-rate emission reductions for all Parties, irrespective of cost-effectiveness. The Protocol on Heavy Metals and the Protocol on Persistent Organic Pollutants (POPs) of 1998 can also be regarded as first-phase protocols. The 1994 Oslo Protocol (the second Sulphur Protocol) was the first effects-based protocol. Integrated assessment modelling came into play calculating cost-optimized emission ceilings in order to meet certain intermediate goals towards attainment of critical loads for acidification.

The successful experience with integrated assessment modelling led to the decision to use it again for the review of the Protocol on Nitrogen Oxides (NOx), which gradually grew into a combined review of the Protocol on VOCs and the second Sulphur Protocol. The resulting masterpiece, the Gothenburg Protocol, was directed to abate acidification, eutrophication and ground-level ozone (vegetation and human health) and addressed four substances (SO_2 , NOx, ammonia (NH_3) and VOCs). Targets were set for all four environmental problems and cost-effective emission ceilings were calculated for each pollutant. Subsequently, these calculated ceilings were negotiated.

Reorganization

Even before the Gothenburg Protocol was finalized and adopted in December 1999 the Convention started thinking of life after the Protocol. The Protocol on Heavy Metals, the Protocol on POPs and the Gothenburg Protocols addressed practically all the transboundary air pollutants, apart from particulate matter, and it would be some years before these protocols entered into force and met their targets. So no new protocols were foreseen at that time for the forthcoming years. It was decided therefore that emphasis should go towards consolidation of what was achieved, and implementation and review of the existing protocols. Compliance with obligations by the Parties to protocols was seen as a major challenge. This strategy led to a reorganization of the Convention's working groups, task forces, expert groups as well as some of the scientific centres. The resulting structure continues to develop (see figure 10.1) to reflect and address the priorities ahead.

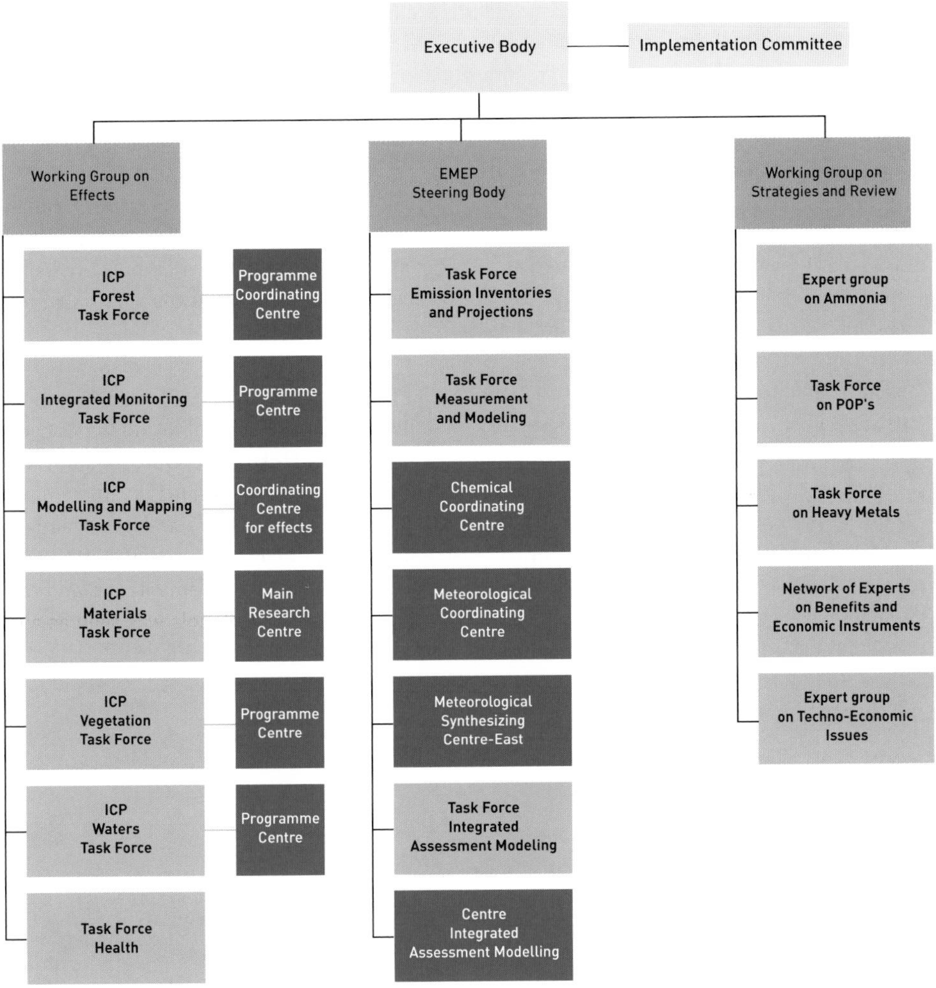

- Executive Body — Implementation Committee
  - Working Group on Effects
    - ICP Forest Task Force — Programme Coordinating Centre
    - ICP Integrated Monitoring Task Force — Programme Centre
    - ICP Modelling and Mapping Task Force — Coordinating Centre for effects
    - ICP Materials Task Force — Main Research Centre
    - ICP Vegetation Task Force — Programme Centre
    - ICP Waters Task Force — Programme Centre
    - Task Force Health
  - EMEP Steering Body
    - Task Force Emission Inventories and Projections
    - Task Force Measurement and Modeling
    - Chemical Coordinating Centre
    - Meteorological Coordinating Centre
    - Meteorological Synthesizing Centre-East
    - Task Force Integrated Assessment Modeling
    - Centre Integrated Assessment Modelling
  - Working Group on Strategies and Review
    - Expert group on Ammonia
    - Task Force on POP's
    - Task Force on Heavy Metals
    - Network of Experts on Benefits and Economic Instruments
    - Expert group on Techno-Economic Issues

Figure 10.1. The current organizational set-up of the Convention on Long-range Transboundary Air Pollution

Strategy

After the adoption and signing of the Gothenburg Protocol, a workshop, held in April 2000 in Saltsjöbaden, Sweden, formulated the future needs for regional air pollution strategies.

It concluded that the most important elements for future strategies were:

- Health would become more important, especially as a consequence of the growing concerns about exposure to particulate matter;
- Given the rising interest in health-related exposure to pollutants, urban air quality problems would need to be part of a regional approach to air pollution control;
- Non-technical measures as well as measures to combat climate change had to be addressed and should lead to more cost-optimal solutions;

- Policy indicators that were appealing to both the public and politicians should be developed to explain the benefits of air pollution abatement with regard to human health and nature; and
- Cost-benefit analysis would be more important to quantify both the damage from air pollution and also the benefits of pollution abatement in physical as well as in monetary terms.

To address these elements a large work programme was set up to prepare for the review of the Gothenburg Protocol following its entry into force.

Gothenburg workshop

Currently, it is expected that the Gothenburg Protocol will enter into force at the beginning of 2005. Therefore, a follow-up to the Saltsjöbaden workshop is organized for October 2004 in Gothenburg, Sweden. This workshop on "Review and Assessment of European Air Pollution Policies" aims at discussing possible objectives and targets for human health and environmental effects for the medium term, 2010-2020, as well as the long term. The workshop will consider the development of the Convention's strategy for the review of the Gothenburg Protocol as well as the European Commission's Clean Air for Europe (CAFE) programme for the preparation of its thematic strategy. The strategy to be proposed by the European Commission in July 2005 will include, inter alia, a review of the EU National Emission Ceilings (NEC) Directive and air quality directives. The advances in science, especially with respect to health and particles, new dispersion models from EMEP, changing energy pathways and the Kyoto Protocol as well as dynamic modelling will be discussed. The workshop will evaluate how these might be used to develop new strategies. The workshop provides an example of the continuing close interaction between science and policy. It will seek to coordinate further the future strategies for the two most important air pollution abatement frameworks in Europe: the Convention and EU legislation.

The Convention and the European Union

Up to ten years ago international air pollution policy in Europe was relatively simple. The Convention dealt with strategies to reduce air pollution that affected the environment UNECE-wide, especially the effects of acidification. This resulted in protocols for which certain reduction percentages were agreed together with emission limit values for mobile and stationary sources, fuel standards and BAT. The EU worked on air quality standards and issued directives on emission reductions for various mobile sources (cars, heavy-duty vehicles, etc.) and stationary sources (large combustion plant, waste incineration, etc.). The European Community had become a Party to the Convention and to a number of its protocols. The Convention's emission reduction obligations and the EU air quality standards were not linked to ensure that implementing obligations for mobile and stationary sources would automatically achieve the necessary emission reductions and the air quality standards.

The second Sulphur Protocol and the EU15

In the mid-1990s two things happened that changed things dramatically. The first was the finalization of the second Sulphur Protocol, the 1994 Oslo Protocol, and the second was the entry into the European Community of Sweden, Finland and Austria.

The Oslo Protocol was the first effects-based protocol; it was negotiated on the basis of the critical loads approach (see chapter 5). Integrated assessment, using computer models, linked environmental effects, in terms of exceedances of critical loads, to national emissions and calculated the pollutant controls needed to decrease exceedances. This approach made it possible to achieve agreed benefits at minimal overall cost by setting country-specific ceilings for sulphur emissions. The approach was attractive, but more complex.

In another way, complexity was further increased by the EU enlargement from 12 to 15 members. Attracted by the effect-based approach, which was reinforced through pressure from the three new members, the European Commission developed an acidification strategy largely underpinned by the Convention's work on the Oslo Protocol. At the same time, the European Commission was charged with drawing up an ozone abatement strategy and proposing environmental objectives for ozone. The Convention had also put the ozone problem on its agenda, giving health protection a much greater prominence in its policy-making process.

The Convention's Task Force on Integrated Assessment Modelling and the European Commission's ozone working group both used the same modelling tools, considered the available data and scrutinized model results. There was some consistency in their approaches as many people were involved in both groups, while the programmes of the Convention's Working Group on Effects provided both groups with the necessary information on ozone effects on vegetation and ecosystems and advice on appropriate indicators. The choice of a suitable ozone indicator for health impacts was provided through joint activities between the Convention and the World Health Organization (WHO) while the ozone working group also discussed the issue.

Although there were differences in the ambition levels of the emission ceilings set, for some EU States they were slightly higher in the Gothenburg Protocol than in the NEC Directive, both instruments were based on the same technical and scientific information. They made use of the Convention's scientific networks and the European Commission's project-oriented funding. So not only did the complexity with respect to science and policy tools increase, the interaction between the two policy frameworks also became more complex.

Complementing and cooperating

The air pollution policies of the Convention and of the EU are moving ever closer. Furthermore, the EU - recently enlarged to 25 countries - encompasses a large part of Europe. Yet, one should not fall into the obvious trap that only one regime could or should survive. Both now work closely together. They are heavily dependent upon each other and complement each other's strong and weak points. Of course, there are obvious differences between the two such as the geographical size of the regions that they cover, the institutions themselves and their compliance regimes. But both address transboundary air pollution in Europe and they work together to achieve common goals. They use one another's work but address different work items to avoid duplication and waste of resources. In considering the scientific and technical work, there is a clear difference between the working processes of the Convention and those of the EU.

The Convention with its well-developed structure and networks delivers work through:

- EMEP: estimating emission inventories and projections and maintaining the emissions database, monitoring pollutant deposition and concentrations, modelling transport of air pollution and integrated assessment modelling;
- The Working Group on Effects and its international cooperative programmes (ICPs): monitoring of effects, developing dose-response relationships, estimating and mapping critical loads and their exceedances, modelling of effects with time (dynamic modelling);
- The development of policy tools: the critical loads approach and integrated assessment modelling.

The EU activities have been more project-based, have tended to consider each pollutant separately, have been driven by provisions in existing air quality legislation and underpinned financially by a budget allocated to specific studies. To overcome fragmentation of the policy-making process and to reap the benefits from the links between different environmental problems, the Commission launched its CAFE programme. This aims at a more integrated approach that covers several effects and several pollutants. Examples of projects under CAFE are:

- The WHO review of its air quality guidelines: this will be used to evaluate the air quality standards in the EU daughter directives;
- The City Delta project: this is attempting to link local air pollution levels and their effects with regional air pollution policy; and
- A cost-benefit analysis: this will calculate benefits, in monetary terms, by comparing the costs of abatement measures with the resulting benefits.

Given the adoption of the multi-effects, multi-pollutants approach by both the Convention and CAFE, there should be even more common ground for work in the future. The practices of the past are expected to continue functioning in the future. The Convention will use the outputs from EU projects and EU will use the network results and tools of the Convention.

Technology and the enlarged EU

As far as air pollution abatement policies are concerned, in general the Convention and EU have complementary activities and obligations. Since the 1990s the EU has taken the lead in developing specific technical emission reduction measures; the Convention has often included these in its protocols thus promoting further harmonization across the UNECE region. The two organizations have "played leapfrog" in strengthening technological obligations and the Convention has increased the area over which such obligations take effect. Although since 1 May 2004 the EU has encompassed 25 countries, it should not be forgotten that to the East there are a further 20 Parties to the Convention. And it is not only to the East that the Convention has additional value. It also stretches West across the North Atlantic to play an important role in harmonizing technology through that subregion also.

Developments

In the Convention's scientific networks and groups many topics are currently being addressed. The developments of five of the most important are discussed below.

Health

The Convention places more emphasis on human health and will continue to do so. Evidence is growing that current levels of (ground-level) ozone and particulate matter cause significant health problems; a quarter of a million people die prematurely in Europe as a result. Particle emissions (primary particles) and the formation of particles in the air (secondary particles or aerosols) are large-scale problems like acidification and photochemical pollution. So, it is logical that the Convention should address these in its future review of the Gothenburg Protocol. Already the RAINS model is being prepared to calculate scenarios for particulate matter. It is incorporating data on activities that emit particles, the levels of pollutants that are precursors of secondary aerosols, the transport of these pollutants, the possibilities for abatement measures and the associated costs.

More emphasis on health does not mean that the Convention will neglect the environment. Acidification is not yet solved even though exceedances of critical loads are decreasing as a result of abatement measures and they will continue to do so. Eutrophication due to deposition of nitrogen compounds is a great threat to biodiversity and will be so for decades to come. "Background" ozone levels, the levels that are due to emissions across the Northern hemisphere and measured throughout the year between high ozone episodes, are rising slightly year by year; these give cause for concern as the concentrations are approaching levels known to damage plants. Nature is not neglected but, as a consequence of the perceived decreased pressure of pollution on the environment, pressure from society to protect nature has also weakened. The reverse is true for human health issues; the increased attention on them reflects this.

Agriculture and products

Acidification was the original focus for the Convention and expertise was concentrated on emissions from fuel combustion. When eutrophication emerged as an environmental problem, ammonia came into the picture and agricultural knowledge was added to the expertise of the Convention. Although they had already featured in the Protocol on VOCs, products from industry and agriculture were important in the development of the Protocol on Heavy Metals and the Protocol on POPs. World Trade Organization rules did not prevent these Protocols including measures on substances and products. There are limitations to adding substances and products to the Protocols which are defined by procedures described in the Protocols themselves as well as in associated decisions of the Executive Body, but the issue will receive renewed attention now that the Protocols have entered into force (in 2003) and their reviews have started.

Changing the scales

When the Convention focused on acidification it considered transboundary air pollution though the EMEP European model, which had a modelling grid size of 150 km x 150 km. Even before the Gothenburg Protocol was negotiated critical loads data were available at much higher resolution, so it was felt that modelling deposition at higher resolution would give a better indication of critical loads exceedances. EMEP has now developed a deposition model using grids of 50 km x 50 km and with an increased number of air layers.

Downscaling further to urban background or even street level, which would be needed to include human exposure to air quality levels into integrated assessment modelling, is something that would overstretch the EMEP model. The question also arises whether the Convention, which has always worked on transboundary air pollution, should address "typical" local problems. However, a significa part of the air pollution levels even in cities (the so-called urban background, which includes secondary pollutants such as ozone and secondary particles such as ammonium nitrate and sulphate has a transboundary origin. Therefore, the Convention has a responsibility to address at least part of the local air quality problem.

To extend the Convention's effects-based approach to particulate matter, it is essential to deal with th scale at which people are most affected, that is in urban areas. The European Commission's Auto-oil programme, which used a number of pilot cities, and the more recent City Delta project, may be able to indicate to what extent it is cost-effective to implement reduction measures at a city scale. This would need to be related to or supplemented by Europe-wide action to reduce the exposure of populations to particulate matter.

There is recent evidence that existing EU limit values, for example for particulate matter, are particularly difficult to meet in urban areas and this has fuelled discussions within the CAFE programme. Might there be a way around the difficulties of attaining a uniform air quality standard i urban hot spots without preventing improvements elsewhere? Again, elements developed by the Convention, like the gap-closure approach, could help the EU to supplement its traditional concept o simple limit values so that maximum health benefits could be achieved in a cost-effective way.

Moving away from the European scale, the Convention increasingly focuses attention on the Atlantic and on the global movement of pollution. "Background" (global) ozone levels are rising and mercur and POPs are being dispersed across the Northern hemisphere. Hemispheric models are being developed by the EMEP Meteorological Synthesizing Centre-East (see figure 10.2). Further expansion of modelling to the global scale will be necessary to reap benefits from integrating the problems of ai pollution with those of climate change.

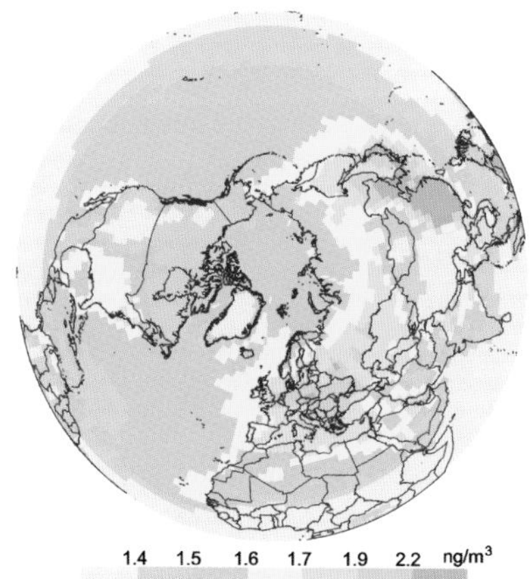

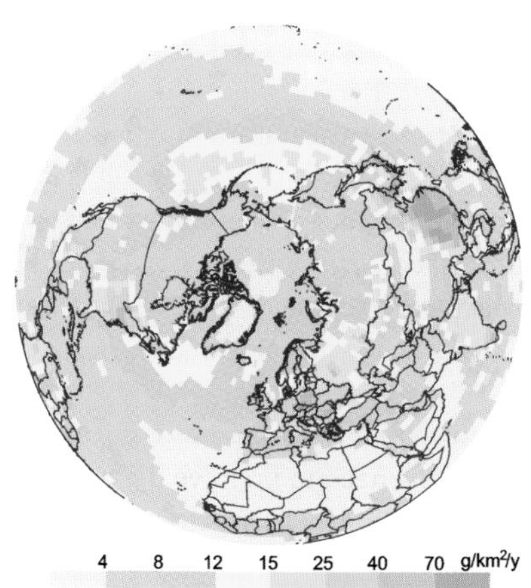

Figure 10.2. Mean annual concentration of total gaseous mercury in surface air (left) and total annual deposition flux o mercury (right) in the Northern hemisphere (1996)
Source: MSC-East

Cost-benefit analysis

Damage estimates related to air pollution are often compared with abatement costs. A reduction in air pollution results in less damage, a benefit that can be compared with the costs of the reduction. Besides the cost-benefit analysis assessing the environmental benefits, monetary benefit calculations were made for the implementation of the Gothenburg Protocol. This was the first time that monetary cost-benefit analyses played a role in the negotiation of an international environmental agreement. The results showed that almost all countries benefited from abating air pollution as required by the Gothenburg Protocol; benefits were two to five times the calculated abatement costs. However, not all damage can be expressed in terms of money and real costs are usually lower than those predicted by the integrated assessment models, so the benefits are generally even greater than estimates suggest.

Environmental cost-benefit analyses expressed in purely monetary terms are a special type of cost-benefit analysis. Some may argue that human life or biodiversity does not have a price. Other critics point out that those bearing the costs do not receive the benefits. Despite these criticisms monetary cost-benefit analyses are likely to become more and more important. Currently the methodology developed under the Convention is being further elaborated under the CAFE programme.

Dynamic modelling

Critical loads for acidification and eutrophication used for the Gothenburg Protocol were based on "steady state" models. These calculate the critical (deposition) load which is sustainable in the long term, i.e. one that does not lead to harmful imbalances in soil and water chemistry. Deposition exceeding critical loads will ultimately affect the health of forests, vegetation and surface waters. At the time of the adoption of the Gothenburg Protocol it was recognized that there was a need to assess the long-term effects of deposition changes in order to understand the sustainability of deposition loads. Therefore, increasing attention has been given to assessing delays in recovery, both in regions where critical loads are no longer exceeded and in regions where there is still excess deposition. For this, dynamic models have been developed under the Working Group on Effects for use with integrated assessment models.

Further needs

The developments above are mostly scientific or technical and they demonstrate the way that the Convention can respond to such issues. Here the developments considered are those that are necessary because of changing circumstances or the need to raise the profile of activities under the Convention.

Quality of emissions data

There is a need to improve the overall quality of emission inventories and emission projections. In 2002, the Convention's emission inventory guidelines were harmonized with those of the United Nations Framework Convention on Climate Change. Despite the emissions guidelines and the emission inventory guidebook that assist countries in calculating their emissions and projections, the emission data reported by countries are not always comparable. The possibilities for data checks are limited and data recalculations by countries themselves sometimes show great differences with earlier data. Better quality emissions data and an insight into how data are calculated are needed, especially now that obligations are becoming more stringent. Furthermore, to achieve a stronger compliance regime an important step is to increase the quality of the reported data. Already work is under way to develop quality assurance programmes under the Convention. A software tool devised by the EMEP Meteorological Synthesizing Centre-West checks the completeness of data submitted by each countr Countries are informed about missing data and are invited to correct omissions.

This is just the first step to better quality assurance and quality control (QA/QC) of emission data. The Task Force on Emission Inventories and Projections proposed an inventory improvement programme in 2003. It set about drawing up procedures for reviewing inventories and is developing standardized format for informative inventory reporting. Such inventory reports should indicate the methodologies used and include any assumptions, uncertainties, recalculations and QA/QC applied. In 2004 a more extended review is being made, based on the results of the voluntary review held in 2003. This should result in the reporting of better emission data.

In the future, as obligations in protocols become more demanding, it may be considered necessary t validate emission data through verification by independent auditors. Such a procedure already exists, for example, under the United Nations Framework Convention on Climate Change.

Setting indicators for human health and biodiversity

Integrating air pollution policies has many advantages not least the cost savings. Air pollution policy measures are expensive and it is important for industry, the general public and politicians to understand that they are getting value for money. Therefore, the understanding of the results of integrated assessment modelling should not be restricted to a few specialists. To appreciate the benefits, indicators should be used to demonstrate the results. Various indicators may help relate emissions to effects on human health and the environment.

For health, work is showing how illnesses (morbidity) and premature death (mortality) due to air pollution can be expressed as "disability-adjusted life years" or, more simply, the loss of healthy life years. However, this concept is not widely accepted, so we continue to use the more traditional health indicators, e.g. the number of people exposed to high concentrations, the numbers of hospital admissions, the number of premature deaths.

For natural ecosystems, critical loads are generally related to the physical-chemical state in soils and surface waters. When chemical changes occur as a result of critical loads being exceeded, there will b effects on the flora and fauna, e.g. changes in biodiversity. For the Netherlands, calculations have linked the abundance of plant species (a nature quality index) with the causes of biodiversity loss (se figure 10.3). In past decades 45% of the nature quality index was lost. About 55% of this was due mainly to air pollution, 15% to a lowering of groundwater levels and 10% to the reduction and fragmentation of natural areas. Since the last two causes are considered important in the Netherland the contribution of air pollution in other countries will probably be higher.

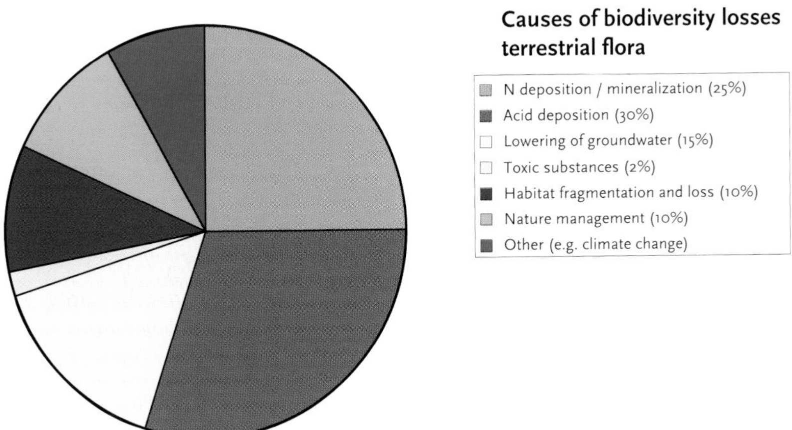

Figure 10.3. Relative causes of total biodiversity loss for terrestrial flora in the Netherlands during the past decades, expressed as the average abundance of plant species relative to unpolluted natural ecosystems

Source: RIVM

Such relationships between acid and nitrogen deposition and biodiversity need to be established. The first step might be to use critical loads for biodiversity and calculate accepted pressure-based indicators. For example, estimate the percentage areas of (specific) natural ecosystems where deposition exceeds the level for sustainable biodiversity, and calculate the level of that excess (figure 10.4 (a) and (b)). The second step would express the effects of air pollution in terms of suitable effects indicators, for example showing changes in ecosystem properties such as species abundance (figure 10.4 (c)) or extinction rates. The use of such biodiversity indicators may link air pollution regulation and international biodiversity goals such as those of the EU Habitats Directive and the 1992 Convention on Biological Diversity. Until such a concept is fully developed and accepted, indicators such as percentage areas of ecosystems where deposition exceeds the levels for sustainable biodiversity, together with estimates of the exceedance, should prove appealing.

Communications

At present, in EU countries especially, interest in the Convention seems to have waned. EU activities and climate change attract a great deal of attention from the media, the public and politicians. The Convention lacks an active communication strategy to increase its profile and to address this it held a workshop on communications in 2003. A journalist from Reuters summed up the general feeling when he wondered how is was possible that a convention as successful as the Convention on Long-range Transboundary Air Pollution was receiving so little media attention.

One reason for the lack of an effective communication strategy lies in how the Convention operates: Parties are responsible for the work under the Convention. They are also responsible if work is not done. There is no institution behind the Convention and the small UNECE secretariat in Geneva simply supports the work of the Parties in the various Convention bodies.

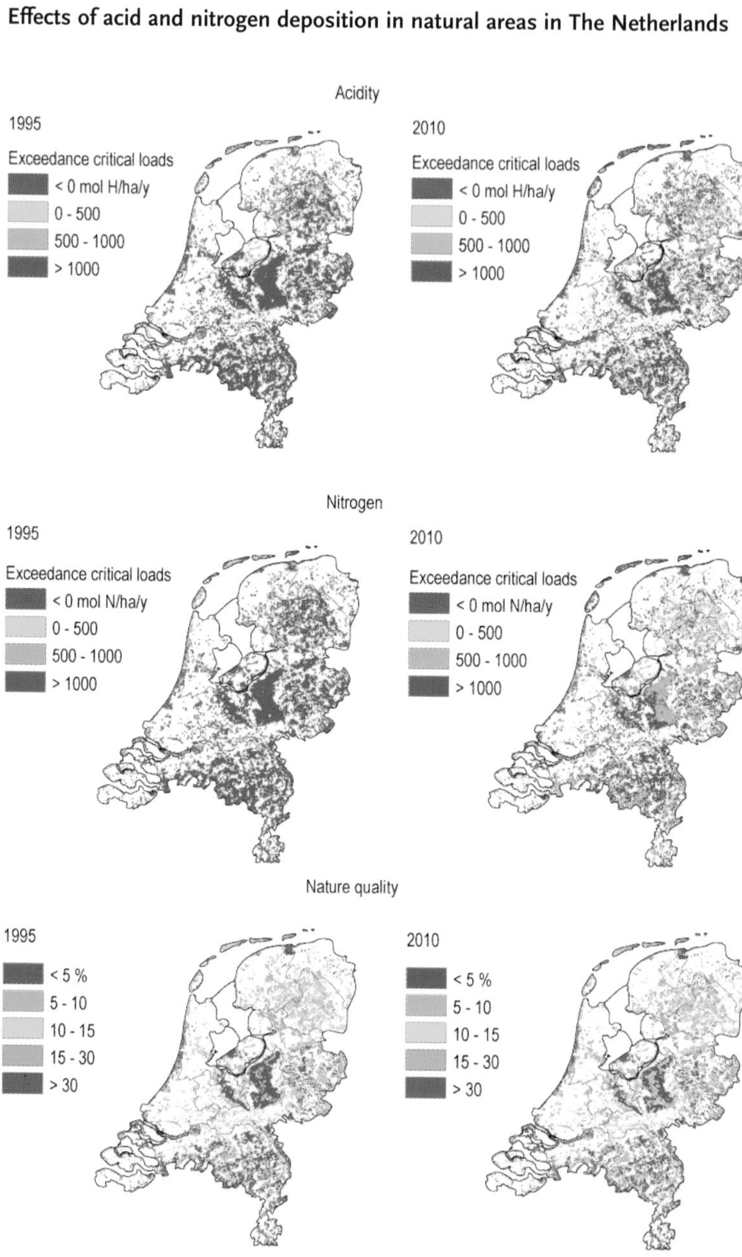

Effects of acid and nitrogen deposition in natural areas in The Netherlands

Acidity

1995

Exceedance critical loads
< 0 mol H/ha/y
0 - 500
500 - 1000
> 1000

2010

Exceedance critical loads
< 0 mol H/ha/y
0 - 500
500 - 1000
> 1000

Nitrogen

1995

Exceedance critical loads
< 0 mol N/ha/y
0 - 500
500 - 1000
> 1000

2010

Exceedance critical loads
< 0 mol N/ha/y
0 - 500
500 - 1000
> 1000

Nature quality

1995

< 5 %
5 - 10
10 - 15
15 - 30
> 30

2010

< 5 %
5 - 10
10 - 15
15 - 30
> 30

Figure 10.4. Accumulated exceedances of critical loads for biodiversity in the Netherlands for (a) acid deposition and (b) nitrogen deposition, together with (c) the resulting combined effect on biodiversity presented as the average plant species abundance relative to unpolluted natural ecosystems

Source: RIVM

At the 2003 workshop many valid reasons were put forward for implementing a long-term communication strategy for the Convention. Unfortunately, as yet, no country has taken the lead for developing and implementing a strategy. As a result, it is only the Convention secretariat and some voluntary contributions from individuals and Parties that are maintaining communications, for example, through the Convention's web site, on the basis of existing resources. Future communications would benefit much, not only from a Party or Parties taking more leadership, but also from improved contributions from national experts.

The 25th anniversary of the Convention provides a significant occasion for communicating its effectiveness and benefits. Several publications will document the achievements of the Convention as well as highlight the continuing need for measures to abate air pollution.

Challenges

The Convention is working on many topics and Parties have a clear idea of how to address several of them. However, some issues are much more difficult, complex or even controversial. These are the challenges for the future.

Particulate matter

If particulate matter is to be included in the review and possible revision of the Gothenburg Protocol it will be a major challenge. Many aspects of linking emissions of particulates to effects are poorly understood or quantified:

- Emission inventories have difficulty including natural emissions;
- Atmospheric transport models have difficulties matching the concentrations that are being monitored. Contributions from natural emissions (e.g. sea salt) and resuspended dust are not fully understood;
- Health standards for particulates are still under development. Although it is recognized that particulate matter causes many health problems, the links between health effects and those particles responsible are unclear;
- Monitoring of small particles (PM2.5, particulates less than 2.5 micrometre in diameter) is difficult and experience of such monitoring is limited.

There will need to be a good deal of work and innovation to include particulate matter in future air pollution strategies. One approach might be to set an emission ceiling for anthropogenic emissions of PM10 and/or PM2.5 plus technical obligations (best available technology / techniques, emission limit values). Currently, many believe that particles should be included in any revision of the Gothenburg Protocol, not least because additional health-related objectives for particulate matter are likely to further lower the existing emissions ceilings for their precursors. If particles are included in such a revision, some serious thought should be given to considering the Protocol on Heavy Metals at the same time to ensure heavy metal particles are addressed in a harmonized way.

Air pollution and climate change

Air pollution and anthropogenic climate change (i.e. global warming) are closely connected in a number of ways. Both are caused to a large extent by the burning of fossil fuels; sulphur and nitrogen oxides (NOx) cause air pollution, carbon dioxide (CO_2) contributes to global warming. In addition, agriculture influences both acidification and eutrophication (through NOx and ammonia emissions) and climate change (through emissions of methane (CH_4), nitrous oxide and CO_2). Forestry also plays a role, but can act as a source of VOC emissions and a sink for the greenhouse gas CO_2.

In addition to sharing a number of sources, climate change and air pollution also share some gases. Air pollutants such as NOx, VOC and CH_4 (precursors of ozone) and aerosols/fine particulates not only affect air quality but also contribute to global warming.

It is interesting to note that almost half of all "heat-related deaths" in Western Europe during the summer of 2003 were attributed to air pollution with ozone and fine particulates. Both of these are also important greenhouse gases. In fact, in the Northern hemisphere, ozone is the second most important greenhouse gas after CO_2. But neither ozone nor aerosols/fine particulates are covered by the Kyoto Protocol.

In addition to the above links, there are also synergies related to effects. Biodiversity is threatened by rising temperatures and changing precipitation patterns (climate change) as well as by acid and nitrogen deposition (air pollution).

Early in 2003 the Convention organized a workshop on linkages and synergies of regional and global emission control to explore how air pollution and climate change were linked and how they might be addressed together. The workshop concluded that it was worthwhile continuing to explore the synergies and trade-offs and the Netherlands has provided funding for the Centre for Integrated Assessment Modelling to develop the RAINS model to include the greenhouse gases covered by the Kyoto Protocol, including their abatement measures and costs. The extended model should be able to indicate the benefits of adjusting energy policy to meet both air pollution objectives and those for climate change at the same time (see figure 10.5).

The first model runs give a good indication of how the extended RAINS model works and how it might be used for integrating policies for air pollution and climate change. Calculations show that with the right choices, European climate policies can lead to significant cost savings for traditional air pollution policies and they would provide additional health benefits (e.g. fewer premature deaths from $PM_{2.5}$). There are also plans to extend the RAINS-ASIA model (for Asian countries) to cover climate change, to see whether the European results might apply to countries such as China and India. The models and results are to be presented to the Conference of the Parties to the United Nations Framework Convention on Climate Change at the end of 2004.

The insights obtained from the extended RAINS model will provide input to the 4th Assessment Report of the Intergovernmental Panel on Climate Change. This will give further prominence to the integration of climate and air pollution policies.

For acidification and air quality, the issue of integration is likely be addressed by the Convention in its review and possible revision of the Gothenburg Protocol and by the CAFE programme for possible amendments to the air quality daughter directives and the NEC Directive.

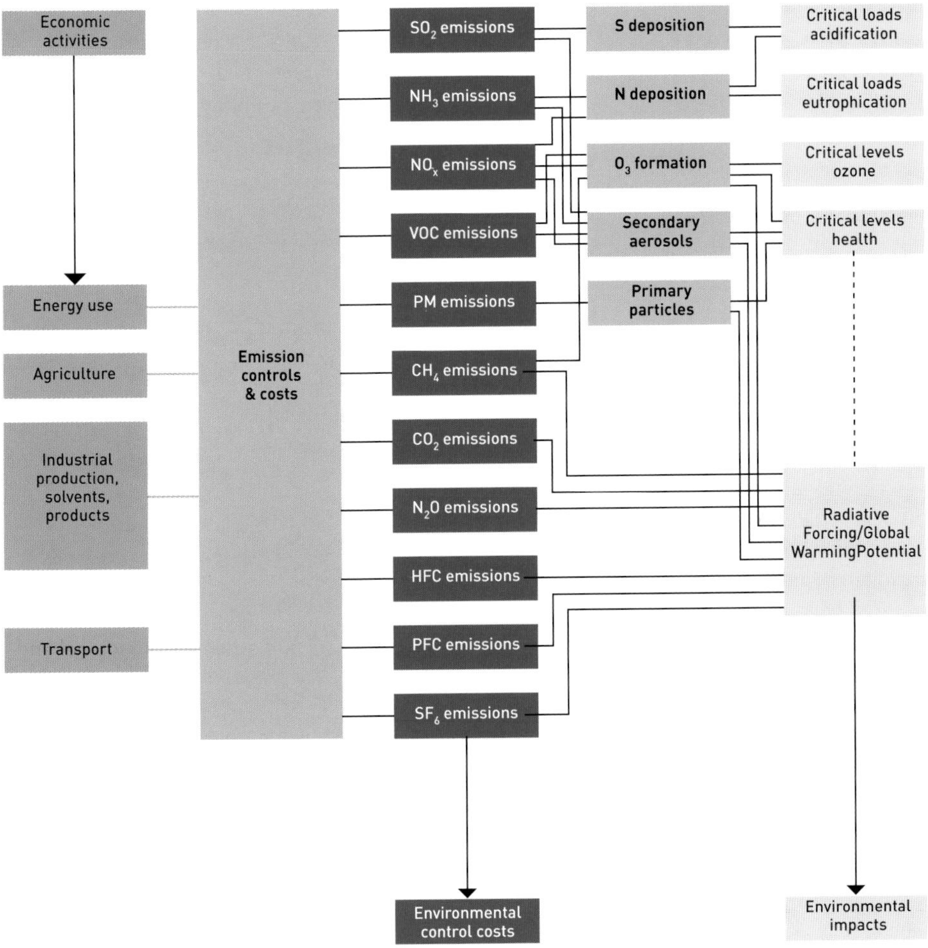

Figure 10.5. Diagram of the RAINS model, including greenhouse gases

Source: IIASA

Ratification and compliance

Roughly 4-5 years usually pass between the signing of a protocol and its entry into force. Obligations in the protocols such as meeting emission ceilings and emission limit values are generally timed to take effect even later. Technologies listed in their annexes are sometimes out of date even before their application becomes obligatory. But revision of a protocol cannot start before its entry into force, so technical annexes cannot be changed until that time.

Some countries often ratify a protocol early, while others consistently ratify late or not at all (table 10.1). This is not a very positive sign for the implementation process. Perhaps the Executive Body should more regularly call upon Parties to ratify the protocols.

Table 10.1. The Protocol Ratification Index (8 September 2004) is a measure of the rate at which countries sign and ratify protocols. Ratification gives a country a score, e.g. 6 if the country is the sixth to ratify. A country that is a Signatory but has not ratified scores the total number of Signatories. Non-Signatories score the number of Parties to the Convention (49). Totals are given for all eight protocols and for the last three. The ranking is based on the last three protocols

	EMEP	85 Sulphur	NOx	VOC	94 Sulphur	HM	POP	Multi-effect	Total	Overall ranking	Total last 3	Ranking last 3
Norway	2	13	7	1	2	2	2	2	31	1	6	1
Sweden	6	4	11	2	3	3	3	3	35	2	9	2
Luxembourg	23	16	13	4	4	4	4	1	69	4	9	2
Netherlands	11	6	7	3	1	6	5	5	44	3	16	4
Denmark	14	5	21	14	10	10	7	4	85	6	21	5
Finland	15	7	10	5	18	5	12	12	84	5	29	6
Czech Republic	33	20	20	16	7	12	10	9	127	8	31	7
European Community	16	49	23	49	15	9	21	11	193	17	41	8
Romania	40	49	49	49	49	16	16	10	278	27	42	9
Canada	12	1	17	49	8	1	1	49	138	11	51	10
Switzerland	5	17	12	7	12	7	6	49	115	7	62	11
Slovenia	31	49	49	49	16	17	49	7	267	25	73	12
Republic of Moldova	49	49	49	49	49	13	13	49	320	33	75	13
Slovakia	34	21	22	18	14	14	14	49	186	16	77	14
Bulgaria	17	11	1	17	49	21	8	49	173	14	78	15
France	24	3	5	15	6	11	19	49	132	9	79	16
Austria	19	15	9	10	19	19	11	49	151	12	79	16
Cyprus	29	49	49	49	49	15	15	49	304	30	79	16
Germany	18	14	15	11	17	22	9	49	155	13	80	19
Liechtenstein	3	2	24	8	11	20	18	49	135	10	87	20
Lithuania	41	49	49	49	49	49	49	6	341	35	104	21
United States	1	49	4	49	49	8	49	49	258	22	106	22
Latvia	35	49	49	49	49	49	49	8	337	34	106	22
Hungary	4	10	18	13	24	49	17	49	184	15	115	24
Monaco	37	49	49	21	25	18	49	49	297	28	116	25
Iceland	49	49	49	49	49	49	20	49	363	38	118	26
United Kingdom	6	49	14	9	5	49	49	49	230	18	147	27
Italy	28	19	19	12	21	49	49	49	246	19	147	27
Spain	22	49	16	6	9	49	49	49	249	20	147	27
Belgium	21	18	28	20	23	49	49	49	257	21	147	27
Russian Federation	8	8	3	49	49	49	49	49	264	23	147	27
Belarus	10	8	2	49	49	49	49	49	265	24	147	27
Ukraine	9	12	6	49	49	49	49	49	272	26	147	27
Estonia	39	22	27	19	49	49	49	49	303	29	147	27
Greece	25	49	26	49	13	49	49	49	309	31	147	27
Ireland	20	49	25	49	20	49	49	49	310	32	147	27
Croatia	32	49	49	49	22	49	49	49	348	36	147	27
Turkey	13	49	49	49	49	49	49	49	356	37	147	27
Poland	26	49	49	49	49	49	49	49	369	39	147	27
Portugal	27	49	49	49	49	49	49	49	370	40	147	27
Bosnia and Herzegovina	30	49	49	49	49	49	49	49	373	41	147	27
Malta	36	49	49	49	49	49	49	49	379	42	147	27
Serbia and Montenegro	38	49	49	49	49	49	49	49	381	43	147	27
Kazakhstan	49	49	49	49	49	49	49	49	392	44	147	27
Armenia	49	49	49	49	49	49	49	49	392	44	147	27
Azerbaijan	49	49	49	49	49	49	49	49	392	44	147	27
Georgia	49	49	49	49	49	49	49	49	392	44	147	27
Kyrgyzstan	49	49	49	49	49	49	49	49	392	44	147	27
The FYR of Macedonia	49	49	49	49	49	49	49	49	392	44	147	27

In the EU, States do not "ratify" directives. The European Commission proposes legislation and, provided the Council and the European Parliament agree, obligations take effect for all members on a specified date. The European Commission has the power under the Treaty of European Union to ensure that the member States comply with their obligations. It could be argued that national input to the content of directives is smaller than to the content of protocols to the Convention, and that the subsequent control of compliance by the Commission is tougher than under the Convention.

In the Convention's early years there was no call or need for a compliance regime. In time the need for introducing a compliance system grew stronger and in 1997 the Executive Body established the Implementation Committee (see chapter 8).

It should be noted that the Convention and its protocols make little reference to compliance. How to deal with this remains the problem of the Executive Body and this does not have a large investigation organization working for it. The Executive Body chose not to seek a punitive route for dealing with non-compliance. It believed that gentle pressure including "naming and shaming" was the best approach. Under the terms of some of the protocols, Parties have access to various mechanisms for settling disputes, including arbitration and submission of the dispute to the International Court of Justice. But such action is unprecedented in the Convention's history and would be considered inappropriate by most.

Despite the Implementation Committee's and the Executive Body's apparent lack of teeth, they have managed to scrutinize Parties' compliance, identify cases of non-compliance and, in most instances, successfully encouraged non-complying Parties to meet their obligations. There is, however, still a long way to go before the Convention's implementation and compliance regime is as effective as it could, and should, be. A few Parties still do not take their obligations seriously and the Executive Body and the Implementation Committee must continue to seek new ways of exerting more effective pressure on Parties to ensure that they meet their obligations. Furthermore, compliance with some obligations relies upon Parties' own reports, e.g. emissions are calculated by the Parties themselves. To develop the compliance regime further, a system of auditing performance could be introduced such as that negotiated in 2001 for the Kyoto Protocol.

Bright sky

This chapter started by characterizing the Convention as science-based, science-policy interactive, innovative and "of the countries and for the countries". These qualities have provided a strong and active convention that has proved very successful and productive.

Stepping stone or breeding ground

As noted above the EU has used policies and tools developed under the Convention and the Convention has built upon work by EU. Such an interchange of ideas and results is quite common and the Convention has provided a good example to other bodies and agreements, not all of them associated with air pollution.

For air pollution the Convention serves as an example of how countries can organize themselves to address transboundary problems. There are various initiatives in other regions of the world where groups of countries are discussing, either under a formal agreement or more informally as a network, their problems of air pollution often with a view to seeking measures for improvement. The Convention, either through its Parties or through its secretariat, has links with many of these and the Executive Body has encouraged "outreach" activities to assist these regions with their problems. Sweden, through its Regional Air Pollution in Developing Countries project, is using the Convention as an example for developing monitoring, effect studies, and modelling and policy development in several regions. The secretariat and some of the Convention's programme centres have good links with the Acid Deposition Monitoring Network in East Asia.

As yet there have been no major initiatives to deal with air pollution at a global scale even though very long-range transport of pollutants is of increasing concern. However, the International Union of Air Pollution Prevention and Environmental Protection Associations has recently brought together representatives from the various regional agreements and networks so that they can discuss their common interests. It has been proposed that such meetings should take place regularly.

The Convention's work on heavy metals and POPs has prompted, and provided direction for, worldwide action. An initiative by the United Nations Environment Programme (UNEP) resulted in the 2001 Stockholm Convention on POPs. The development of that Convention followed very much the path that was laid by the Protocol on POPs; 12 of the 16 substances currently in the Protocol are also in the Stockholm Convention. In a somewhat similar way following on from the adoption of the Protocol on Heavy Metals, the UNEP Governing Council initiated the Global Mercury Assessment, the results of which were presented to it in 2003. Following on from this, the Governing Council in 2005 will decide on further action or measures, including legally binding or non-legally binding instruments, to address the global mercury problem.

In the light of its interregional activities and in particular its work on heavy metals and POPs, the Convention might be thought of as a stepping stone or even a breeding ground for more global action. It has certainly stimulated and encouraged action far outside the UNECE region. But more work is still needed to deal with issues at a global level. The Convention and its Parties are aware of this and will continue to play an active role sharing the knowledge and experience gained over the past 25 years.

Value added

In the past the Convention has led the way in fighting air pollution; with the EU and its other Parties it will continue to do so in the coming decades. The role of the Convention is vital, not only in Europe but across the UNECE region in North America and Central Asia. Stretching West and East of the EU, the Convention includes nations of great economic and social disparity. Even so, it has always been able to bridge political differences and we hope it will continue to do so.

Air pollution in the UNECE region has decreased considerably over the past 25 years and the Convention is a major contributor to this. But there is still much to be done before air pollution reaches sustainable levels or, as expressed in the Gothenburg Protocol, critical levels and critical loads The Convention will remain important and the future looks bright for its combat for Blue Skies.

Acknowledgements
I would like to thank Messrs. Richard Ballaman, Mike Chadwick, Helmut Hojeski, Volkert Keizer, Martin Lutz and Kaj Sanders for commenting on drafts of the text.